Heroines

Remarkable and Inspiring Women

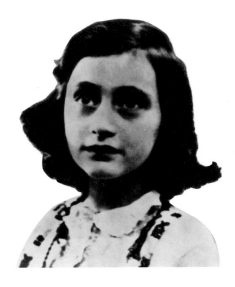

Heroines

REMARKABLE AND INSPIRING WOMEN

An Illustrated Anthology
of Essays by Women Writers

A *Saraband* Book

Copyright © 1995 Saraband Inc.
Essay by Marge Piercy copyright © 1995 Middlemarsh, Inc.
Design copyright © Ziga Design

ISBN 1-887354-01-8

10 9 8 7 6 5 4 3 2 1

Printed in China

General Editor: Sara Hunt
Associate Editor: Julia Banks

For Chloe, Rachel, Kate, Linda, Maureen, and Eve

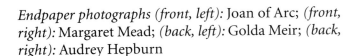

Endpaper photographs (front, left): Joan of Arc; *(front,
right):* Margaret Mead; *(back, left):* Golda Meir; *(back,
right):* Audrey Hepburn

Page 1: Helen Keller

Page 2 (top row): Marie Curie, Audrey Hepburn, Harriet
Tubman; *(center):* Emmeline Pankhurst; *(bottom row):*
Christine de Pisan, Anne Frank, Amelia Earhart

Page 3 (left to right): Rigoberta Menchú, Wilma Rudolph,
Cleopatra

This page (above): Rosa Parks; *(below):* Tina Turner

The Contributors

Jane Anderson lives in Connecticut where she runs a business. She is a writer with a long-standing interest in English literature and women's history.

Joan Halimah Brooks writes poetry, plays and film screenplays. Her publications include *My Soul's Journey*, a poetry collection, and the play *What Will Tomorrow Bring?*.

Denise Clay is a freelance writer on African art and history. She studied at the University of London's School of Oriental and African Studies.

Diane Cole is the author of *After Great Pain: A New Life Emerges*, a memoir of loss and renewal.

Maria Costantino, author of numerous books including *Georgia O'Keeffe* (1994), is an art history and film studies lecturer in England.

Andrea Feld, the former managing editor of *Bride's* magazine, is a writer in New York City.

Andrea Hopkins has written several books on medieval and early English history, including *Courtly Love* (1994), and works for Oxford University Press, England.

Rachel Hunt is a former legal aid family and childcare lawyer in Yorkshire, England, with a special interest in the learning disabled.

Sydney Johnson, a freelance writer based in New York City, has a long-standing interest in women's history; she contributes profiles of women scientists to *The Sciences* magazine.

Holly Lloyd is a writer and former editorial fellow at *Mother Jones* magazine in San Francisco.

Catherine Mooney publishes environmental guidebooks and writes magazine features on women's interest subjects. She is based in York, England.

Ruth B. Moynihan teaches at the University of Connecticut and has written frequently on the history of American women. Her books include *Rebel for Rights: Abigail Scott Duniway* (1983), *So Much to be Done: Women Settlers on the Frontier*, and *Second to None: A Documentary History of American Women* (1994).

Margaret Mulvihill is the author of three novels, a biography of Charlotte Despard, and many articles and books on women's history. She was 1989 Writing Fellow at the University of East Anglia, England. She is currently working on her fourth novel.

Amy Nutt is a writer and reporter for *Sports Illustrated* with a special interest in the history of women in sports.

Marge Piercy, a bestselling author, writes novels (including *Vida, Woman on the Edge of Time, Braided Lives, The Longings of Women*), poetry (eleven collections published), nonfiction, and criticism. She lives in Wellfleet, Massachusetts.

Cathy Porter is a London-based writer and a translator of Russian fiction and plays. She has written biographies of both Alexandra Kollontai and Larissa Reisner.

Holly Regier, former magazine writer and editor, is a career counselor and is currently studying for a Masters degree in social work.

Catsou Roberts is a curator and critic of contemporary art. She is currently working and living in Paris.

Robin Langley Sommer, author of numerous nonfiction books, including a biography of Nien Cheng for children, is a freelance writer and editor.

Nadine Spencer has written several books and articles on women's and Canadian history. She is based in Vancouver, Canada.

Carla van Splunteren is a freelance writer, editor and translator who lives in Amsterdam, Holland.

Eleni Stylianou is Lecturer in Inflammatory Cell Biology at the University Hospital, Queen's Medical Centre, Nottingham, England. She has written articles and profiles on women in science for various publications.

Brenda Wilkinson grew up in Waycross, Georgia, before the Civil Rights Era. Her first novel, *Ludell,* was a National Book Award nominee; she has written adult and young adult nonfiction on African American affairs.

Ellen Williams and **Annie Roberts** are human rights activists who volunteer for Amnesty International.

Contents

Introduction

These profiles of remarkable and inspiring women seek to identify those qualities that make a heroine, whether or not she has become renowned. It is certain that a great many heroines have been lost to us in the unwritten pages of history—not only those women who distinguished themselves by great courage, learning, or enterprise, but those who lived and died in obscurity, giving fully of themselves in their own small spheres of influence.

History, largely recorded by men and concerning for the most part "great men," battles, and events of political and strategic importance, has left us with scant details of daily life—particularly for women—in earlier centuries. We read of women whose qualities set them apart from traditional norms for their

sex: the strong-willed Amazons, ambitious Cleopatra, militant Boudicca, and women who ruled by virtue of their birth. Until recently, it was far likelier that a woman would become famous as a seductress than as a scientist, writer, reformer, or saint. Her avenues to power and worldly esteem were drastically limited. However, the long struggle for equality has made us more aware of the quiet courage and tenacity of everyday heroines who seek to improve conditions for themselves and those around them, as well as the more public strengths of charismatic figures like suffragist Susan B. Anthony, who declared, "Failure is impossible!" This century's heroines include women like "Mother" Clara Hale: dedicated, selfless and determined to help the vulnerable; someone whose extraordinary qualities would not have been recorded had she lived in an earlier age.

Some of the women profiled here are much better known in their own countries than they are in the wider world. This is true of the Australian foundress Mary MacKillop, who was excommunicated for her views on the role of women in the Roman Catholic Church in 1871 and beatified in 1995 for her work among the poor of the island continent; and of English-Canadian writer Susanna Moodie, who spent most of her life as a pioneer in Upper Canada.

Some women who were heroines in their own place and time have been largely forgotten, like African tribeswoman Nzinga Mbande, who resisted Portuguese colonialism in the early 1600s. Courageous Grace Darling, who helped rescue survivors of the shipwrecked steamer *Forfarshire* near Longstone Lighthouse, was a household name in Victorian England, but few outside England had heard of her until Jessica Mitford published her entertaining biography *Grace Had an English Heart* in 1988. Similarly, Ida Lewis, the keeper of Newport, Rhode Island's, Lime Rock Lighthouse who rescued many endangered sailors during her long career, aroused great admiration during the nineteenth century but is almost forgotten today.

Aside from the difficulty in recovering details on women from the past, a true picture of current events, too, can be elusive. Chai Ling, student leader during the Tiananmen Square rebellion in 1989, was revered as a heroine in the immediate aftermath of the event, but has faded from the public eye as conflicting accounts of the rebellion have raised doubts about her role as a spokeswoman for the participants. Her story, as those of others surrounded by controversy, confusion, or manipulative press coverage, may never be definitively told.

Considerations of space have precluded the inclusion of countless heroines whose stories are as inspiring as those included here. Brilliant writer Sigrid Undset, Danish-born Norwegian novelist and winner of the 1928 Nobel Prize for literature for *Kristin Lavransdatter*, broke new ground for feminism. Fearless Lakshmi Bai led the province of Jhansi during the Indian Rebellion of the 1850s. Equally remarkable women were medieval stonemason Sabina von Steinbach, whose work adorns the Cathedral of Strasbourg; nineteenth-century African-American antislavery campaigner Sojourner Truth; Mairead Corrigan and Betty Williams, joint winners of the Nobel Peace Prize in 1977 for their work in founding the Ulster Peace Movement; early twentieth-century Italian education reformer Maria Montessori; and Komyo, a devout Buddhist who founded charitable institutions for the sick and starving in eighth-century Japan—to name but a few. Their strengths and achievements, and those of other heroines in all fields of endeavor, are mirrored in the lives of some of the women featured. From the rich, almost endless variety of women who could be considered heroines— those whose stories have been preserved—a small but diverse selection has been made to represent role models of many kinds.

Pocahontas, whose real name was Matoaka, was one of the few Native American women to win a place in the history books when she interceded for the life of Captain John Smith of the Jamestown, Virginia, Colony in 1608. Her story, like that of Sacajawea who guided Lewis and Clark in their famous expedition in the American West in 1804-6, was recorded because of her actions assisting white men. Although both were clearly extraordinary women, they can be found in standard history texts, while Sarah Winnemucca,

Above: Pocahontas   Above left: Maria Montessori
Opposite: Chai Ling

who did not achieve as much recognition for her life-long activism on behalf of her own Paiute tribe, has been chosen for inclusion here.

Many women have experienced persecution, even hatred, when their convictions clashed head-on with the establishments of their day. We have only to think of the tribulations of English suffragists Emmeline, Christabel, and Sylvia Pankhurst, or their American counterparts, including Elizabeth Cady Stanton. Irish-American labor organizer "Mother" Jones antagonized the powerful business interests of her day, and novelist Radclyffe Hall was vilified for her candid and personal account of lesbian love in *The Well of Loneliness*, which resulted in an obscenity trial that tested England's laws on freedom of the press. German artist and sculptor Käthe Kollwitz saw her work banned by two repressive governments—the kaiser's (in 1898) and the Nazis' (in 1936)—because of her impassioned protests against social injustice. Novelist George Eliot (Mary Ann Evans) made enemies with her incisive portraits of moral, political, and intellectual hypocrisy in Victorian England. Dutch physician Aletta Jacobs outraged Amsterdam when she opened the world's first birth-control clinic in 1882, and Margaret Sanger broke American laws to establish such clinics in the United States, then successfully challenged those laws to win a series of favorable court decisions. Adversity is no stranger to women who have questioned, much less flouted, the conventional wisdom.

Media personalities and performing artists today are in a unique position to serve as role models and spokeswomen on contemporary issues, whether they actively campaign on behalf of a particular cause or simply fight their personal battles under the glare of the public eye. Elizabeth Taylor has worked tirelessly to raise public awareness of AIDS. Glenda Jackson, one of this century's most highly acclaimed actresses, has become a formidable politician. Actress Audrey Hepburn combined her successful film career with a long-term commitment to the United Nations Children's Fund on behalf of underprivileged and endangered children all over the world, a cause also espoused by Britain's Princess Royal, Anne. The involvement of these high-profile women has generated huge publicity for their causes. Jazz singer Billie Holiday struggled with depression and drugs,

and Tina Turner, the dynamic singer and actress, overcame domestic violence and drug abuse to regain her independence and revitalize her career. Both women increased public awareness of these everyday problems and inspired ordinary women who suffered with them.

Some women bring "female" perspectives of nurturing, conservation, and harmony to challenge such "male" pursuits as industrial and scientific progress, and warfare. Both Anita Roddick and Rachel Carson were pioneers in the field of environmentalism, pointing out the wastefulness and danger of plundering limited natural resources and polluting the air, earth, and water. Austrian nuclear physicist Lise Meitner made important discoveries in nuclear fission, then fought unsuccessfully against using this knowledge to develop the nuclear bomb.

Women in politics and civil rights movements are just beginning to find their strength and make their influence felt. It is only a century since the first woman was elected to the status of cabinet member—Alexandra Kollontai, who served in the government that followed the Russian Revolution. Ukrainian-born Golda Meir emigrated to Palestine in 1921 and joined the World Zionist Movement in 1929. During the 1930s she toured Europe and the United States on behalf of the Zionist movement and the Jewish Agency for Palestine. She was a member of Ben Gurion's faction during the struggle for Israeli nationhood and signed the Proclamation of Independence in 1948. Her career as a stateswoman culminated in her service as prime minister from 1969 to 1974, making her the first woman prime minister who achieved the office in her own right, without family connections assisting her path to power.

In Ireland, Charlotte Despard worked tirelessly for women's suffrage and Irish Independence, and Polish-born German socialist Rosa Luxemburg inspired her movement by her powerful writings (many of which were written while she was in prison). Today, women like Nien Cheng, Rigoberta Menchú, and Aung San Suu Kyi have suffered imprisonment, torture, and violence against their families to uphold the cause of human rights against despotic governments.

Throughout history, women of deep spirituality, conviction and compassion have worked to alleviate the suffering caused by poverty, bigotry, illness, homelessness, and disenfranchisement. St. Margaret, Queen of Scotland in the eleventh century, Mary MacKillop,

and Mother Teresa of Calcutta expressed their devotion by selfless care for the least fortunate of their fellow creatures. Marian Wright Edelman lobbies ceaselessly for those who have no voice of their own—underprivileged and endangered children. Helen Keller's remarkable success in her struggle to communicate brought hope and opportunity to those with learning disabilities. Countless lives have been touched, even transformed, by their example.

The role of women varies greatly by culture, as it has varied over time within a given culture. Today, the obstacles to women pursuing careers and independent lives in most countries have diminished. It is still unusual for a woman to become a mathematician, but the barriers are less severe than they were for Sonya Kovalevsky in nineteenth-century Russia. In some cultures, though, the role of women remains tightly circumscribed by the strictures of religion and tradition, and for this reason, the strengths of individual women are unknown beyond their immediate circles.

One of the contributors to this book, Catherine Mooney, wrote her essays shortly before giving birth to her first child. The experience of childbirth, and the dedication and professionalism of the hospital staff, prompted her to comment on the potential for heroism in all women. She wrote: "Women's heroism is a quiet, vast, ineffable underpinning energy, unnoticed, for the most part, like the colour green, but essential." Diverse heroines portrayed here, from those in quiet, everyday pursuit of selfless goals, to others who aimed for extraordinary achievements, demonstrate aspects of this essential energy. The women who contributed their thoughts and feelings to this anthology bring a wealth of knowledge and insight into their various subjects. They do not claim perfection for their heroines, nor would all agree with everything that is written here. Rather, these essays form a kind of mosaic of those qualities that have inspired respect and admiration, and have shown by their example the truth in the rousing statement of Jeanne d'Albret (1528-1572, mother of Henri IV of France): "Nothing is impossible to a valiant heart."

Sara Hunt

Opposite: Billie Holiday   Left: Mary MacKillop

Hatshepsut

Hatshepsut was the daughter of the great warrior Pharaoh Thutmose I, and his queen, the Theban princess Ahmose. Thutmose himself was not of royal blood and came to the throne through his wife. On his death he was succeeded by Thutmose II, his son by another wife. Thutmose II married his half sister Hatshepsut; she was the heiress so, like his father, he gained the throne through her. Though Hatshepsut was the queen, Thutmose II, like all pharaohs, had a number of wives, and one of these gave birth to

his son, Thutmose III. When Thutmose II died in 1504, this son was still a little boy not old enough to rule. Hatshepsut then became official co-regent with her stepson/nephew. Until then records of her life are few and sketchy. For the next twenty years, however, she ruled effectively alone, and within seven years she declared herself to be the pharaoh, independently of Thutmose III. She prevented him from assuming rule when he was old enough to do so; she did not marry him to her own daughter, his half sister Nefru-Re. Instead she built up a formidable network of favored officials and ministers whose interests were identified with hers. These key administrators helped her retain power for twenty years.

When he eventually came to power, Thutmose III became a very great pharaoh, a fearsome warrior, a general of genius, and also a ruler of judgment and wisdom. He probably spent his youthful time in the army acquiring the martial skills of sword, spear, and chariot for which he was later renowned. Soon after he came to power, Thutmose began to have all records of his stepmother systematically destroyed. Her name was chiseled out of all inscriptions, her images defaced from all reliefs, even from her own funerary temple at Dayr al-Bahrī, and her statues there were spitefully smashed to pieces. The statue on the opposite page was painstakingly reassembled from thousands of fragments found dumped in a quarry near the temple/tomb. It and several other statues had been thrown down, then its eyes gouged out, the sacred serpent hacked from the brow, and then thoroughly pulverized until it was nothing but rubble. What did Hatshepsut do to inspire such fury?

Her twenty-year rule was peaceful, in contrast to the incessant military campaigns of her father, husband, and stepson after her. She concentrated instead on the establishment of peaceful trading and the improvement of Egyptian agriculture, architecture, and the arts. She was highly intelligent and able and was the only woman who succeeded in reigning as pharaoh in her own right. Hatshepsut declared her-

self divinely begotten (by Amon Re) and adopted the ceremonial (male) dress of the Pharaohs, including the false beard. She appointed and enabled a number of brilliant administrators who assisted her in holding off the ambitions of her stepson; one of these, Sen-en-Mut, was a special favorite, and it has been suggested that he was also her lover. Hatshepsut sent a major sea expedition to Punt to establish trading agreements in gold, furs, ebony, and myrrh trees. She received rich tributes from the neighboring states of Libya, Nubia, and various Asian countries that had been conquered by her father. She instituted an extensive building program, which included restoring her father's great hall at Thebes (Karnak) where she added four huge inscribed obelisks and a chapel; the temple of Speos Artemidos at Beni-Hasan, and the magnificent temple at Dayr al-Bahrī, which was intended as a funerary monument for herself and her father. There are no records of the last few years of her life, and we do not know exactly how or when she died.

Andrea Hopkins

Cleopatra

Cleopatra was born in 69 B.C., the third daughter of King Ptolemy XII of Egypt. The rulers of Egypt at this time were Greek and had descended directly from the first Ptolemy, one of Alexander the Great's generals, who had become king of Egypt in 323 B.C. on Alexander's death. Although Egypt was not the mighty empire it had once been, it was still a very wealthy country; by the time of Cleopatra's father, the Romans had found it desirable to annex it to the Roman Empire. They didn't invade and conquer Egypt, but pursued their usual course of supporting "client" kings in exchange for favors—usually financial favors. The later Ptolemies did not hold onto their thrones easily, and Ptolemy XII was no exception: in 59 B.C. he agreed to pay the Roman triumvirate of Julius Caesar, Pompey the Great, and Crassus the enormous sum of six thousand talents in exchange for their firm recognition of his right to the throne. Even this was not enough to quell all the plots against him, and in 57 B.C. he went to Rome again for military aid. While he was gone his eldest daughter, also named Cleopatra (the VI) seized his throne; she was soon assassinated, and her place was taken by the next daughter, Berenice. With the help of the Roman general Gabinus, one of whose staff officers was Mark Antony, Ptolemy was restored to power and had Berenice executed. So at an early age Cleopatra had had hard lessons in the treachery of family members and the need for strict measures to retain power.

Cleopatra came to the throne in 51 B.C., ruling jointly with her younger brother Ptolemy XIII. The Ptolemies had adopted the pharaohs' practice of royal intermarriage, and this brother and sister were supposed to rule as man and wife. Cleopatra was eighteen, Ptolemy ten; she had enough of a mind of her own not to go along willingly with everything decreed by the young king's advisers and the couple soon quarreled. Cleopatra fled the royal palace and recruited an army of her own; civil war followed. Meanwhile, the triumvirate in Rome had also split apart into civil war; Julius Caesar was the victor and arrived at Alexandria in 48 B.C. looking for Pompey, whom he had just defeated at the battle of Pharsalus. Pompey had had good relations with Egypt and fled there hoping for support. The Egyptians preferred to support the winner and presented Caesar, much to his disgust, with Pompey's head. Caesar stayed, ostensibly to reconcile the warring factions, but also to collect the money owed to Rome by Ptolemy XII for his restoration. He was in the royal palace with Ptolemy XIII and his chief adviser, the eunuch Pothinus. Cleopatra snuck in past the guards—tradition has it by being rolled up in a carpet. Whether that is true or not, there is no doubt that the fifty-two-year-old Caesar succumbed to her charms (she was twenty-one) and thereafter took her side in the dispute. Having received reinforcements from Rome, he defeated an Egyptian army that was preparing to place yet another sister, Arsinoe, on the throne, had Pothinus executed, and, Ptolemy XIII having drowned in the Nile meanwhile, married Cleopatra to her youngest brother, the twelve-year-old Ptolemy XIV, and declared them joint rulers. Cleopatra was effectively the sole ruler from this date onwards, though she never claimed the throne in her own name. Caesar left three legions in Alexandria to help Cleopatra keep control and departed for Rome. Shortly afterwards Cleopatra gave birth to a son, whom she named Ptolemy Caesar (known as Caesarion). She claimed (and later, Antony claimed) that Caesar was the father of this boy, but Caesar never acknowledged this publicly.

Caesar returned to Rome in 46 B.C. after further military campaigns abroad and celebrated four Triumphs (ceremonies of a returning victorious general); Cleopatra's captured sister Arsinoe appeared in one of these celebrations, loaded with chains. Cleopatra herself soon followed Caesar to Rome, officially to negotiate a treaty, and was established in a villa belonging to him, together with her husband/brother. Caesar accorded her royal status and had a large gilded statue of her placed in his Temple of Venus. Cleopatra remained in Rome for over a year, until Caesar was assassinated in March 44 B.C., when she immediately returned to Egypt. Shortly afterwards young Ptolemy XIV was also assassinated, tradition has it on Cleopatra's orders. She then declared herself joint ruler with her three-year-old son, Ptolemy XV Caesar. The next three years were devoted to a consolidation of power. Despite internal difficulties brought on by famine and unrest and threats from outside, Cleopatra governed her country effectively and began once more to amass wealth.

In 41 B.C. Mark Antony returned to Egypt. He was enjoying an uneasy division of power with Caesar's great-nephew and heir, Octavius. Mark Antony was now about forty years old, and determined to mount an invasion of the vast and wealthy Parthian empire.

As usual, a Roman general determined to raise funds and troops for a military campaign turned to Egypt. Antony summoned Cleopatra to Tarsus to negotiate what aid she could give him. It was a magnificent opportunity, and Cleopatra made the most of it, sailing into Tarsus up the river Cydnus in a barge of astounding opulence, immortalized by Shakespeare. Antony and Cleopatra became lovers and formed an enduring mutual alliance; she provided financial backing for his Parthian campaign, and he had various political rivals of hers executed, including her sister Arsinoe who had once again proclaimed herself queen from exile at Ephesus. They spent the winter together at Alexandria, according to Latin historians, abandoning themselves to every sensual pleasure, founding a society of "inimitable livers."

Meanwhile, in Italy, Antony's wife Fulvia and brother Lucius had raised a rebellion against Octavius and been defeated. They fled to Greece where Antony, on hearing the news, joined them. Fulvia then conveniently died, and Antony, returning to Rome, was reconciled with Octavius and married his sister Octavia as a sign of their new alliance. Not long after the wedding Cleopatra gave birth to twins, Mark Antony's children. He was to remain away for over three years, during which time Cleopatra again concentrated on her job. Plutarch claims that she was the only Ptolemaic ruler who bothered to learn to speak Egyptian—the court spoke Greek—and was careful to observe the religious rites of her subjects, calling herself daughter of Ra. Records remain of various trade agreements she negotiated which give the impression not of an idle voluptuary but of a shrewd, intelligent businesswoman.

At the end of the three years, Antony seems to have decided that further association with Octavius was pointless. He returned to Alexandria and, from then on, the recorded facts imply that a growing passion for Cleopatra affected his judgment. The first thing he did on his return in 37 was to marry her—an outrageous and deliberate insult to Octavia and Octavius that could not be overlooked. In 36 he set off on his Parthian campaign, leaving Cleopatra pregnant again. The campaign was an expensive failure; Antony lost almost half his men and gained no territory. He refused to be deterred and raised money and troops for new campaigns in 35 and 34.

Octavius had been busy convincing the Romans that Antony had been corrupted by Cleopatra and "gone native," forgetting his allegiance to Rome and acting as the tool of a vicious female tyrant. On his return from Armenia, Antony and Cleopatra celebrated an extravagant Triumph in Alexandria which fueled Roman fears about his intentions. Seated on olden thrones, the couple declared themselves to be gods—she Isis and he Dionysus/Osiris—in the famous Donations of Alexandria. Cleopatra was declared Queen of queens and her son Caesarion King of kings. Antony declared Caesarion to be Julius Caesar's legitimate son and heir (which would disinherit Octavius), and both Caesarion and Antony's three children by Cleopatra were declared kings and queens and granted territories. Some of these territories, like Judaea and Syria, were provinces of the Roman Empire ruled by local client kings, and some, like Parthia, had not yet been conquered.

On hearing this, Octavius illegally seized Antony's will from the temple of the Vestal Virgins and revealed

brilliant admiral Agrippa in the naval battle of Actium. It was a total disaster, with over three quarters of their fleet destroyed or abandoned.

Cleopatra's main priority was to escape with her massive treasure, which she succeeded in doing, although her premature departure from the battle was seen by later historians as cowardly flight. Antony too, escaped, but to further news of disaster; Canidius with the army had encountered Octavius, and all the soldiers, demoralized by the defeat of Actium, had defected to Octavius before a blow had been struck. Antony seems to have been completely shattered by these reversals, but Cleopatra still hoped to fight another day. She spent the following months (while Octavius was in Rome trying to pay his soldiers) raising money and making plans for escape. In 30 Octavius set out for Egypt; every ally of Antony and Cleopatra had made terms with him. Cleopatra sent messages to Octavius offering to abdicate if he would allow her children to reign in her place. Octavius ignored the messages. Cleopatra had all her treasure carried into her mausoleum and shut herself in with her attendants. Antony, believing her to be dead, fell on his sword, but he did not manage to inflict an instantly mortal wound. He had himself carried to the monument and hoisted up into it, where he died in Cleopatra's arms. Octavius now took possession of Alexandria, and Cleopatra was taken prisoner. Though kept under close guard at all times, she succeeded in killing herself, traditionally by the bite of a venomous asp. The Greek historian Plutarch, who had access to the papers of her personal physician, is not clear on this point, but does record that she dressed herself in full royal regalia to die, and that her body was unmarked except for two scratches on her arms. Octavius honored her final request to be buried with Antony. She was thirty-nine.

Cleopatra's story has been so romanticized by later writers that it is hard to recover the historical personality behind the myth. Despite the extremely bad press she got from Latin historians, however, she was certainly a remarkably strong woman and a gifted leader, who managed not only to manipulate famous Romans to her advantage, but to rule successfully for over twenty difficult years.

Andrea Hopkins

to the uneasy Romans that he had bestowed Roman territories on Cleopatra and her children and planned to found the capital of his own empire in Alexandria. Cleopatra was portrayed as a temptress who had destroyed Antony's reason; and in 32 B.C. it was on Cleopatra, alone, that the Roman senate, at Octavius's instigation, declared war. Despite his overweening ambitions, Antony was not without his supporters in Rome, and hundreds of senators, including the two acting consuls, fled to join him. Thanks to Cleopatra's massive wealth they had amassed a huge fleet and an enormous army of over one hundred thousand men. They waited in Greece for Octavius to come to them. There Antony engaged Octavius's

Boudicca

oudicca was the wife of Prasutagus, king of the Iceni. Though this tribe was both numerous and powerful, they had come to an arrangement with the Romans quite early on in the history of Roman Britain: Prasutagus was a "client" king, acknowledging the overlordship of the emperor. The emperor in this case was Nero, not noted for paternalistic trustworthiness. Britain had only been a Roman province for seventeen years, and the British were not convinced that it was either desirable or inevitable to remain so. Under Nero the local officials were brutal and rapacious. They treated the British with contempt and extorted huge taxes from them.

Boudicca and Prasutagus had no sons, only two daughters, Camorra and Tasca. Though nothing in British law and custom prevented a daughter from inheriting royal status, it was not permissible under Roman law. Prasutagus anticipated difficulties with the Roman authorities, which he tried to circumvent in his will by dividing his considerable estate equally between the emperor and his two daughters, with a direct appeal to the emperor to protect them and support their rights.

This appeal fell on deaf ears. The Roman officers assumed that in the absence of a male heir they could take over the entire estate; Roman historian Tacitus, somewhat sympathetic to the wrongs suffered by the Britons, noted that "Kingdom and household alike were plundered like prizes of war…for a start, his widow Boudicca was flogged and their daughters raped. The chieftains of the Iceni were deprived of their family estates as if the whole country had been handed over to the Romans. The king's own relatives were treated as slaves."

Within months the outraged Boudicca had united the Iceni with another tribe, the Trinobantes, and other smaller groups in a rebellion against the despised Roman regime. They had chosen a very good time to make their stand: the governor of Britain, Gaius Suetonius Paulinus, was away on a campaign in north Wales with the bulk of the army. One thing that had especially annoyed the Britons was the establishment of communities of retired soldiers. One of these was on Trinobantes land at Camelodumun (Colchester). Roman veterans were given estates of land as a pension without any regard for any Briton who might already own the land. At Camelodunum there was also a temple to the divine Claudius, the emperor who had finally completed the conquest of Britain. This temple added insult to injury, as the British were forced to pay for its priests and ceremonies. The veterans appealed for help when they heard of the uprising; they received a relief force of only two hundred men. They and the local garrison tried to make a defense in the temple, but everyone in the town was massacred by the gleeful British. The hated temple was burned to the ground.

The Romans retaliated by sending an entire division against the rebels but the division was humiliatingly defeated. The infantry were all killed, and the commander and the cavalry only survived by running away and sheltering in their camp. The British then marched on London. Meanwhile, Suetonius had come hurrying back from Wales and had reached London, but his intelligence reported that he was so vastly outnumbered by the rebels — whose initial success had encouraged many others to join them — that it would be suicide to remain. Ignoring the pleas of the citizens, he and the army abandoned the city to its fate. London was sacked and its population massacred — not merely Romans, but also "romanized" natives. Next the British turned to the small town of Verulamium (St. Albans) and accomplished the same thing. Tacitus reports that the rebels bypassed forts and defended settlements and chose to attack peaceable civilian populations where there would be plentiful goods to loot; as no prisoners were taken, deaths were estimated at seventy thousand.

Suetonius managed to gather together all the available troops in the south of England and carefully chose a narrow valley to deploy them in his attack on the British. In this position the British could not make good use of their superior numbers, since only as many as could fit into the valley could engage the Romans at any one time. Tacitus reported that Boudicca rode her chariot around the British troops before the battle, encouraging them by reminding them what they were fighting for — the right to a decent life and liberty, and to be free of tyranny and enslavement by the arrogant invaders. Clearly she was an inspiring leader and an impressive woman with her flowing red hair and powerful figure.

However, the Romans were victorious, and as they were eager to avenge the civilian massacres perpetrated by the British, slaughtered the defeated Britons indiscriminately. Boudicca and her daughters escaped the battlefield but afterwards poisoned themselves to avoid capture.

Although the immediate retribution for the rebellion was swift and cruel, the British refused to give in and resume normal life. They continued to make war for another year, after which Suetonius was succeeded by Publius Petronius Turpilianus. The new governor perceived that the stubborn British would not be intimidated by force and changed the policy to one of appeasement, improving the conditions for natives under Roman rule and laying a foundation for three hundred years of Roman occupation. So Boudicca did not die in vain.

Andrea Hopkins

Hypatia

ypatia was the last in a long line of distinguished mathematicians who taught at the University of Alexandria; the lineage began with with Euclid, the Greek father of geometry, brought to Alexandria by Ptolemy I in 306 B.C.

It was Hypatia's good fortune to grow up in the cosmopolitan city of Alexandria (founded by Alexander the Great) on the Mediterranean coast of Egypt. Her father, Theon, a mathematics professor who later became head of the University of Alexandria, was in a position to offer her the best possible education for that era. It was not unusual for Greek women to study mathematics, but Hypatia was by far the most outstanding woman to do so.

An enlightened man, Theon set the highest standards of perfection (educating the whole person in the Greek tradition) for his daughter, born around 370 A.D. He taught her mathematics and tutored her in other subjects he considered essential, including philosophy and rhetoric. Part of every day was devoted to physical activity, and she learned how to row, swim, ride, and hike. He encouraged her to be independent of established religion, telling her, "Reserve your right to think, for even to think wrongly is better than not to think at all."

Hypatia was a willing student. Strikingly beautiful, she was a brilliant mathematician whose skill would eventually surpass her father. He sent her abroad to continue her studies; it was in Athens, Greece, where she was studying with Plutarch the Younger and his daughter Asclepigenia, that she began to establish her reputation as a mathematician. When she returned to Alexandria, she was asked to teach mathematics and philosophy at the university.

A charismatic teacher, she attracted a wide following among young students who came from Europe, Asia, and Africa to attend her lectures. She also wrote a number of commentaries on mathematical works to be used as texts for her courses. Of the few that have survived, the most famous are *On the Astronomical Canon of Diophantus* and *On the Conics of Apollonius.*

Her following was not limited to university students. The well-known philosopher Synesius of Cyrene, who later became the Bishop of Ptolemais, was a frequent correspondent, asking for scientific advice. From his letters it appears that she invented the astrolabe, an earlier version of the sextant, and the hydroscope, used in determining the gravity of liquids. Historians including Socrates praised her scholarship and her character.

Scholars not only came to the university, but they visited her at her home, which became an intellectual center in Alexandria. Although she had many suitors, Hypatia never married, claiming that she was "wedded to the truth." She did, however, have several affairs, which led to much speculation over the years, including a rumor that she had been married to Isidorus of Gaza.

As a philosopher she was so well known that letters addressed simply to "The Philosopher" were automatically delivered to her.

Unfortunately, the school of scientific rationalism, neo-Platonism, to which she belonged was considered heretical to Cyril. He had become the patriarch of Alexandria in 412 and inflamed popular opinion against all those opposed to Christian doctrine.

Hypatia became a prominent target of his ire. The public certainly knew who she was. Jealous of her popularity, he proclaimed her a heretic, but his attacks were motivated by secular considerations as well. She was a good friend of Orestes, the prefect of Egypt, Cyril's main political rival. At his urging a crowd of fanatics attacked her in 417 A.D. as she was driving her chariot to the university. After pulling out her hair, they brutally tortured her to death.

Although Orestes tried to get the Roman authorities to investigate her murder, no one was ever charged. Orestes fled Alexandria himself shortly afterward, and efforts to solve the case were foiled by a curious lack of witnesses. Cyril, who would become

St. Cyril, claimed that she was alive in Athens, and the prefect who replaced Orestes finally accepted the official story.

If she had been a Christian, she would have been celebrated as a martyr. But the church canonized Cyril, while Hypatia's contributions to mathematics and science were obscured by her tragic early death. According to Carl Boyer in his *History of Mathematics* (1985), "No other city has been the center of mathematical activity for so long a period as was Alexandria." Many believe that Hypatia's death marked the end of Alexandria as a mathematical center.

Annoyed that Raphael had neglected to include Hypatia in his painting the *School of Athens*, H.J. Mozans paid tribute to her enduring contributions in his book *Women in Science* (1913). Describing her as "the chiefest glory of her sex," he continued: "In profundity of knowledge and variety of attainments she had few peers among her contemporaries and she is entitled to a conspicuous place among such luminaries of science as Ptolemy, Euclid, Apollonius, Diophantus and Hipparchus."

Sydney Johnson

St. Margaret of Scotland

argaret of Scotland, queen and saint, was born in about 1046. Her grandfather had been King Edmund Ironside of England, who lost his kingdom to the Danish invader King Cnut; Cnut is credited with sending Edmund's young sons into exile after his death. Tradition has it that they spent their exile at the royal court of Hungary, where Margaret was born and grew up, daughter of prince Edward the Exile. Her biographer later described her as beautiful, intelligent, and exceptionally devout. She received a good education and a taste for elegant living and beautiful clothes.

Edward's son and Margaret's brother Edgar the Atheling was elected king by the nobles of England after King Harold's death at the Battle of Hastings in 1066, but William the Conqueror was in the stronger position, and Edgar was forced to acknowledge William as king and relinquish his own claim. As the last surviving member of the Anglo-Saxon royal family, he was still a potential focus for disaffection and a threat to William; so in 1067 he fled, with his mother and his sisters, to the court of King Malcolm III of Scotland.

To Margaret, the royal court of Scotland must have come as something of a shock. It was considerably less refined in manners and standard of living than continental courts, and when King Malcolm fell in love with her and declared his intention to marry her, she was initially less than thrilled. There seems little doubt that this was a love match (at least on his side), because as princess of a dispossessed royal family, Margaret could bring no useful political allegiance or a great dowry of lands and income to her husband. Malcolm's own lords tried to dissuade him from marrying her. Margaret herself said that she wished to become a nun. But Malcolm pressured her brother Edgar to persuade Margaret to marry him. As a refugee dependent on Malcolm for protection, Edgar had little choice. So Margaret married the king of Scotland in 1069 or 1070, at Dunfermline, where they later founded an abbey to commemorate the event.

The marriage of the learned, pious English princess and the rough Celtic warrior was unexpectedly happy. Margaret clearly possessed a good deal of quiet determination, and she set about a series of ecclesiastical and domestic reforms that made her widely respected during her own lifetime and led to her canonization after death. The Scottish Church was a Celtic foundation and differed from the Roman Church in various crucial observances. Margaret, with the assistance of two English monks sent her by the Archbishop of Canterbury and the agreement of her husband (who acted as interpreter), held a council for the reform of the Scottish Church. It sat for three days and made new regulations to bring the church more in line with Roman practice.

Margaret's fame rested chiefly on her achievements in traditional female roles—as a wife and mother, as a patron of the church and of the arts, and as a powerful influence at her husband's court rather than a power in her own right. She had great influence over Malcolm, who was rather a rough diamond. He had never learned to read or write and hadn't thought much about religion, but he came to value what she valued. He gave her beautifully bound and decorated books as gifts; one of these, a small Gospel with exquisite miniatures of the Evangelists and illuminated initials, is in the Bodleian library at Oxford. Through Malcolm's respect for her Margaret was able to introduce many English customs to his court. This did not always meet with approval from his chieftains, who respected the ways of their forefathers even if they were lacking in polish. Margaret had eight children, and was very concerned to bring them up well. Her daughter Matilda later married King Henry I of England, and two of her sons, Alexander and David, became outstanding kings of Scotland.

She was personally very devout: she prayed with such intensity as to produce tears; she fasted until she became weak; she was especially concerned to

each side. She excelled at needlework and embroidery and donated several magnificent altar-cloths and ecclesiastical vestments to various religious foundations; she and Malcolm built churches, founded and endowed abbeys, and she rebuilt the ruined abbey of Iona.

Margaret had foreknowledge of her own death, having had a lingering illness which almost completely confined her to bed for six months beforehand. As she was dying her husband and eldest son were killed while on a raid into England against King William Rufus, who had confiscated Edgar Atheling's estates. Her son Edgar wished to protect Margaret from the knowledge of their deaths, but she forced him to tell her before she died, humble and penitent, on November 16, 1093. She and Malcolm were buried beside one another at Dunfermline.

After the usual investigation into her life and miracles, she was canonised in 1250 by Pope Innocent IV and her body "translated" into a beautiful shrine. One of the legends attached to her name says that on this occasion her body became impossibly heavy and could not be carried—Margaret's way of letting her people know that she refused to be moved without her beloved husband.

aid homeless children, feeding them with her own spoon; she regularly washed the feet of the poor (a symbolic rather than strictly useful act, imitating Christ in showing humility); she ransomed Anglo-Saxon prisoners with her own money; she supported numbers of hermits. She paid for the passage of pilgrims across the Firth of Forth at what is now known as Queensferry and built guest houses for them on

Andrea Hopkins

Hildegard of Bingen

Hildegard was a remarkable woman whose powers made her respected beyond any other churchwoman of the middle ages, though she was never canonized. Hildegard was the tenth child of the Count of Spanheim and was destined for a career in the church from an early age. Members of her family had risen to prominence in the church; her aunt Jutta of Spanheim was the abbess of the Benedictine monastery of Disibodenberg. When Hildegard was only eight she became a servitor to an anchoress living near this monastery, where she was educated and which she entered at the age of fourteen. She succeeded her aunt as abbess in 1136.

Hildegard had been experiencing revelations from God since she was about three years old. In 1141 when she was forty-three she reported to her confessor that her health had broken down because she refused a divine command to commit her visions to writing. The confessor sensibly advised her to obey the command, and she began writing her first collection of revelations, *Scivias* (*Scito vias domini, or Know the Ways of the Lord*) with the help of her nuns. This work became so impressive that her confessor informed the archbishop of Mainz about it, and in 1148 a committee of theologians investigated Hildegard and her visions. Hildegard was formally declared to be the recipient of authentic divine revelations, an endorsement which was to have profound consequences for the rest of her life. Scivias was finished in 1152; it consisted of 26 visions, astonishingly bold in concept and scope, moving from creation to judgment day and examining all aspects of human life including the Church, God's relationship with his creatures, and the means of redemption. Hildegard's idea of God's love for his people was radical: she saw this love and the power of creation as an essentially feminine, nurturing, sustaining care. All her writings are characterized by bold ideas, encompassing grand themes and attempting to explain the large mysteries of life. Scivias made her a celebrity; from this time on she was regarded as an authority and consulted on all kinds of matters by both church and secular leaders. She even toured German cities preaching, and explaining her prophetic visions.

In about 1147 a divine vision instructed her to leave Disibodenberg with eighteen of her nuns and found a new convent at Rupertsberg near Bingen. Later in life she wrote to her nuns explaining how she managed to achieve this and to persuade patrons to part with the land and revenues necessary to found new convent.

"Afterwards I returned under God's guidance to Disibodenberg, the community I had left by permission, and I made this proposal to all those living there — that not only our place of residence, but all the real estate attached to it by deed of gift, should not remain with them but should be released to us. In this practical business I was solely concerned with the salvation of our souls and the discipline commanded by our rule.

I then shared with the abbot what I had received in a true vision: 'The bright streaming light speaks: "You ought to be the father over the ghostly care of this spiritual nursery garden for my daughters. The gifts willed to them do not belong to you or to your brothers; on the contrary, your monastery should be your shelter." But if you want to grow stubborn in your opposition and gnash your teeth against us, you…are like the sons of Belial and you have not the justice of God before your eyes. Therefore, God's judgment will destroy you!'

When I, lowly creature that I am, had demanded from the abbot in these words to be made free of the place and to retain the endowments made to my daughters, all of these things, both great and humble, judged favorably of them, so that it was clearly God's will that all this should be legally fixed in writing."

ing publicly. Her reputation was so preeminent that her advice was sought by bishops and princes on secular as well as spiritual matters.

Her surviving writings testify to an extraordinary mind. Hildegard wrote two further books of visions and several saints' lives. She also wrote two scientific treatises, one on medicine and one on natural history, in which she shows both powerful creative imagination and sound scientific thought. She anticipates by centuries several important scientific theories: she suggested that blood circulates around the body, that there is a connection between sugar and diabetics, and that the brain transmits its commands to the body via nerves. She was very well read in the medical theory of her day, but she was able to contribute creative new ideas. She also wrote a symphony, *Symphony armonie celestium revelationum* (*Symphony of the harmony of the Heavenly Revelation*), which consisted of a cycle of seventy-seven songs for performance on the feast days of the Virgin and of local saints. This symphony is still performed and has more creative harmonic variety than most Gregorian chants.

In 1178 at the age of eighty Hildegard became involved in a dispute with local Church officials from Mainz about the burial of a local nobleman in the abbey cemetery. The most serious ecclesiastical sanction, an interdict, was placed on the abbey. As usual, Hildegard went over the bishop's authority and appealed to her archbishop in Rome—by once again referring to the divine authority that assuredly attended

It is clear from this what a formidable weapon the official acceptance of her divine authority had given her. Anything she wanted, if she claimed that she had been instructed to do it as a Divine revelation, had a powerful sanction; anyone who opposed her was thwarting the will of God. Hildegard continued to exploit this unanswerable authority for the rest of her life, successfully opposing the male hierarchy of the established church on several occasions, and always appealing to her status as a confirmed genuine mystic. She had a long and not always amicable correspondence with the great St. Bernard of Clairvaux; she also wrote to secular and religious leaders, fearlessly reproving them for injustice or bad government if she thought they deserved it. She went on tours of major German cities, preaching and teach-

her visions, she persuaded him to lift the interdict and settle the dispute in her favor. Shortly after this Hildegard died, famed and honored. Proceedings to canonize her were begun in 1227 but never completed. She is, however, considered a saint and honored in some local German churches.

Andrea Hopkins

Eleanor of Aquitaine

 leanor was one of the outstanding personalities of the twelfth century: a great noblewoman, an enthusiastic patron of the arts, an indefatigable politician and power broker.

She was the granddaughter of the famous Duke William IX, crusader and troubadour. In 1115 William defied both religious and secular authorities by carrying off Dangereuse, the Viscountess of Chatellerault. His passion was reciprocated and she remained at his court; his wife Philippa retired, outraged, to the Abbey of Fontevrault. Though they could never marry (William had already been excommunicated for other offenses, but his sentence was extended by this crime), they allied themselves as closely as they could by marrying Dangereuse's daughter Aenor to William's eldest son in 1121. Eleanor (originally Alia-Aenor, the other Aenor) was born the following year.

Eleanor was born to wealth and high estate, but her importance increased many times on the death of her brother William and her mother in 1130. Suddenly Eleanor was the heiress of the regions of Poitou, Aquitaine, and Gascony— almost one third of France. Her father showed no hurry to remarry and beget a male heir. He made one attempt in 1136 but was thwarted when Count William of Angoulême abducted and married the lady. The following year, nervous and depressed, William made a pilgrimage to the shrine of St. James at Compostella in Spain; there he was taken ill and died on Good Friday 1137.

Before leaving he had made arrangements with King Louis the Fat of France (Louis VI) to marry Eleanor to his eldest son Louis. The marriage was hastily celebrated on July 25; only one week later Louis VI died, and sixteen-year-old Louis and fifteen-year-old Eleanor became the king and queen of France.

The marriage was not a success. Eleanor, spirited, educated, and beautiful, was disappointed in her gentle, pious husband who, until the death of his elder brother Philippe, had intended to join the Church. Louis was often guided by his mother, the formidable dowager Queen Adelaide, and Abbot Suger of Saint-Denis, the most eminent churchman in Paris. Eleanor was not without influence, however. Louis was very fond of her, at least initially. She imported courtiers, troubadours, minstrels, and musicians from the gayer courts of the South to the grim royal palace and permanently changed its culture. Eleanor also compelled Louis to assert her claim to Toulouse, to which her father's mother Philippa had been the heiress. The present Count Raymond, in possession of the fief, proved impossible to dislodge, however.

Eleanor and Louis had no children for eight years, but in 1145 Eleanor gave birth to a daughter, Marie. Later that same year she and Louis committed themselves to the ill-fated Second Crusade, which was then being preached by the great Bernard of Clairvaux. It was not unusual for women to accompany their husbands on crusade; a crusade was a kind of pilgrimage, as each crusader took a vow to worship in the Church of the Holy Sepulchre (even if this meant conquering Jerusalem first). Several noble ladies followed Eleanor's example, and this gave rise to a later legend that she armed herself and them in the guise of Amazons. The crusaders set off to reach the Holy Land overland in June 1147.

While Eleanor and Louis were being lavishly entertained in Constantinople by Emperor Manuel Comnenus, the German army of their ally, the Holy Roman Emperor Conrad, was annihilated at the disastrous battle of Dorylaeum. Inadequate supplies, bad leadership, and constant harassment from their Turkish enemies slowed Louis's army in its perilous advance towards Antioch. Eventually they reached it by sea in March 1148. Prince Raymond of Antioch was Eleanor's uncle. Raymond was tall, handsome, virile, and only eight years older than Eleanor. She had known him from her childhood and was delighted to be welcomed to a civilized court that reminded her of her home. Whether or not she and Raymond ever formed an improper liaison, their undoubted affection and intimacy made Louis passionately jealous and caused a massive scandal.

Eleanor refused to accompany Louis on his journey and asked for a divorce on the grounds that they were too closely related to one another, and that God's displeasure was manifested by their having had only one daughter in their eleven years of marriage. Louis responded by abducting Eleanor from Raymond's palace prior to a hasty departure. A long stay at Jerusalem followed, marked by only one abortive and costly military action, an ill-timed siege of Damascus that ended in a rout of the crusaders. In April 1149 the sad remnants of Louis's army embarked for home in only two ships. Eleanor sailed in one and Louis in the other.

On the way home from the failed crusade, Louis and Eleanor visited Pope Eugenius at Tusculum to consult him about their marital difficulties. The pope declared that the marriage was legal and must at all costs be preserved, and even went to the length of personally escorting the estranged couple to bed. Perhaps his advice did have some effect, for Eleanor became pregnant soon afterwards; but once again she gave birth to a girl, Alice. This was a piece of luck for Eleanor because it lent strength to the idea of a divorce. Eleanor was now twenty-eight years old, and it was thought unlikely that she was capable of bearing a son. In March 1152 a church council presided over by the Archbishop of Rheims declared the marriage dissolved. According to the settlement agreed at this council, Eleanor retained her territories and Louis retained the children.

Both parties had the right to remarry. Eleanor took advantage of this provision with extraordinary speed. Europe was scandalized when she married the young Duke of Normandy, Henry Plantagenet, less than eight weeks after the annulment of her marriage. Not only was Henry eleven years her junior, but he was more closely related to her than Louis. Louis, predictably, was furious, and invaded Normandy in the

company of other nobles angered by the marriage; but they were no match for the energetic young duke. The following year Henry invaded England. His mother, the Empress Matilda, was the legitimate queen of England and had been waging a civil war against the usurping King Stephen for almost twenty years. Fortune favored Henry, and after the death of Stephen's son Eustace, Henry was declared heir to the English throne. The same year, Eleanor gave birth to a son. King Stephen died in 1154, and Henry and Eleanor became king and queen of the biggest empire in Europe. The early years of their marriage seem to have been reasonably happy. They ruled jointly, though they were often apart for long periods of traveling around their huge domains. Eleanor bore the virile Henry eight children (of which five were sons) in twelve years, finishing up with John in 1166, when she was forty-four years old. She spent much of her time in France as Henry's regent, traveling through her lands of Poitou and Aquitaine and Henry's of Anjou and Normandy. She still had not forgotten her claim to the county of Toulouse and persuaded Henry to attack it in 1159. Most of her time was spent in her beloved Aquitaine, where she formed once again a court famed for its brilliance, attracting the most accomplished poets, troubadours, and musicians.

As the years passed Eleanor and Henry began to lead increasingly separate lives, and Eleanor began to focus her energies on her children. Henry fell in love with his mistress Rosamund Clifford, and Eleanor gathered her children (except John, whom she seems not to have liked very much) around her at Poitiers. There she was joined in 1170 by the daughter she had scarcely known—Marie, now Countess of Champagne and a notable literary patron in her own right. Together they presided over a court culture of unrivaled sophistication which would influence the literary tastes of western Europe for centuries to come.

As Eleanor identified more and more with the interests of her children, she came into conflict with Henry. She persuaded him to invest her favorite son Richard with the duchy of Aquitaine in 1170, but generally her desire to give her sons territories and responsibilities of their own conflicted with Henry's to consolidate authority in the hands of the central monarchy. This policy of Henry's rankled particularly with his oldest surviving son, Henry. He was crowned as Henry the Young King in 1170 but had no real power, and it is clear that Eleanor helped and encouraged the young Henry, Richard, and Geoffrey to rebel against their father in 1173.

He did not forgive Eleanor and kept her a virtual prisoner until his death sixteen years later. The Young King had died prematurely in 1183; Richard continued to plague his father with rebellions and reconciliations until Henry's famous energy was exhausted, and he died, aged only fifty-five, in 1189.

Eleanor was almost seventy years old when she was released from custody in Salisbury castle, but she leapt into action with all the energy and enthusiasm of her younger days, promoting the interests of the absent Richard by touring England collecting oaths of allegiance in his name. She also issued an amnesty for all prisoners at this time. When Richard was held hostage by Duke Leopold of Austria in 1193, it was Eleanor who actively prevented John and Philip-Augustus of France from invading the country, and she (not Robin Hood) supervised the collection and delivery of Richard's ransom money, on his own instructions. She was also very active in promoting the interests of her family by marriage; in 1200, after seeing that John was reconciled with Philip-Augustus and recognized as king of England, she traveled all the way to Castile to bring back her granddaughter Blanche as a bride for Philip's son Louis, the future Louis VIII.

Exhausted by this journey, she retired temporarily to her favorite abbey of Fontevrault, but was obliged to come out again in 1202 when war broke out between John and Philip. Eleanor was attempting to secure Aquitaine and was staying in the poorly defended castle of Mirebeau when she was suddenly besieged by John's archenemies Arthur of Brittany and Hugh de Lusignan. All seemed lost, but John made a forced march overnight to come to her rescue, capturing all the besieging force with scarcely a man lost on his own side. This experience seems to have been a profound shock to Eleanor, and she retired once again to Fontevrault, where she died two years later on April 1, 1204. She was buried in the Abbey, between her husband King Henry II and her son Richard Coeur de Lion.

Andrea Hopkins

Christine de Pisan

Christine de Pisan was the only known professional author in medieval Europe who was a woman. She was a celebrated writer in her day, although her work was somewhat neglected until interest in feminist studies revived her importance.

Christine was born in Venice in 1364. Her father, Tomaso de Pizzano, was a physician and astrologer who advised the government of Venice. He became so famous that both Louis I of Hungary and Charles V of France invited him to visit their courts. He decided to go to France, attracted by the intellectual splendors of the University of Paris and the reputation of King Charles for wisdom and learning. Charles found his new physician/astrologer so indispensable that he refused to let him leave and insisted that he stay per-

manently in France and bring his family from Italy. Christine recorded in her autobiographical *Vision of Christine* how she was presented at the Louvre Palace to Charles V as a child of five, bundled up in her strange, Italian clothes. She never left France.

She received an excellent education and could read both French and Italian, and possibly Latin as well. Her father was a great success at court, and Charles V came to rely on him not only as physician and astrologer but also as an adviser on matters of policy and affairs of state. In addition to his salary as court astrologer, Tomaso received many valuable gifts from the king, including annuities and property. Tomaso's position at court made Christine a desirable match, and he selected a husband for her carefully. His choice fell on Étienne du Castel, a young gentleman from Picardy who had a post as court secretary.

Christine was married to him in 1380 at the age of fifteen; the marriage was an exceptionally happy one. Unfortunately for the de Pisans, King Charles V died later that year at the early age of forty-four. Most of the lucrative annuities Tomaso received depended on the personal patronage of the king, and the new king discontinued them. Tomaso still received a salary for his post as court astrologer, but it was much reduced (as was Étienne's); when Tomaso died after a long illness he left debts behind him.

Étienne died too, very suddenly, in the autumn of 1390, leaving Christine a widow at twenty-five with three small children, a niece, and her mother to support. Even the small amount to be inherited from Étienne was the subject of dispute, and Christine was involved in a series of lawsuits to defend her property. Loyalty and responsibility to her family prevented Christine from entering a convent and possibly also from remarrying. She decided to try to earn a living as a writer, and applied herself to a course of training in history, science, and poetry. She began by writing love poems, songs, and ballads around 1393. These were very well received and she was encouraged to continue. By the late 1390s she was earning her living as a writer.

Part of the reason we know so much about Christine de Pisan is that many of her works contain autobiographical details, something quite rare among medieval writers. Her major works began with her long poem *The Changes of Fortune*, in which she used examples from her own life as well as those of more famous characters to show how fortune can cast down the prosperous and raise up the humble. She followed the contemporary fashion for allegory with *The Epistles of Othea*, a collection of ninety-nine allegorical tales each with its own interpretation. She wrote *The Road of Long Study* next, and by 1404 had achieved such renown that she was invited by Philip the Bold, duke of Burgundy, to write a biography of his dead brother, King Charles V. This she did triumphantly: *The Book of the Deeds and Good Manners of the Wise King Charles V* is an invaluable if somewhat flattering first-hand account of the king and his court. She followed this with the autobiographical *Vision of Christine*, written in 1405.

This volume was partly written to silence her critics, for Christine had become involved in one of the

of the City of Ladies (1405), a collection of stories about heroines of the past, and *The Book of the Three Virtues* (also known as *The Treasury of the City of Ladies*) (1406), a manual of instruction for women in all walks of life on how to be virtuous and happy.

Christine was patronized by some of the greatest lords and ladies of medieval Europe, including the Dukes of Burgundy, Berry, Brabant, and Limburg, King Charles VI, and especially his wife Queen Isabella of Bavaria. Christine concerned herself with serious topics as well. Devoted to France, she was horrified by the civil strife that broke out after the assassination of Louis of Orléans, and wrote *Lamentations on the Civil War* in 1410. She also dealt with topics more traditionally handled by men in her *Book of Feats of Arms and Chivalry*, which was later one of the first books to be printed in English.

most heated literary debates of the day. The great majority of writing in the middle ages was done by men, and much of it was openly misogynistic. One of the greatest successes of the previous century had been the allegorical poem *The Romance of the Rose*, begun by Guillaume de Loris and completed by Jean de Meun. In the latter's hands the poem ceased to be a delicate exploration of how to win a woman's affection and became a much more cynical account of seduction. Christine contributed to the controversy (whether or not de Meun's work was slanderous or true) with her poem "Letter to the God of Love" in 1399, daringly and wittily defending the reputation of women from de Meun's scurrilous satire. The debate between Christine and two opposing camps of clerical writers went on for three years, and Christine soon found herself the foremost apologist of feminine virtue, writing her most famous works *The Book*

With the renewal of hostilities with England in the second phase of the Hundred Years' War, she was devastated by the disastrous Battle of Agincourt in 1415, and in 1418 she retired to live in a convent. Only a few short prayers survive from the years between 1418 and 1429, when she took up her pen once more to write the joyful *Hymn to Joan of Arc*, inspired by Joan's early victories. Here was a woman worthy of Christine's ideals—an exemplar of feminine heroism, working to achieve stability in France. After 1429 we know nothing more; the date and place of Christine's death are not recorded.

Andrea Hopkins

Joan of Arc

Joan of Arc, patriotic heroine, visionary, military figurehead, and saint, was a most extraordinary person. To understand her significance it is necessary to take a brief look at the situation in France at the time when she came to prominence in 1429. The king, Charles VI, had become insane in 1392 and thereafter had only periods of lucidity. His cousins, the dukes of Burgundy and Orléans, were each as wealthy and powerful as the king, and their sons became mortal enemies whose power struggles made France vulnerable to English invaders. This was the last phase of the Hundred Years' War, when powerful commanders were consolidating King Henry V of England's victories in the name of his infant son

Henry VI. The English controlled most of northwestern France and much of the south. Philip the Good, duke of Burgundy, had allied himself with the English and supported little king Henry's claim to the throne of France.

Charles VI died in 1422, and Charles VII had himself crowned king; but by the Treaty of Troyes (1420) both his parents recognized Henry as the rightful heir. His mother, the infamous Queen Isabella of Bavaria, was enjoying the protection of the Duke of Burgundy and had no hesitation in declaring her own son to be illegitimate. Burgundy held Paris, and Charles, supported by Dunois, the illegitimate half brother of the Duke of Orléans (Orléans himself had been taken prisoner at the Battle of Agincourt and was to remain unransomed in England for twenty-five years), held a much weaker position with a makeshift court at Mehun-sur-Yèvre. The English seemed invincible, and the cause of France hopeless.

At this point Joan came on the scene. For years there had been rumors of a prophecy that after an evil woman had betrayed France to her enemies (Isabella, presumably), the country would be saved by a pure maid from Lorraine. Joan's appearance therefore fulfilled popular expectations. Joan's family was a reasonably well-to-do peasant family, living in the village of Domrémy in Lorraine. She had three brothers, Jacques, Jean, and Philippe, and a sister, Catherine. She was never taught to read and write, but she was very religious from her early childhood and familiar with the popular legends of the saints. She was also strong, healthy, and athletic; later eyewitnesses attest to her robust physique. From the age of thirteen Joan had heard supernatural "voices," which she later identified as those of Saint Margaret, Saint Catherine, and Saint Michael the Archangel.

At first these heavenly voices only told her to be a good girl and go to church, but soon they began to tell her that she was destined to be God's instrument in saving France from the English. Joan understood that she was to dedicate her life to this purpose and

her to the captain; but Baudricourt was not impressed, and sent her home again with a message that her father should give her a good spanking. Then the English went on an offensive and began taking towns and villages in the Meuse valley; Domrémy itself was sacked and burned; Vaucouleurs was the last outpost loyal to the French crown. In January 1429 Joan returned. In the atmosphere of fear and doubt her calm conviction won her two devoted supporters—Jean de Metz and Bertrand de Poulengy—and Baudricourt himself, unsure of whether this strange girl was really sent by God to save the French or a lunatic, allowed these two men at arms and four archers to accompany her to Chinon to meet the Dauphin. At this point Joan began to dress in men's clothes—obviously for safety on the journey. This seemed much more shockingly unnatural in the fifteenth century than it does today, and one of the repeated accusations against her at her trial was that contrary to the laws of nature and modesty, she had assumed male attire.

This journey of over three hundred miles, partly through enemy-held territory, was accomplished in eleven days. At Chinon there was a delay while the Dauphin decided whether or not he should see her. When at last she was admitted to his audience chamber her passionate conviction assured the majority of the court that she was indeed "the Maid" (La Pucelle) chosen by God to save France. An eyewitness later testified that "she went up to the king with great humility and simplicity like a poor shepherd girl" and with a trembling voice said, "Most illustrious Sire Dauphin, I have come and God has sent me to bring help to the kingdom and to you." The Dauphin believed her but wise caution prompted him to have her examined carefully by a panel of prominent religious leaders. Accordingly, she went to Poitiers and her claims were thoroughly investigated by the Archbishop Regnault of Rheims, the bishop of Poitiers, the inquisitor of Toulouse, a professor of theology from the University of Paris, and numerous others. This was the first of three very detailed investigations of her life, her character, and her divine revelations. It was very important to be sure that Joan was divinely inspired and not deluded by the devil. The committee at Poitiers decided in her favor. She also submitted to a physical examination to determine whether she was really a virgin—this was carried out by the Dauphin's

voluntarily made a vow of chastity. She acquired at this time a reputation for piety for the length of time and intensity with which she prayed in church. All witnesses agree, however, that she was stolid, sober, and unhysterical.

Joan gradually came to identify her mission of saving France as having two focal points: first, the Dauphin must be crowned king at Rheims, and second, the besieged city of Orléans must be relieved and the English driven out. Her voices told her that she must fight for France, although she protested that she was only a girl and could neither ride nor fight. The voices persisted that if she trusted in God she would be able to do all that was necessary. She must "go to France" (Lorraine was part of the German empire at this time); and she must lead the Dauphin to Rheims, the traditional coronation place of French kings, to be crowned. Finally, the voices instructed her to go to the king's representative in the district, the captain Robert de Baudricourt, at Vaucouleurs, who would provide her with an escort to the Dauphin. She made one attempt in May 1428, persuading her mother's cousin to bring

mother-in-law Queen Yolande of Sicily and her ladies. Joan's mission was then officially endorsed by the King's Council.

It speaks volumes for the power of her personality that Joan managed not only to convince the soldiers in the army and the common people of France (who were after all just waiting for "the Maid" to appear) but the king's chief military commanders, Dunois and the Duke d'Alençon, who were intelligent, hardened, even somewhat cynical men. The soldiers took fire from her conviction, and a string of successful military engagements followed. First, as promised, she raised the siege of Orléans. Joan was given splendid white armor, a banner bearing the cross of Lorraine (later adopted by de Gaulle during World War II as the badge of the Free French), and a war-horse. A witness wrote that "she bears the weight and burden of armor incredibly well"—men trained for years to be fit enough to ride and fight wearing armor. Many others testified that she was fearless leading her men into battle. The army arrived at Orléans in the evening, and Joan rode into the town with Dunois on her left at the head of their troops, in full armor, carrying banners; they were received with joyful enthusiasm by the townspeople, who regarded her as their savior. Dunois then returned to Blois to fetch reinforcements, and on May 4 Joan took part in her first battle.

The English were not in a very good position; a force of about five thousand men were spread out around the city walls, concentrated inside small makeshift forts called redoubts. They weren't able to prevent the French from entering and leaving Orléans, and their blockade of supplies via the Loire, which cut their forces in two, was not efficient either. Joan played a critical part in capturing the series of redoubts in early May, because her confidence and energy inspired the French soldiers to act decisively in a

way in which their cautious commanders did not. During the attack on the redoubt of Les Tourelles Joan was wounded in the neck by an arrow, but after field treatment returned to the front line; the soldiers who had lost confidence when they thought her dead attacked with new courage and took the redoubt. It was the decisive action of the relief, and Dunois himself attributed it to the intervention of the Maid, who had persuaded him to renew the attack when he had been on the point of calling it off. The day after this the English army withdrew; Orléans was liberated. This pattern was repeated in successive engagements; the French soldiers fought with new energy and confidence, while the English soldiers were demoralized and plainly terrified of the Maid's supposed supernatural powers. The towns of Jargeau, Meung, and Beaugency were captured from the English in rapid succession; the Duke of Suffolk was captured and his army destroyed. The English commanders Talbot and Fastolf were approaching with a new army from Paris; the French engaged them at the Battle of Patay and won a decisive victory. Again Joan was later credited with persuading the cavalry commander La Hire to make a charge against the English archers before they had succeeded in erecting a defensive line of stakes— a case where he who hesitated would indeed have been lost. This is not necessarily a sign of great military genius in Joan, as all her recorded words are in favor

of immediate action, as opposed to the waiting game so often favored by the commanders. The cavalry had favorable conditions to mount a devastating charge, and the English were destroyed before they could get off a single shot. Talbot was taken prisoner, and Fastolf fled ignominiously to Paris while his army was butchered behind him.

If the French had chosen to follow up this advantage and march on Paris at once, history might have been very different; but instead it was decided to move to Rheims and crown the Dauphin in the Abbey of Saint Rémy. This area belonged to the Burgundians, but because the towns were considered loyal they had not been garrisoned with English soldiers; one after another they yielded to the French almost without a blow being struck, such was their awe at Joan's achievements and reputation; Troyes, Châlons, and Rheims itself opened their gates in July 1429. Charles was crowned in Rheims, and the momentum continued with the towns of Soissons, Laon, Compiègne, Senlis, Beauvais, and Creil changing their allegiance. Then the regent Duke of Bedford received reinforcements from England, and the French commanders had another attack of caution; a period of inactivity followed, during which Joan unwisely persuaded some French commanders to make a raid on Paris. This was a failure, and Joan herself was wounded again, which injured her reputation. She played no further part in the progress of the war from a military point of view. In March 1430 she again led a small force of volunteers to relieve the town of Compiègne which was being besieged by an Anglo-Burgundian force; on May 23 she was surrounded and captured.

The Burgundian commander, Jean de Luxembourg, set her ransom at ten thousand gold crowns — a phenomenal sum for that time — and when King Charles

made no attempt to pay it, he handed her over to the English. Joan made two unsuccessful attempts to escape when she heard what was planned, in one of which she dropped sixty feet from a tower window without injury. The Duke of Bedford permitted her to be handed over to the Church for examination; all the inquisitors and judges were selected by Bedford; learned theologians from the University of Paris and ecclesiastics loyal to Burgundy or to England, they were all hostile to Joan. The chief judge was Pierre Cauchon, bishop of Beauvais, who led an investigation and trial that was scandalous for its illegality even at the time, but it was certainly a genuine expression of outrage at what Joan had done.

Aside from their horror at Joan's unnatural and unfeminine behavior, these clerics committed to the Anglo-Burgundian cause were enraged by Joan's explicit connection of her divine revelations to her political goal. It was completely unthinkable to them that what she claimed could be true — that God was really on the side of the French and against the English. It was therefore very important to them to discredit Joan, and they concentrated on trying to break her down and make it appear that she was a witch — demonically and not divinely inspired, a heretic, a schismatic, a blasphemer.

Joan's conduct during this ordeal was truly heroic. She spoke with straightforward candor to her accusers, just as she had when addressing dukes and counts at the height of her acclaim; she refused to be intimidated even though she was kept in appalling conditions and had no one to help or counsel her. Her prison was a room in one of the towers of Rouen castle; here she was kept chained at the neck, wrist, and ankle, attached to a block of wood, and allowed no privacy. Her warders were five English soldiers who habitually abused and assaulted her. In court she was continually interrogated by panels of inquisitors, all hostile to her, all well versed in the skills of dialectic, hoping to trip her into betraying herself. On more than one occasion, they threatened her with torture, but when Cauchon seriously moved that it should be tried, he was fortunately outvoted by his fellow judges. In all, the nineteen-year-old Joan was pitted against the combined forces of sixty priors, bishops, and canons for a period of almost a year, and it is a great tribute to her that they did not succeed in breaking her will until almost the end of that time.

In May 1431 Joan was finally badgered into "signing" (making a cross, since she could not write) a recantation. She was taken to the cemetary of the abbey of St. Ouen, where the pyre for her execution had been constructed; and here she seems to have experienced her first doubts. She said that she would submit to the Church's authority and agree with what they wanted her to say; she was then presented with a document listing a shortened version of the twelve main charges against her, including a confession that she had lied in claiming that she had been visited by angels and by Saints Margaret and Catherine. It seems clear that Joan believed that by doing this she would be removed from English custody and spend the rest of her life in a church prison doing penance and praying; this was what Cauchon had promised. But instead she was taken back to her old prison with its English soldiers. Her head was shaved, she was given women's clothes to wear (all through the trial she had insisted on retaining her male clothing), and she was chained up again. Three days later she had reverted to her men's clothes. The soldiers had assaulted her again and badly beaten her, but she was clear in her mind that her recantation was wrong, so she withdrew it. She explained that her voices had told her that it was wrong for her to deny them and to say that her previous inspired actions had been the devil's work. She knew the consequences of her words: "If I say that God sent me, I shall be condemned, but God really did send me." This was all Cauchon needed.

On May 30 Joan was dressed in a long white shift and a mitre-shaped hat bearing the words "Heretic, Relapsed, Apostate, Idolater." She was taken on a cart to the Old Market square in Rouen. There an enormous pyre and stake had been constructed. Joan was permitted to pray for half an hour after the sentence had been read. She asked for a crucifix, and an English soldier bound two sticks together and placed it in her hands. She put it inside her shift, then begged that another crucifix should be brought from the church and held up in front of her so that she could see it as long as she lived. She was bound to the stake and the pyre was ignited. Despite the previous enthusiasm of the crowd, many now wept, including the judges. Eyewitnesses agreed that Joan did not scream or groan, but continued to pray and to call on Jesus from the midst of the flames until she died. This made a deep impression on the crowd, and many were convinced that they had killed a genuine holy woman.

Just over twenty years later the Hundred Years' War ended for good with the battle of Chatillon. King Charles had begun a new investigation in 1449, with the intention of overturning the verdict of Joan's trial. It was important that someone who had been closely associated with his rise to power and the success of the war should be cleared of the disgraceful charges of sorcery, heresy, and blasphemy. In November 1455 a new Trial of Rehabilitation opened and took evidence from over one hundred and fifty witnesses who had known Joan, fought with her, or seen her in action. Not surprisingly, it found that the previous trial had been invalid on legal grounds, but even if it had not, its conclusions were false because Joan was clearly a true Christian of exemplary piety. The new trial did not pronounce on whether Joan's visions were genuine, but historically it is clear that Joan's contribution to the war effort was decisive precisely because she convinced the French that they were morally in the right and that God was on their side.

In the nineteenth century Joan's reputation grew and a movement was begun to have her canonized. Not for having received divine revelations—about which the Church remains tactfully quiet—but for her piety, purity, her selfless dedication to God's will, her bravery in battle, and her still greater bravery during her terrible martyrdom. Joan was declared a saint on May 9, 1920, by Pope Benedict XV. For the modern age, apart from the consideration of her religious faith, Joan remains an outstanding figure of feminine achievement and a truly inspirational heroine.

Andrea Hopkins

Elizabeth I

The last one thousand years of British sovereignty have seen the coronation of just seven queens among twenty kings. Yet two of the female monarchs, Victoria and Elizabeth I, have lent their names most resoundingly to eras of English history, and did so as much through the power and influence of their personalities as through the cultural circumstances that prevailed during their reign.

When we think of the Elizabethan age, we do so almost romantically: it is recorded as a time of commercial and geographic expansion and artistic expression. The English cultural Renaissance flowered with such literary blooms as Shakespeare, Edmund Spenser and Ben Jonson, while men of vast political scope — such as Francis Drake and Walter Raleigh (whatever one may think of their privateering exploits) — bestrode the nation.

Yet when Elizabeth inherited the kingdom in 1588 at the age of twenty-five it was burdened with colossal foreign debts and torn with the religious strife caused by the persecution of Protestants during the five-year reign of her Catholic half sister, Mary. It even appeared that Spain and France had more robust claims to the throne than Elizabeth, whose title was uncertain. For the transformation of this beleaguered province into the international power England became at the time of her death, we must look to the character and powerful impetus of its queen.

For the first twenty-five years of her life it often seemed unlikely that she would survive, let alone reign. Her mother, Ann Boleyn, had been executed for adultery by her father, Henry VIII, when the infant Elizabeth was not yet three years of age. Henry, intent on producing a male heir, had tried to deprive his young daughter of her rights of succession. After her

father's death and during the reigns of her sickly half brother Edward VI and half sister Mary Tudor, she was surrounded by plot, intrigue, and danger. A harmless affair with Admiral Seymour when she was fifteen cost her lover his life and enveloped her in a scandal that must have caused her to subdue thereafter whatever natural passion she had allowed herself to express. And when she was imprisoned in the Tower of London for her alleged plot in the Wyatt Rebellion against Mary, she lived under constant threat of the axe.

So although the young princess who acceded to the throne, described as "comely rather than handsome," with fair hair, fine eyes, and delicate olive complexion, might have seemed of delicate mettle to her subjects, her natural talents, inclinations, and dreams had been tempered in a crucible of bitter experience that had forced her to learn quickly the arts of prudence, self-repression, and mistrust. Intelligent and

quick-witted she undoubtedly was (she spoke French and Italian as well as English, in addition to Latin and Greek), but she also had had to learn to survive, to pit her wits against her enemies and had acquired a worldly wisdom beyond her years—especially in her ability to interpret her subjects' aspirations and those of her court. Inexperienced in statesmanship she may well have been, but there can be no doubt that she had every attribute of a monarch.

The most significant achievement of the first year of her reign was to establish the Act of Supremacy enforcing Protestantism by law. This was no makepeace measure to attempt to heal the wounds caused by Mary's ruthless enforcement of Catholicism (for which she was dubbed Bloody Mary), but was both an act of courage and politically astute. In so doing she began a process of alienation of Catholic Spain whose king, Philip II, had been married to Mary and now sought Elizabeth's hand.

It is no small mark of her courage and independence that she never sought the safe harbor of a foreign marriage (and therefore potentially a joining and strengthening of forces) but preferred instead to use her spinsterhood and marriage potential as a sort of pawn in an international game which she almost invariably won. There is no doubt that the Virgin Queen was none such and that she had her affections and *amours* (the Earls of Leicester and of Essex to name but two), but she recognized that even an English husband would have limited her regal scope, and in this she did not wish to be compromised.

In short, Elizabeth was more likely to conquer than to woo, and chose to extend and strengthen her kingdom through colonial expansion rather than by means of an expedient marriage. It is impossible to condone the policy of those sixteenth- and seventeenth-century European monarchs who plundered the Caribbean and the so-called New World in expeditions dubbed explorative and glorious which were little more than privateering. But one cannot resist harboring a sneaking admiration for the young queen who first snubbed the king of Spain's offer of marriage, then sent her rough sea captains to plunder and antagonize his ill-gotten territories and defeat the huge Armada warships he sent in retaliation.

She was capable of being equally vigorous in her home rule—although she had suffered enough personally at the hands of an autocratic ruler to choose to act with restraint rather than ruthlessness, given a choice. This was the policy she tried to adopt with Mary Stuart, heir presumptive to the thrones of both Scotland and England who, although a tragic figure, was in some measure to blame for her end. Elizabeth, fearing with justification that Mary would eventually lead a rebellion to depose her, kept her imprisoned for eighteen years. Mary Stuart was indeed a thorn in the queen's side, and only her involvement in one conspiracy too many forced the queen to consent to her execution, after much persuasion from parliament (she went into mourning and ordered a public burial for her "kinswoman").

The vigor and courage of Elizabeth's policies at home and abroad are particularly ironic given the determination of her father to beget a male heir. It is true to say that he had virtually precipitated the Reformation in England by divorcing Catherine of Aragon, his wife of twenty years, and marrying Ann Boleyn who he hoped would provide him with a son (after her execution he sought political safety—and doubtless other satisfactions—in five further marriages before dying of syphilis). However, it was to be his fiery young female child, Elizabeth, who would prove his most worthy successor—going one step beyond her father by successfully consolidating her reign through the *avoidance* of marriage.

Elizabeth was a hugely popular monarch in a way our modern minds would find difficult to comprehend. Although this was in some part due to the glorious age she nourished and patronized (it was during her reign that Francis Drake circumnavigated the globe and, though he plundered as he went, it seems that as the first Englishman to perform this feat he was as acclaimed as the queen who had supported him), more significant that this mere achievement was the way she fitted into the Elizabethan world view. This was one of immense orderliness at the center of which was the notion of a fixed hierarchy in which the divinely appointed monarch bestrode both the terrestrial and celestial world with infallible and absolute rule over the mundane and spiritual well-being of his or her subjects.

Elizabeth was bred as well as born to accept this dual authority: although she had little time for metaphysics and the niceties of dogma which, in her experience, she saw led to persecution and dissent, she nevertheless recognized the value of religious stability and believed that the benefits bestowed on her subjects during her reign were the direct result of her sovereignty's divine ordination. Similarly, although she was highly intelligent and exceptionally well read, it was her fostering of a stable society in England rather than her direct patronage of the arts which enabled the great flowering of literature and drama to take place.

At the end of her life much of her power was spent and she had lost, through natural causes or the executioner's axe, many of her closest advisers, lovers, and friends. But she had brought a nation back to life, and the positive effects of her reign were to be felt for many decades to come.

Catherine Mooney

Nzinga Mbande

Nzinga Mbande, Queen of Ndongo and Matamba, African peoples on the frontier of Portuguese colonial expansion in northwestern Angola, balanced leadership in war with diplomacy in a sustained campaign of resistance that eventually forced the invaders to make peace on her terms. Her remarkable life story has inspired her successors and is the basis for many legends and oral stories throughout Africa.

By the early seventeenth century the Portuguese controlled a large area of the central African coast and the hinterland of what is now Angola, but their position was increasingly threatened by Dutch forces. To the north the Catholic kings of the Kongo, Alvare II and his successor Pedro II, were attempting to reduce their dependence on Portugal by appeals and treaties with the Vatican and its Spanish allies. Portuguese attempts to subdue Angola had begun in 1575, and after nearly forty years of intermittent warfare looked to be on the verge of final success.

Nzinga's father, the ngola (ruler) Kiluanji of the kingdom of Ndongo, had traded peacefully with the Portuguese until 1581 when war broke out over land disputes. Nzinga, one of five children of Kiluanji, was born during this war. Her father was effective in fighting off the Portuguese, but was a tyrant; he was deposed and killed in 1618. His eldest son, though considered illegitimate, became ngola. On taking power the ngola Mbandi killed his main rival, Nzinga's son.

The Ndongo forces were defeated by Portuguese troops and slave traders in alliance with African raiders from the interior. Mbandi was forced to retreat to an island. Nevertheless disruption continued, trade was impossible and the Portuguese governor was instructed to make peace.

Mbandi sent for his sister Nzinga for assistance in dealing with the Portuguese. After the assassination of her son she had moved with her husband and sisters to Matamba, a neighboring territory. The meeting between Nzinga and the Portuguese representative, the new governor of Luanda (pictured here in a con-temporary engraving), produced one of the most powerful stories about Nzinga. The orchestration of her arrival at the meeting held at the governor's residence is a triumph of clever diplomacy: preceded by musicians and accompanied by a retinue of servants, Nzinga did not appear to be anything but a royal diplomat, much less a messenger from a conquered people. Upon entering the chamber she noticed there was only one chair, and that for the governor. She gestured to a serving woman who dropped to her hands and knees to form a seat for Nzinga.

Nzinga negotiated a treaty which restored the kingdom to its 1604 territories in exchange for the return of Portuguese prisoners and help with the slave trade and with efforts to conquer the Jaga. The Jaga were a roving band of cannibals, mostly escaped slaves and criminals. However, Portuguese compliance was delayed as a rebellion by the Kongo led to the dismissal of the governor.

In 1623 the Ndongo king died suddenly on his island refuge, apparently as a result of poisoning, possibly by Nzinga. Nzinga Mbande succeeded her brother to the throne and at once sent messages to the Portuguese capital Luanda demanding that the terms of the treaty be carried out. Dutch attacks, including the burning of six ships in Luanda harbor in June 1624, diverted the attention of Portuguese officials to the coast. Nzinga adopted various strategies to rebuild her army, forming alliances to incorporate groups of raiders (including the Jaga), giving asylum to slaves who escaped Portuguese territory, and luring away African soldiers from the Portuguese forces with offers of land. Although alarmed by the increasing number of vassal chieftains rebelling to join Nzinga, the Portuguese were unable to move against her for a further year. In 1626 the governor provoked Nzinga to attack by proclaiming a Ndongo chief to be the legitimate king and having him crowned as Phillip I of Ndongo. The Portuguese army at Luanda was mobilized to counterattack.

At first the assault was successful. Nzinga's island

stronghold was captured and the new king installed. Nzinga, however, escaped capture and rallied her army with popular support. The Portuguese were obliged to withdraw to protect Luanda from an anticipated Dutch attack, allowing Nzinga to displace Phillip and briefly regain her territories. A second Portuguese invasion, this time aimed primarily at capturing or killing Nzinga, forced her to flee again the following year. She was pursued through the neighboring Matamba kingdom and only escaped by spreading false rumors that she had been killed. Once again, however, Nzinga was able to recover from an apparently disastrous position. By 1630 she had enlisted the help of the ruler of the Jaga raiders with a promise of marriage and used the support of his warriors to take over the Matamba kingdom. From there she harassed the colonists and the Ndongo king, retaking much of her old territory by 1635.

In 1639 emissaries seeking a settlement were sent to Nzinga after the council in Lisbon ruled that Portugal had failed to implement its earlier treaty. Local Portuguese representatives were unwilling to comply with the promised peace so Nzinga continued to disrupt trade with the colony. Just as the governor in Luanda decided to return to all-out war, a renewed assault by the Dutch led to the fall of Luanda in August 1641. Nzinga was the most prominent African ruler in a large-scale alliance with the Dutch which continued to drive back the Portuguese, inflicting a series of defeats over the following years. However, the Dutch were to prove only temporary allies. The final Portuguese stronghold in the region, Masangano, was on the brink of falling in August 1648 when Luanda was recaptured by a large Portuguese fleet sent from Brazil. The Dutch rapidly conceded the area to Portugal and withdrew, leaving their local allies to fight on alone. A massacre of the chiefs in the Luanda region followed their defeat, but, like the Kongo, Nzinga was still strong enough to negotiate a settlement. She dragged out negotiations for eight years before finally agreeing a treaty in which she gave up the western part of her territory but remained independent, escaping the tribute payments imposed on vassal rulers. In the five years of peace before her death in 1663 Nzinga converted to Catholicism and allowed a mission to be established in her capital.

At a time when established order was falling apart in the face of slave trading and repeated colonial invasions and kings were short-lived and kingdoms fragile, Nzinga Mbande ruled her people for forty years, sustaining their resistance against overwhelming odds. Three hundred years later she was revered as a symbol of Angolan independence in their renewed and lengthy fight to overthrow colonial rule.

Denise Clay

Amina Sarauniya Zazzua

Although many queens are remembered in local oral histories throughout western Africa, Amina, a sixteenth-century queen of the region of Zazzua in northern Nigeria now known as Zaria, has become more widely known as an example of female achievement in a predominantly patriarchal society.

Zazzua is one of a small number of competing Hausa city states that dominated central trans-Saharan trade following the collapse of the Songhai empire to the west in the mid-sixteenth century. Shifting patterns of alliance and warfare allowed Zazzua to build up great wealth through the trade of leatherwork, kola, cloth, horses, salt, and imported metals until its conquest by the reformist Islamic jihad of Uthman dan Podio early in the eighteenth century. This conquest imposed orthodox Islamic practices of patrilineal descent and wife seclusion on previously more open societies.

Our knowledge of the reign of Amina is drawn from local historical traditions and later references in Arabic manuscripts. In keeping with the historical practice of the time, these sources are primarily concerned with glorifying the ruler's military victories and have passed on little firm information on most other aspects of her life.

Amina was born during the reign of Sarkin (king) Zazzau Nohir, around 1533. She was probably a granddaughter of the ruler. As we might expect of a future ruler, traditions record that her childhood was different from that of other Hausa princesses. As soon as she was able to she would leave her nurses and crawl into the court, sitting at the king's side as he administered the city. As she grew up she insisted on remaining at the court, learning the skills of its warriors as well as its officials.

After the death of the Sarkin and a short-lived successor, power was apparently seized by Amina's mother, known as Bakwa of Turunku. Bakwa is the only other female ruler recorded by Zazzua tradition but little is known about the circumstances of her accession or the details of her reign. At about the age of sixteen Amina was given the title of Magajiya, or heir apparent, making her responsible for a ward in the city and entitling her to attend daily councils with the other officials. At this period she is supposed to have rejected any marriage offers from suitors including both wealthy Zazzua nobles and the kings of neighboring states. Instead she preferred to train with the warriors, although her mother's reign was noted for its peace and prosperity.

Warfare returned following the death of Bakwa around 1566. The ten-year reign of her younger brother Karama was marked by continual conflict in which Amina emerged as the leading warrior of the Zazzua cavalry. Her military achievements earned her great wealth and power. On the death of Karama Amina was appointed queen. Her reign was dominated by warfare that expanded the domain of Zazzua to its largest extent ever.

Traditions relate that her first military expedition set off three months after her accession and that she continued to fight until her death. At this period military activity was not primarily aimed at establishing permanent occupation of territory. Instead it focused on capturing prisoners and goods, forcing the local rulers to accept vassal status and permit Hausa traders and immigrants safe passage. This often necessitated repeated attack every few years as the intimidatory effect of previous raids wore off. Amina led these raids well beyond the Hausa-speaking region as far as the powerful Nupe kingdom on the Niger river to the southwest and the Kwararafa of the Benue river valley to the southeast. According to Zazzua history she never spent more than three months in succession in her capital, continuing suc-

cessful campaigns against new enemies throughout her thirty-four-year reign.

Amina is regarded as the instigator of the fortified earthen city walls that characterized the Hausa city states since this period. It is reported that wherever she established an army camp she would order the building of a defensive wall. Towns later grew up on the camp sites within these walled areas. Major Hausa cities, including Zazzua, retained these walled defenses until the colonial occupation began early this cen-tury and remains still; known as "ganuwar Amina," Amina's walls can still be seen in many.

Today Amina is seen as both a heroic figure in Nigerian history and an inspirational figure in a cul-ture where womens' aspirations for equal status and political responsibility are frequently opposed by ref-erence to "natural" roles.

Denise Clay

Aphra Behn

Were Aphra Behn the heroine of one of her novels rather than the narrator, readers would hunger for more facts to flesh out the tantalizingly skeletal life story of this extraordinary literary figure. She was the first woman to write prolifically for the English stage, the reputed mistress of the Earl of Rochester, and an erstwhile (if ill-paid) spy in Antwerp. We want to know more than the inscription on the marble slab in Westminster Abbey gives us: "Mrs. Aphra Behn. Died April 16, 1689. *Here lies a proof that wit can never be defence enough against mortality.*"

There are more questions than answers surrounding the part of Aphra's life before her literary work became publicly acclaimed. We are not even sure of the spelling of her name (Aphra, Aphora, Astrea, or Ann?). Several accounts deem her to have been born, in 1640, of fairly lowly parentage in Canterbury, England, but this does not match with the later image of a confident, self-assured woman, exceptionally well schooled in literature and languages (she published translations of French scientific and philosophical works) hobnobbing with aristocrats and royalty, and sure enough of her talents and status to publish some of the most vigorous and biting political poetry of the period.

Only two sets of facts present themselves with any degree of certainty, and fortunately they appear to reveal something useful of the character of the exceptional Mrs. Behn. First, as a young child she probably emigrated to Surinam with her family (her successful novel *Oroônoko* was set there) and married before returning (although it seems her husband was soon discarded, as there is no subsequent mention of him). Secondly, she acted for King Charles II as a spy in Antwerp, although she was not well paid for her endeavors and narrowly escaped ending up in a debtor's prison.

Although these events paint a colorful picture of the early life of the woman who would later wield a pen with such decisive and worldly authority, it is more fair to focus on the achievements of the mature Aphra—something she herself would probably have preferred. After all, during her life she had to rise above both the criticism of those who condemned her writing as "flawed because female" and the false praise of those who tried to marginalize her work (quite inaccurately) as expressing "a delicate understanding of the mysteries of nature, women and love." She was none of this, and did not want to be judged thus. It is only right and fitting that we should value her as she wished to be recognized "for the masculine part, the poet in me…to tread in those successful paths my predecessors have so long thrived in…. If I must not, because of my sex, have this freedom, but that you will usurp all to yourselves; I lay down my quill."

The end of the Puritan epoch and the restoration of the monarchy in England created an atmosphere of libertine living which took its lead from the court. Aphra Behn embraced this way of life; the prefaces to her plays reveal a vigorous, amorous, and convivial woman who enjoyed good company and was acquainted with both the most important people in the newly restored theater (which had been banned during the days of Cromwell) and with the most important intellectuals of her day, including John Dryden.

She wrote at least seventeen bawdy and comic plays which were performed by the Duke's Theatre Company (under royal patronage) and were hugely successful. However, she had to suffer accusations of plagiarism from those who believed that her dramas must have been written by a man, and she recognized that her work would be more greatly appreciated if the audience thought it had been penned by a male hand.

However, what is most heroic about Mrs. Behn is less her considerable talent than a quality of self-awareness and assurance which enabled her to rise above the social precedents of her age and speak with a voice of calm, clear authority on political and social matters. It is impossible to decant her political views into a twentieth-century bottle and expect them to appear unclouded to our modern eyes, but taken within the context of her time, her royalist beliefs in the power of absolute monarchy and her detestation of the rising emphasis on commercial trade as an end in itself was a courageous one. Likewise, her aspiration toward a golden, classical age, sexually and socially liberated, was expressed with an admirable consistency and confidence.

It is probably fair to say that her example is more inspiring to twentieth-century writers than to those of previous centuries. Although many contemporary male dramatists shared her political views and literary achievements, no female author was to soar so high having overcome financial hardship and professional criticism for centuries yet to come. To have done so while enjoying a strong and robust life full of food, wine, pleasure, intelligent conversation, and distinguished lovers is a rare and, let us admit, enviable achievement for a writer of either gender in any age.

Catherine Mooney

Catherine the Great

In January 1744 an obscure young German princess, Sophia of Anhalt-Zerbst, arrived in Moscow. She had been summoned by the empress Elizabeth as a consort for her sickly nephew, the future Tsar Peter III. Slender, dark, fifteen years of age, and precociously intelligent, Sophia was described in contemporary reports as "neither pretty nor plain." Only a particularly firm cast of jawline and mouth gave some indication of the prodigious and purposeful will which was to be so characteristic of the future Empress Catherine the Great.

Her introduction to court life was anything but empowering: her husband was a philanderer (successfully so in spite of the disfigurements of small

pox) and was no intellectual or social match for his bright, bored, young wife. The marriage was probably not consummated, in spite of the fact that a court lady was employed to invigilate over the couple on their wedding night. Empress Elizabeth blamed Catherine, as she was then renamed, for her failure to produce an heir, the principal reason she had been summoned to marry the sickly Peter. But Catherine's mettle was far above that of a mere breeding machine—albeit that of emperors. Vastly ambitious, she recognized that her boorish husband was the key to achieving her aims. She humored him while taking secret lovers to allay her sexual appetite. She had several children by these lovers; her first son, Paul, was borne away in triumph by Elizabeth who was unaware of the child's paternity.

Meanwhile, Catherine espoused the traditions, language, and religion of her adopted country, recognizing rightly that this would be the key to the peoples' deeply conservative hearts. She played a tactical game of allegiance and political maneuvering with such skill that when Peter was deposed shortly after becoming emperor she had apparently played no part in the conspiracies that had overthrown him. Ever the tactician and show-woman, she marched in triumph to St. Petersburg at the head of her army, clad in the uniform of a guard and riding a white charger. Her subsequent coronation was an affair of unprecedented opulence.

It is difficult today to appreciate or admire the power of a female personality which, through sheer willpower and confidence in the scope of its abilities, can shape itself into the most powerful monarch in Europe. Her life had not been without tragedy or difficulty—her early years at court were fraught with danger, and her daughter had died while still an infant—but the strength of her nature fashioned the circumstances of her life into something vast, grand, baroque and, therefore, awe-inspiring.

The driving force in her life was her apparently boundless ambition. Consequently, her actions as

QUEEN CATHERINE'S DREAM.

empress were frequently more façade than substance. She collated a huge work, the *Nakaz*, which was intended to embody and create legislation for the whole of the Russian system of government and to prescribe alleviation for the appalling suffering and slavery of the Russian peasant serfs. The work was of such magnitude that Voltaire, whose friendship Catherine had courted as a means of achieving favorable reports of her empire in Europe, described it as "the most beautiful monument of the century." In practice it proved too cumbersome to implement and became another emblem of her self-aggrandizement: the serfs continued to suffer, ultimately losing more freedom during the course of her reign that they had for some considerable time previously.

A foreigner and a usurper, she had to fight to maintain the position of power that she had achieved through the help of friends who were often her lovers. She is frequently perceived as being a libertine, although her practice was to take lovers sequentially rather than concurrently, first submitting them to a medical examination to check that they were free of venereal disease, then assessing their sexual prowess with the help of a lady-in-waiting. After their services were no longer required, sometimes after a period of some years, these companions were amicably retired to the country with vast wealth and estates. The bestowal of a palace on a lover of Catherine the Great generally signified upheaval at court and the appearance of a new favorite.

She eschewed marriage, not only because her lovers almost universally lacked the qualities she would require in a ruling consort, but because her appetite for power far exceeded her desire for an equal partner; she intended to rule her empire alone. Only one man, Grigory Potemkin, came close to being a match for the empress. She described this extraordinary man as "one of the greatest, the most strange and the most amusing eccentrics of this iron age." Certainly his ability as soldier and administrator added to her renown (Catherine's foreign policy was far more impressive and successful than her home rule). But when the quarrelsome passion of their relationship threatened to impede the harmony of their co-regency, they agreed that Potemkin should remain her partner and co-regent but choose a succession of lovers for her who would be loyal to them both. The arrangement worked and, when Potemkin died some twenty years later, Catherine, by then in her early sixties, never recovered from the loss of her dearest partner and friend.

It is difficult to wholly admire Catherine's achievements in reviving a splendor and opulence in Russian culture considering that the impetus for such display was the vanity of self-promotion, and that the majority of her subjects toiled in slavery. But that can only be part of the story. In the same way that her jewels were celebrated throughout Europe (she wore a crown of diamonds at state events) while in private she dressed simply in a kaftan, Catherine's façade was upheld by a finer and stronger spirit, without which her achievements could not have endured or been so skillfully executed.

Her reign represented a golden age of art and architecture in Russia, and the theater flourished under her patronage. All her life she had had a genuine ambition to be a writer and a dramatist and her literary works alone amount to some twelve large volumes. For all her industry, however, she was devoid of talent, and her real cultural contribution was to introduce new ideas and to foster learning.

This and her foreign policy of expansionism placed a heavy financial burden on her subjects, and inflation soared during her reign. At the time of her death, her subjects had become disenchanted with their glittering empress. She died suddenly on November 6, 1796, still planning to fulfill Potemkin's dreams of reviving the lost kingdom of Byzantium.

Catherine Mooney

Pauline Léon and Claire Lacombe

auline Léon and Claire Lacombe were friends who worked together politically, and for a brief time during the French Revolution they created a political organization of working-class women.

Pauline Léon was born in Paris in 1768, the daughter of a chocolate maker. After her father's death, she ran the chocolate business and enjoyed much more independence than most unmarried women— or married women, of course. At the taking of the Bastille in 1789, she was twenty-one. By 1791 she turns up as a leader of working women rioting against royalist supporters. In March 1791 she was petitioning the government for permission to drill and arm a band of more than three hundred women whose names were attached to the petition. We can locate her at the storming of the Tuileries when the king was finally overthrown.

Claire Lacombe was born in 1765 at Pamiers, a small town on the Ariege river near the Pyrenees and not far from the red brick city of Toulouse. She left home to become an actress and was reasonably successful in the provinces. Exactly when she came to Paris is unclear. In any event, she met Pauline Léon shortly after arriving and they began to work together.

Both women did something considered shocking: they made public speeches. Claire seems to have been the better speaker. She was the one who attracted attention because of her beauty. All actresses were outside the law and the Church, but she particularly aroused malicious gossip. She worked with a number of men politically and was close to the radical worker's priest Jacques Roux, so her name was linked with them, although there is no evidence to suggest Roux had any interest in sex with Claire or with anyone else.

Claire's affairs, however many or few they were, seemed to mean little to her in comparison to friendship and to politics. She lived with the young Enragé Theophile Leclerc for some months, but stepped aside when Pauline fell in love with him. She went on working daily with Pauline and seems to have accepted the new relationship without a fuss, indeed without caring particularly. Pauline and Theophile were married shortly afterward, but only prison separated the friends.

In 1793, they started the Society of Revolutionary

Economic issues were important to them, but they also wanted to vote in local government. Some of them had simply taken that right and done so. They wanted education for their children and for themselves. They wanted the price of bread controlled so they could feed their families. They wanted direct and open democracy.

Their militancy, their arming themselves, and their lack of hesitation in attacking men and their privileges rendered them unpopular among the men in power. Robespierre turned against them and began to consider them dangerous. The market women were stirred up against them and they were suppressed. Soon afterwards, it was legally forbidden for women to meet publicly or to form independent groups. Pauline and Claire were thrown into prison. Women were shoved back out of the political arena. Under Napoleon, women lost most of the rights they had fought for and gained.

To read the attacks upon these women by contemporary legislators is to see the terror they aroused by refusing to behave passively, for they assumed they were full human beings and full citizens, and they believed that the rhetoric of the revolution about equality and freedom applied to them as well as to men.

Pauline and Claire were pushed out of history and back into obscurity. It took many generations of women to begin to achieve what the Revolutionary Republican Women strove for. Pauline Léon and Claire Lacombe are examples of how brave and farsighted women disregarded by society can be, if there is any opening for their abilities.

Marge Piercy

Opposite: a meeting of the Society of Revolutionary Republican Women   Above: Claire Lacombe

Republican Women. It was the first political organization we know of composed only of women, directed by women, its agenda and actions set by women. Its stated aims were to defend the revolution, frustrate the schemes of its enemies including aristocrats and speculators, and demand various political and economic rights for women. During the insurrection of May 31 to June 2, 1793, the Revolutionary Republican Women supported the Mountain (the Jacobin left in the National Convention) against the Girondins. This support took the form of marches, petitions, and direct intimidating action. Unlike other groups composed largely or partly of women, they were not well-to-do. They were not ladies in any sense. They carried pikes and pistols and they were experienced street-fighters. They even invented a kind of uniform for themselves, composed of red trousers, red bonnet, and tricolor ribbon so that they could move more quickly and militantly on their days of action and to give themselves a kind of authority women had never enjoyed.

Mary Wollstonecraft

In 1667 John Milton wrote "Paradise Lost," in which the poet has Eve "with perfect beauty adorn'd," addressing Adam:

My author and disposeer, what thou biddest
Unargued I obey; so God ordains,
God is thy law, thou mine: to know no more
Is woman's happiest knowledge and her praise.

In 1792 Mary Wollstonecraft wrote *A Vindication of the Rights of Woman* in which she set forth what was fallacious about this line of reasoning, applied it to all women and all men, and endeavored ardently to change society.

Mary Wollstonecraft, born in 1759, was a phenomenon of her time: a responsible, caring woman philosopher and writer who perceived that there could be no liberty or happiness for anyone as long as women were ruled by men. In an early work, *Thoughts on the Education of Daughters*, Mary set forth many of her ideas about women, which she continued to develop in her mature work.

Today, browsing through *A Vindication*, one is constantly amazed by the date of publication. Here is a woman, writing in 1792, who believed that society regards women as the property of men; that women are weak and shallow because they have not had the proper education and because men wish to dominate them, desiring only that they be soft and beautiful; that it is as bad for a man's character to be a tyrant as a king and from this tyranny come all the evils of the world; that it is important for boys and girls to have equal training of minds and bodies; that women's perfectibility is the same as man's;.....that women should have the right to vote, to become financially independent, to enter the professions.

Mary's sense of grievance, while certainly appropriate, may well have been fostered by the rather chilly way she was treated by her parents, who favored her older brother Ned. Ned got much more affection than his little sister, and when their grandfather died,

Ned got one-third of his estate; Mary and her two younger sisters received nothing. Mary cared for her mother in her last illness and took responsibility for her two sisters, helping them find work in the only fields open to women: together, they started a school and worked as governesses.

Mary's male mentor, sponsor, friend, and publisher was Joseph Johnson, the center of an intellectual group in London which included the poet Blake, writer Thomas Christie, and Henry Fuseli, an artist and scholar. Johnson rescued Mary from her other occupations and provided her with a structure in which to write. He paid her rent, saw to it her bills were paid, got her a maid, and in general left her free to write, an amazing arrangement for the time, and one that worked out well for both parties. The friendship was real and lasted until the end of Mary's life.

During this time she became an acknowledged writer, and with the publication of *A Vindication of the Rights of Woman* she found herself famous.

Mary was subject to depressions; a contributing cause seems to have been her unsuccessful relationships with men. She felt she was capable of great passion, but like many women who have done and now do pioneering work with feminist concerns, the course of true love did not run smoothly. Mary tended to fall in love, as she did with Henry Fuseli, who was indeed married but an unregenerate flirt, whole-heartedly and unflaggingly, making demands which the object of her affection often would not meet. At one point she rather innocently (but outrageously) demanded to be made a member of Fuseli's household; she needed to see him every day. The request, of course, was summarily dismissed by Sophia, Fuseli's wife.

The French Revolution coincided with this period of Mary's life, and she spent most of 1793 and 1794 in France. Mary's free spirit was stimulated by the freedoms and the ideals of the Revolution, although she was also horrified at the slaughter. When France went to war with England, Mary, continuing to write, stayed on in Paris with a new lover, Gilbert Imlay, with whom she conceived a baby. (And while she was pregnant, wrote a book: *Historical and Moral View of the French Revolution*.) Mary was totally committed to Imlay and for a long time could not recognize that he was not dependable, serious, or responsible. Three months after their daughter Fanny was born, however, he left her. Mary was devastated, the more because their agreed-upon theories gave him (or her) the right to leave the relationship once the feeling was gone. Stoutly, she set out to support her illegitimate child; more and more sadly she contemplated life without him.

Mary's last love, whom she married in 1797 and with whom she had another daughter, was William Godwin. Their courtship is almost amusing, two intellectuals falling all over themselves expressing their love—profound, respectful, and equal, as evidenced in a passage from Godwin's *Memoirs*: "The partiality we conceived for each other, was in that mode, which I have always regarded as the purest and most refined of love... I am not conscious that either party can assume to have been the agent or the patient, the toil-spreader or the prey, in the affair." Godwin understood Mary much better than Imlay or Fuseli and the two settled into an odd but workable relationship wherein they kept separate quarters but shared their evenings. Their daughter was born the same year. Mary did well with the birth; her daughter—who was to become Mary Wollstonecraft Shelley, author of *Frankenstein* (1818)—was fine. Ten days later, however, Mary Wollstonecraft Godwin died at age thirty-seven.

Her clear vision lives on; she is studied in college courses; her works stayed in print long after most of her contemporaries. Reading her now, I wonder how she would have weighed our progress.

Jane Anderson

Susanna Moodie

The century that has elapsed since her death in 1885 has brought new insight into the life and works of English-Canadian writer Susanna Moodie, a pioneer in almost every respect. A Wordsworthian Romantic by education and temperament, she spent most of her life as an immigrant on the Upper Canadian frontier, struggling to reconcile the grandeur and immensity of the natural environment with the relentless toil and tension inherent in frontier life. Her best-known works, *Roughing It in the Bush* (1852) and *Life in the Clearings* (1853), were originally regarded primarily as historical documents, but contemporary critics have focused on their literary value. Indeed, close reading reveals as much about Susanna Moodie the woman and artist as it does about nineteenth-century English Canada.

Born Susanna Strickland in Bungay, Suffolk, in 1803, Moodie moved to Reydon Hall, a mansion near Southwold on the Suffolk coast, at the age of five years. With her brother and four sisters, she was educated by her father in literature, history, nature study, and painting. Five of the six children went on to literary careers, including Agnes and Elizabeth Strickland, authors of *Lives of the Queens of England*, and Catharine Parr Traill, who wrote *The Backwoods of Canada*.

After Moodie's father died in 1818, she and her sisters helped support the family by contributing poetry and children's stories to periodicals. Moodie's first published work was the novel *Spartacus: A Roman Story* (1822), written for young people in the sentimental and didactic vein of the times.

A few years later, she was contributing sketches of Suffolk life to *La belle assemblée*. During this period she became an abolitionist and met her future hus-

band, Dunbar Moodie, a retired British army officer, at the home of poet Thomas Pringle, secretary of the Anti-Slavery Society.

The Moodies married in 1831 and soon experienced financial difficulties in living on the half-pay of a retired soldier, especially when the first of their six children was born in 1832. Emigration to Canada held out the prospect of improved fortune, but Susanna Moodie was devastated by her enforced departure from England, as clearly seen in her introduction to *Roughing It in the Bush*, published twenty years later: "Emigration may, indeed, generally be regarded as an act of severe duty, performed at the expense of personal enjoyment, and accompanied by the sacrifice of those local attachments which stamp the scenes amid which our childhood grew in imperishable characters upon the heart."

The family settled first on a cleared farm in Hamilton Township, in what is now Ontario, but the Moodies did not prosper there, in contrast to others who arrived with more capital or better connections. The continuous influx of new immigrants drove land prices up and wages down. Susanna Moodie was put off by the brash familiarity of "Yankee" settlers who offended her sense of social propriety and by the harsh living conditions she would describe in the sketches and poetry that comprised *Roughing It in the Bush*. In 1834 the Moodies moved to the backwoods settlement of Duoro, near Peterborough, where Susanna's sister Catharine and her brother, Samuel, had settled.

Their attempt at farming failed here, too, and Dunbar Moodie took a position as sheriff of Victoria District in 1840. The family relocated to Belleville, where Susanna Moodie devoted herself to writing for the next fifteen years. During her early years in Canada, she had contributed poems and sketches to such periodicals as the *Canadian Literary Magazine* and the Montreal-based *Literary Garland*. After 1840 she became a leading contributor to the Garland, which published the six Canadian sketches later included in *Roughing It in the Bush*. She and her husband also edited and wrote for the *Victoria Magazine*, a journal intended to educate Canada's working-class people.

In 1852 Moodie signed a contract with the London publisher Richard Bentley, who published the three works describing her immigration and settlement in Canada, the last of which was the autobiographical novel *Flora Lyndsay; or, Passages in an Eventful Life* (1854). Opening upon a young couple's decision to emigrate to Canada, it uses the device of a novel within a novel written by the protagonist en route to the New World. *Flora Lyndsay* is generally considered the weakest of Moodie's three major works. The sketches and poems of the other two books contain astute observations on backwoods and colonial village society, with strong passages reflective of Moodie's romantic response to nature. As Canadian writer Margaret Atwood points out in her book *Survival: A Thematic Guide to Canadian Literature*, Moodie's expectations of nature and her actual experience of it result in the kind of contradiction found in *Roughing It in the Bush*:

> "The aspect of Nature ever did, and I hope ever will, continue 'to shoot marvellous strength into my heart.' As long as we remain true to the Divine Mother, so long will she remain faithful to her suffering children…At that period my love for Canada was a feeling very nearly allied to that which the condemned criminal entertains for his cell—his only hope of escape being through the portals of the grave."

Between the lines of both *Roughing It in the Bush* and *Life in the Clearing* one can read the intensity of Moodie's personal experience and what Margot Northey has called her "long-standing, inward-looking response to her vision of herself as artist." Some critics have argued that she dramatized her vision of herself; others, that she struggled all her life to transcend her "sheltered middle-class veneer." No one has accounted for the long silence that followed publication of the volume of short stories entitled *Matrimonial Speculations* (1854). (It is interesting to note that both this work and the novel that preceded it, *Mark Hurdlestone* (1853), were set in England.) From 1854 Susanna Moodie published nothing until 1868, when the novel *The World Before Them* was published. Although she continued to write for the next twenty years, her life was increasingly marked by illness and poverty until her death in Toronto in 1885. It is only in the last few decades that she has become widely recognized as a significant force in the development of Canadian literature.

Nadine Spencer

Harriet Tubman

Born Araminta Ross in 1820 to Benjamin Ross and Harriet Greene, Harriet Tubman, who adopted her mother's name some years later, was one of eleven children who lived on a slave-breeding plantation owned by Edward Brodas in Bucktown, Maryland. In an autobiography entitled *Harriet Tubman: The Moses of Her People*, Harriet gives an account of her years on the Brodas plantation, and her subsequent escape to freedom.

At the age of seven Harriet began working as a field hand, and by the time she reached eleven years of age had been brutalized by her owner many times. When Harriet was thirteen years old, her skull was fractured with a two-pound weight by an overseer angered by her refusal to help him tie up a slave who had left the field without permission. After awakening from a coma, Harriet discovered that the injury caused extreme dizziness and uncontrollable sleeping spells. At any given moment and without any warning she would fall into a deep sleep from which she could not easily be awakened. Even so, it was Harriet's lot to work as hard as any man in the fields of the Brodas plantation.

Slaves were in constant fear of being sold and separated from their families. Harriet knew well this pain, for she had watched Brodas sell off her two sisters. Now it was her turn. Rumors were spreading that Brodas had plans to sell Harriet and her two brothers to a plantation located in the Deep South. Before this could happen, however, Brodas died. A man named John Stewart took over the plantation and assigned Harriet to the task of working with her father chopping down trees and loading logs for shipment to Baltimore. In 1844 she married a freedman named John Tubman.

Harriet had heard slaves on the plantation talk about an underground railroad that escaped slaves took to freedom. Deep in her heart she longed to be free, and spoke of this longing to her father. Realizing Harriet would never adhere to the rules and protocol of

Harriet Tubman (extreme left) photographed with group of slaves she helped escape

slavery, Benjamin Ross began teaching her how to survive in the woods.

In 1849, after hearing that she had been sold and was to leave the next morning, Harriet decided to go North. Unable to convince John Tubman to join her and afraid that he might reveal her plan, Harriet slipped out while he was asleep, and began her trek to freedom with her two brothers. Her brothers became fearful and turned back, so Harriet made the trip alone. She traveled by night and hid in the woods by day. When she finally reached Pennsylvania, Harriet recounts, "I looked at my hands to see if I was the same person.... I felt like I was in heaven."

With a strong and unwavering faith in God and the help of free blacks and sympathetic whites who were conductors on the Underground Railroad, Harriet would make this trip nineteen more times and successfully lead more than three hundred slaves, including her family, to freedom. There was a forty-thousand-dollar bounty for her capture, and she continued to suffer from sleeping spells, but she kept on in spite of these things. In 1858, when the Fugitive Slave Law was passed making it legal for slave catchers to enter Northern cities, capture runaway slaves,

and return them to their owners, Harriet was not deterred. She led her charges to the borders of Canada. "I never ran my train off the track, and I never lost a passenger." So began the legend of "Black Moses."

During the Civil War Harriet served as a nurse, spy, and scout for the Union Army under Colonel James Montgomery of the Second South Carolina Volunteers. Harriet would don numerous disguises and lead groups of local black men behind Confederate lines. It was reported in the *Boston Commonwealth* on July 10, 1863 that "Col. Montgomery and his gallant band of 300 Black soldiers, under the guidance of a Black woman, dashed into the enemy's country, struck a bold and effective blow, destroying millions of dollars worth of commissary stories, cotton and lordly dwellings…" During this campaign eight hundred slaves were rescued.

After the Civil War, Harriet returned to Auburn, New York, where she had purchased a house and twenty-five acres of land. There she began her work of caring for her parents; campaigning for women's rights; and helping orphans, the elderly, and former slaves. In 1908 Harriet converted her home into the Harriet Tubman Home for Indigent and Aged Negroes from monies she earned from selling fruit and copies of her biography.

Harriet Tubman died in March 1913 at the age of ninety-three and was buried in Ohio with military honors. On July 12, 1914, the people of Auburn, New York, placed a bronze plaque at the entrance of the Cayuga County Courthouse in memory of Harriet Tubman.

A hero is commonly defined as "any person admired for courage and nobility." Harriet Tubman is a hero.

Joan Halimah Brooks

Florence Nightingale and Clara Barton

idely known as pioneering nurses, Nightingale in the Crimean and Barton in the American Civil War, these two remarkable women are less commonly credited for their other lifetime achievements.

Florence Nightingale was born in 1820 to upper-class parents in the Italian city after which she was named. Although she was initially taught by a governess, Florence's father took over her education when she was twelve. Due to his lively and exacting teaching, she received a broader education than most girls of her day.

For Clara Barton, born a year later than Florence, life began in rural Massachusetts. She was also educated at home and was taught by her mother and older brother and sisters. Like Florence, Clara was a good scholar. She began teaching while in her teens and taught for a period of twenty years. In Bordertown, New Jersey, she taught without salary for three months in order to persuade the town to provide free education for all its children. The resulting rapid expansion of the school under her management led the town officials to appoint a male principal to continue the work. As a result, Clara Barton ended her teaching career when she resigned in protest.

Unlike Clara, Florence was unable to pursue a career in her teens. Throughout her youth she craved a regular occupation rather than the social rounds on which she reluctantly accompanied her family. She kept copious notes throughout her life, sometimes in the form of a diary; on February 7, 1837, before turning seventeen, she wrote, "God spoke and called me to His service." It was sixteen frustrated and tormented years, however, before she discovered that nursing the sick and needy was to be her vocation.

Her family was deeply opposed to this. Hospitals in those days were dirty and overcrowded, and nurses had the reputation of being rough, uneducated women. Despite their opposition, in 1851 she enrolled in the Institution of Protestant Deaconesses in Kaiserwerth, Germany, as this was the only place she knew of that provided nursing training for women. In 1853, at age thirty-three, she finally launched her

to go to Scutari. Sidney Herbert, a close friend and then secretary of state at war, appointed her superintendent of nursing at the English military hospitals in Turkey. No woman had previously been employed to nurse wounded soldiers; Florence was given complete authority over nursing staff. On her arrival she found that the hospital was dirty, short of supplies, and lacking in proper organization. The doctors undermined her authority and would not allow her or her staff to enter a ward unless they had a doctor's permission to do so. However, as the numbers of casualties mounted following the Battle of Balaclava, this changed and the doctors had no alternative but to turn to the nurses for help. Florence worked tirelessly to improve army medical care, greatly re-

career by becoming superintendent of the Institution for the Care of Sick Gentlewomen in London. She implemented revolutionary policies that considered the comfort of patients and the well-being of nurses and insisted that any woman, regardless of faith or economic circumstances, could be nursed there.

Florence Nightingale was thirty-four years old when the war that she was to make her mark in, the Crimean War, broke out in March 1854. Cholera had afflicted many British soldiers on the Crimean peninsula and there were also thousands of war casualties. The Turks had given the British a hospital in Scutari, but there were no basic hospital supplies and nurses were lacking. Florence knew that this was what she had prepared for and hastily assembled thirty-eight women

ducing the mortality rate and introducing strict sanitary and nursing standards. While doing her rounds to bring comfort to the sick and wounded, she carried a Turkish lantern containing a single candle. This gave birth to the legend of "The Lady with the Lamp." She often worked all night writing endless letters, reports, and plans for improving hospital administration and reforming the army medical services. She continued to do so even when she caught Crimean fever. She was never to fully recover her physical strength again, and she refused doctors' advice to return to England, only doing so when peace was declared.

Opposite: Florence Nightingale Above: Clara Barton

Florence Nightingale's courage and hard work in the Crimea made her a national heroine and an appropriate welcome awaited her on her return. Yet she deliberately slipped back in to the country undetected and pressed on with her plans to reform the army medical services. In 1855 the Nightingale Fund was launched in England. In total, £45,000 was collected, which she used to start The Nightingale Training School for Nurses at St. Thomas's Hospital in London in 1860. Despite suffering with her health during this time she also succeeded in ensuring that a Royal Commission on the Health of the Army was established. Alongside her work with the Commission, she was asked her views on the organization of hospitals both nationally and internationally and advised the War Office on army medical services in India. Queen Victoria awarded her the Royal Red Cross, and in 1907 King Edward VII conferred on her the prestigious honor of the Order of Merit, the first time it was bestowed on a woman.

At about the time Florence Nightingale was beginning her nursing career, Barton was embarking on a new path after giving up teaching. In 1854 she became the first woman to become an employee of the federal government. She faced sexism in the workplace once again when she encountered considerable hostility from her male colleagues in the U.S. Patent Office where she worked as a clerk. She only stopped working there when political elections in 1856 cost her the position but returned to the Patent Office in 1860, a year before the start of the American Civil War. Although by now Barton was in her forties, she was about to embark on the work that would make her famous.

On the outbreak of the American Civil War in April 1861, Clara Barton was living in Washington. Like others, she was shocked both by the extent of the Union casualties and the lack of nursing care for the sick and wounded. She demonstrated her courage and resourcefulness by deciding, of her own accord,

to try to rectify this. In July, following the Union defeat at the Battle of Bull Run, Clara Barton advertised in a Massachusetts newspaper for medical supplies and food that she could distribute to the injured troops. She used the congressional contacts she had made while working at the U.S. Patent Office and the media to publicize the importance of the donations. The response to the adver-

tisement was so huge that she gave up her job and converted her home into a storehouse. She organized her friends and hired mules and wagons to transport the supplies to the battlefields and front lines. Thus her major contribution was not in organizing nursing care in the way that Florence Nightingale had, but in obtaining and distributing supplies. Like Nightingale, the end of the war in which she had served did not signal the end of her work in caring for the war casualties. She initiated a postwar search for missing soldiers with the endorsement of President Abraham Lincoln. This agency was a first for the U.S. Army, and once again she used newspapers to draw up lists of men whose families considered them missing and sorted through the responses. This effort resulted in her marking during the summer of 1865 the graves of almost thirteen thousand men who had died of disease and starvation in the Andersonville prison camp. She embarked on a postwar lecture circuit to contribute to the costs of this work, giving some three hundred speeches throughout the United States. This tour established her as the premier Civil War nurse, though she acknowledged the similar work done by hundreds of other women.

Following the completion of her Civil War work in 1869 and with her health failing, Clara Barton traveled, for a rest, to Europe. While there however, she became involved in working with the Red Cross during the Franco-Prussian War for which she won acclaim from both sides in the conflict. When she returned to the United States in 1873, she began a campaign to establish an American branch of the Red Cross. The majority of Americans at this time were isolationists, and therefore had refused to sign the Geneva Convention's Red Cross treaty. Her tireless efforts were rewarded almost a decade later in May 1881 when the organization came into formal existence. She became its first director and remained so for the next twenty-three years. She often visited the scenes of calamity herself, particularly during the Spanish-American War of 1898 and oversaw personally the distribution of Red Cross assistance. Under her presidency the Red Cross dealt with several late-nineteenth century natural disasters, including the Johnstown flood. Despite her clear organizational and political skills Barton's hatred of bureaucracy and her frugality resulted in conflicts among board members, largely over finances. In 1904 she resigned her presidency. Even at age eighty-three she turned to a new challenge and spent the remaining eight years of her life organizing the National First Aid Association, and supporting the women's suffrage movement.

Remarkably, both women chose to continue their work, caring for others right up until shortly before their deaths. Florence Nightingale died in her sleep, aged ninety, on August 13, 1910, in Park Lane, London; Clara Barton died at age ninety-one in suburban Washington two years later on April 12, 1912.

Eleni Stylianou

Opposite: Clara Barton   Above: Florence Nightingale

Elizabeth Blackwell and Elizabeth Garrett Anderson

lizabeth Blackwell was the first woman to qualify as a doctor in the United States. With courage and determination, she insisted on a full role for women in medicine, and her career opened the doors of the profession to others.

An unconventional girlhood

Elizabeth Blackwell was born in Bristol, England, in 1821, into a large, progressive family. Elizabeth's father believed in fully educating his daughters as well as his sons, an unusual idea at the time. The Blackwell sisters were taught Latin, Greek, and mathematics, as well as traditional "feminine" subjects such as needlework and French. Some family friends believed that, far from being an advantage, the Blackwell daughters' superior education would ruin their marriage prospects—no self-respecting young man would want a wife who was his intellectual equal.

In 1832 the Blackwells emigrated to America. Some years later, after the death of their father, Elizabeth and her talented sisters set up a private school for girls. Elizabeth wasn't satisifed with teaching as a career, and she had no desire to marry and run a household. As a little girl she had resolved to do something "hard"; as a young woman she decided that this something had to be medicine. In the mid-nineteenth century women were accepted as natural nurses, but the very idea of a qualified female physician or surgeon, even for female patients, was as preposterous as it was shocking. Physically and mentally, no "natural" woman was fit to become a doctor. The young Elizabeth Blackwell's ambition was more than hard.

The first steps

With the backing of her family, Elizabeth began by studying medicine as the private pupil of prominent physicians in Philadelphia. Her teachers were impressed by her capacity for hard work and by her strong stomach. Miss Blackwell coped better with the procedures of the dissection room than many male medical students. But for years no medical school would accept her as a student. Eventually, after she had been rejected by twenty-nine medical schools, she was accepted by the Geneva Medical College in New York State in 1847.

At this stage in her training Elizabeth was still regarded, at best, as a curiosity. She was tolerated as a student, but few people expected her to become a fully licensed doctor. One professor tried to exclude her from an operation on a male patient on the grounds that, even if she were not embarrassed, the other students would be distracted by her presence. Elizabeth firmly told him "all parts of the human body are holy within the sight of God," but tactfully observed alone from the uppermost row of the operating amphitheater. In 1849, when she finally graduated as an M.D. (at the head of her class), thousands of people came to Geneva to watch the awards ceremony.

A setback in Paris

Elizabeth Blackwell's struggle for recognition didn't end with the American diploma. She wanted to enter a leading French hospital in Paris as a graduate surgery student. Paris was considered the medical capital of the world at the time, and there she would learn the most advanced techniques. But the French authorities refused to accept a female student, even one as celebrated as Elizabeth Blackwell now was. Once again

Elizabeth Blackwell

The Blackwell Sisters and the New York Infirmary

Elizabeth's younger sister, Emily Blackwell, also began her training as a doctor around this time. Like Elizabeth, Emily faced many obstacles to her ambition. But Emily managed, eventually, to achieve Elizabeth's original ambition: after some years as a graduate student in Europe Emily Blackwell qualified as a surgeon. In 1857 the Blackwell sisters started the New York Infirmary for Women and Children, a hospital specializing in the care of poor female patients as well as the teaching of female doctors. The medical school grew rapidly, and when she celebrated the twentieth anniversary of her own graduation, Elizabeth could declare that "throughout the Northern States the free and equal entrance of women into the medical profession has been secured."

Elizabeth Blackwell did not rest on her laurels. In 1869, feeling that her presence in England would help pioneering medical Englishwomen, she returned to the country of her birth. As a campaigner in England, Elizabeth Blackwell's slogan was "prevention is better than cure," and she stressed the importance of public health education. In her medical philosophy, as well as her career, Elizabeth Blackwell was ahead of her times. She died in England in 1910. In 1949 the American Medical Women's Association established the Elizabeth Blackwell Medal, presented each year to a woman whose work advanced the role of women in medicine. But no individual woman has ever achieved as much as Elizabeth Blackwell herself.

When she returned to London in 1869 Elizabeth Blackwell, M.D., did what she could to encourage Elizabeth Garrett Anderson, the first woman to qualify as a doctor in England.

A Victorian girlhood

Like Elizabeth Blackwell, Elizabeth Garrett was born into a large family and her liberal father also believed in providing his daughters as well as his sons with a broad education. In 1860, when she was twenty-four, Elizabeth Garrett resolved to become a doctor. Elizabeth Blackwell's success encouraged Elizabeth Garrett in her ambition, but, in practical terms, it wasn't any easier for her to acquire medical training than it had been for the American pioneer.

the courageous young woman took the only way forward. She entered La Maternité, a leading hospital for mothers and children, as a student midwife. While she was working at this hospital she was infected by one of her infant patients and lost the sight in one eye. Sadly, this injury ended her original hope of becoming a surgeon, but soon after her recovery from the eye injury she was invited to attend St. Bartholomew's Hospital in London as a graduate student.

In England Elizabeth Blackwell, M.D., was treated as a heroine. Besides her continuing studies, which took her to most of the major teaching hospitals, she made many important friends, including Florence Nightingale. But when Elizabeth Blackwell returned to America in 1851 she still had to struggle for recognition. In New York, where she started her practice, rentable rooms for a female doctor's surgery were mysteriously hard to find. But Dr. Blackwell was as persistent as ever; within a few years she had established a small but loyal group of patients.

The road to recognition

As a first step Elizabeth Garrett became a student nurse at the Middlesex Hospital in London. But after a year's training as a nurse she was refused permission to continue her training as a doctor. Like Elizabeth Blackwell she studied anatomy as the private pupil of medical professors. While she was at Edinburgh University she was not allowed to use regular teaching hospital facilities, such as the dissection rooms, used by male medical students. On several occasions Miss Elizabeth Garrett had to bring home corpses and dissect them in her own bedroom.

As a woman Elizabeth Garrett could not gain the diploma that would license her to practice as a doctor, no matter how hard she worked or how well she did in the available examinations. But in 1865 she passed the Society of Apothecaries' examination, which meant that she could be listed on the medical register as an L.S.A. With these initials after her name she was able to start her working medical career as the general medical attendant of St. Mary's Dispensary, a London clinic for poor women (later the New Hospital for Women). Then, in 1870, Elizabeth Garrett was granted a French medical degree. Soon she was a lecturer and then the dean of the newly founded London Medical School for Women.

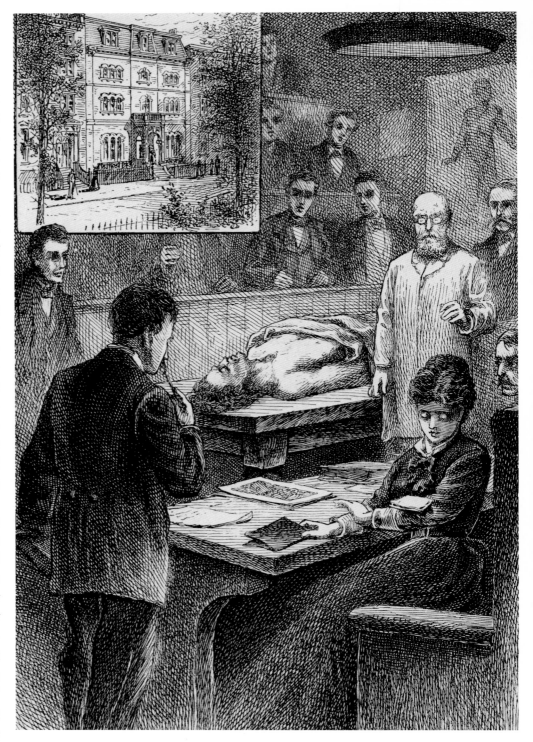

The Cause

First and foremost Elizabeth Garrett was dedicated to medicine, but she saw her work as part of the wider movement for the emancipation of women, "the cause." She met her husband, J.G.S. Anderson, when she was serving as a female member of a school board. Like other feminists, she added his surname to her own, and when she became a mother she did not stop practicing.

Elizabeth Garrett Anderson always supported the campaigns of her equally famous younger sister, Millicent. Millicent Garrett Fawcett was a leader of the British women's suffrage movement. A brilliant and rather formidable woman, Mrs. Fawcett organized the constitutional campaign for votes for women. The ladylike committees and petitions of Mrs. Fawcett's female suffragists contrasted with with the more militant tactics of the better-known suffragettes, who were led by another dynamic widow, Mrs. Emmeline Pankhurst.

For nearly thirty years Elizabeth Garrett Anderson was the only female member of the British Medical Association. Her very existence encouraged young women to train as doctors, and in time her own daughter, Louisa Garrett Anderson, became a surgeon. In 1908 Elizabeth Garrett Anderson scored another first. When she was elected mayor of her hometown, Aldeburgh, the first woman doctor in England also became the first woman mayor in England.

After the First World War broke out in 1914 Elizabeth Garrett Anderson was appointed joint organizer of the British women's hospital corps and chief surgeon of a London military hospital. She died in 1917, a year before the vote was granted to women over thirty. The New Hospital was renamed the Elizabeth Garrett Anderson Hospital in 1918, and under that name it still serves London women.

Margaret Mulvihill

Elizabeth Blackwell (opposite) and Elizabeth Garrett Anderson (above) in the male world of nineteenth-century medicine.

Sonya Kovalevsky

onya Kovalevsky, who believed in omens and portents, might have said she was predestined to be a mathematician, but she had to fight against male prejudice, starting with her autocratic father, General Krukovsky, to achieve her destiny. Passionately Russian, she would spend much of her life in exile, living in Germany, France, and Sweden, because she could neither study nor teach in Russian universities.

Born Moscow in 1850 (some sources have said 1853), Sonya Corvin-Krukovsy had a beloved older sister, Anuita, and a younger brother, Feyda. She always felt that her parents preferred her siblings, which may explain her drive to excel from an early age. When Sonya was six, her father retired from the army to the family estate of Palibino, in a desolate area near the Lithuanian border.

The children were left to entertain themselves, and Sonya diverted herself by staring at the walls of a room which had been papered with her father's old calculus texts until more wallpaper could be sent from St. Petersburg. That was the beginning of her fascination with mathematics. "I passed whole hours before that mysterious wall, trying to decipher even a single phrase, and to discover the order in which the sheets ought to follow each other," she recalled.

That she would be predisposed to mathematics was not surprising. Her great-grandfather was a celebrated mathematician and astronomer. His son, Feodor Feodorovitch Schubert, headed the Russian army's Topographical Corps. Her uncle Piotr, a frequent visitor, spent hours discussing philosophy and mathematics with his niece.

When she was fifteen she convinced her father to let her study with Alexander Nikolaevitch Strannoliubksy at the Naval Academy in St. Petersburg. This celebrated teacher was amazed at the speed with which she understood the concepts of differential calculus. Memories of the strange symbols from her childhood served her well. "The conception of space seemed to have been familiar to me for a long time," she wrote.

Sonya was determined to continue, but her father objected. Although women were not allowed to study in Russian universities, he thought it improper for his daughter to study abroad. Like others in her generation of young Russian aristocrats, she rebelled against parental authority.

With the characteristic ingenuity that was to mark her solutions to male attempts to keep her from becoming a mathematician, she made a marriage of convenience that would enable her to live in Germany. Luckily the man she chose, Vladimir Kovalevsky, a paleontologist at Moscow University, appreciated her talent and willingly agreed to her scheme.

In the spring of 1869 they moved to Heidelberg, where Sonya spent two years listening to lectures given by some of Germany's best known scholars, including Leo Konigsberg. Enchanted by her youth and beauty, people in that old university town turned her into a local celebrity, although it had little effect on her. Still only a teenager, she was more interested in her professor's praise of Karl T. Weierstrass, with whom he had studied and who was known as the "father of mathematical analysis" throughout Europe.

She set out for Berlin alone in 1870, but the university there refused to admit her despite glowing recommendations from her Heidelberg professors. In desperation she asked if Weierstrass would give her private lessons. Although he was reluctant, the professor agreed to consider her case. He tested her with some of the more advanced problems he gave his university students. To his surprise she passed with flying colors, even coming up with some original solutions.

He became her mentor, providing her with his lecture notes, sharing unpublished works, and discussing the latest geometric theories with her. She spent four rigorous years working on her doctoral dissertation, "On the Theory of Partial Differential Equations." When she expressed anxiety about defending her thesis orally before a committee of unknown men, he convinced them to waive that requirement based on the excellence of her written work and the recommendations from various other mathematicians. However, after she received her degree in 1874, Professor Weierstrass was unable to help her obtain work as a university lecturer.

Kovalevsky returned to St. Petersburg where she took a complete break from mathematics, visiting with family and friends. Sonya, who had also considered literature as a career, busied herself writing newspaper articles and the first of several novels. In October 1878 her daughter Fufa was born. However, her marriage fell apart and she realized that she had to leave Russia once again to pursue a career in mathematics.

Still waiting for a teaching position, she was living in Paris when she learned that her husband had committed suicide in the spring of 1883. The news devastated her, but it was followed by good news. A Swedish colleague, Gosta Mittag-Leffler, had finally persuaded the University of Stockholm to allow her to lecture there; he helped raise the money to pay her salary. When she moved to Stockholm in November 1883 with her daughter, she also made friends with his sister, Anna Carlotta Leffler, who would later write Kovalevsky's biography.

In 1888 she achieved her greatest success. On Christmas Eve, the French Academy of Sciences awarded her the prestigious Prix Bordin for her memoir, *On the Problem of the Rotation of a Solid Body about a Fixed Point.* The jury, which was so impressed with the work that they had increased the prize from three thousand to five thousand francs, had not known the winner was a woman until after their decision because each author's name was submitted separately in a sealed envelope to prevent favoritism.

The prize brought the official recognition she had deserved for so long. In 1889 the University of Stockholm finally made her a tenured professor, and on December 2, 1889, she became the first woman Corresponding Member of the Russian Academy of Sciences. However, her triumph was short lived.

Exhausted from the struggle to survive financially and from the extreme effort of writing her prize-winning treatise, she also faced personal loss. In the course of doing the work, she had permanently alienated her lover. Worse still, her sister, Anuita, was dying in Moscow. Although her academic future looked bright, she was profoundly depressed. The round trip between Stockholm and Moscow was grueling and in February 1891, she caught a chill while changing trains and died of influenza several days later at the age of forty-one.

Her premature death took everyone by surprise. Her own papers were totally disorganized and Professor Weierstrass burned all the letters she had sent him over the years. She was buried in Sweden, but Russia honored her posthumously with a postage stamp.

In a touch of macabre irony, four years after her death, her brain was removed, weighed, and found to be heavier than that of the great Hermann von Helmholtz. The motto she gave to her prize-winning work can serve as her epitaph: "Say what you know, do what you must, come what may."

Sydney Johnson

Grace Darling and Ida Lewis

Two nineteenth-century heroines, lighthouse dwellers on opposite sides of the Atlantic Ocean, became famous for their daring sea rescues. The first was Grace Darling, whose father, William Darling, was the keeper of the Longstone Lighthouse in the Farne Islands off the coast of Northumberland, England. William and his wife, Thomasin Horsley Darling, married in 1805 and had nine children; their daughter Grace, born in 1815, was the seventh child.

From childhood, Grace helped with household tasks in the seven rooms of the lighthouse. Her parents taught her to read and write, and she sometimes took the oars of the boat with her father on his travels among the islands. On the night of September 6, 1838, the *Forfarshire*, one of the first luxury steamers, was wrecked on Bib Harcar Rock during a violent storm. Of the sixty people on board, eight crew members and one passenger escaped in the ship's lifeboat and were picked up by a passing sloop.

According to William Darling's journal (actually a logbook): "About 4 am on the 7th, the vessel struck the west point of Harcher's rock, and in fifteen minutes broke through by the paddle-axle, and drowned forty-three persons; nine having previously left in their own boat,…and nine others held on by the wreck and were rescued by the Darlings." Grace might not have been involved in the rescue at all, but her older brothers had moved to the mainland by this time and her younger brother William was fishing at North Sunderland. Thus it was Grace and her father who observed movement on Big Harcar Rock soon after dawn on September 7. With the help of Mrs. Darling, they launched their cable— a short flat-bottomed rowboat used on the northeast coast—and set out through the storm. The rock was about three-quarters of a mile away; when they arrived William Darling had to leap onto the rock while Grace stayed on the oars, rowing back and forth to prevent the boat from being wrecked on the reef.

The nine survivors on the rock were four crew members and five passengers; three people, including two children, had died of exposure and injuries before the Darlings reached them. The boat was too small to take everyone back to Longstone, so one woman and an injured crew member were ferried to the lighthouse first, with three uninjured seamen helping to row. Grace attended to the injured and stayed at the lighthouse while her father and two of the *Forfarshire* crew returned to the rock for the other four survivors. There was no way to recover the bodies until the storm abated, three days later. Meanwhile, nineteen people were sheltered at Longstone Lighthouse, including Grace's brother William and six fishing companions; they had been alerted to the wreck by bursts of gunfire from a lookout in nearby Bamburgh Castle and had returned to help.

The investigation that ensued blamed the wreck on leaking boilers, but the British public was far more interested in the twenty-two-year-old heroine who had gone to the rescue. Initial accounts in the Northumbrian newspapers were picked up and reprinted all over the country. London readers first read the story in *The Times* on September 19. The reporter called Grace's role in the "calamitous case of shipwreck...an instance of heroism and intrepidity on the part of a female unequaled perhaps, certainly not surpassed, by any on record." Queen Victoria sent Grace fifty pounds "as a mark of Her Gracious approbation of your conduct," and a popular song memorialized the deed, with a rousing chorus that declaimed: "But Grace had an English heart,/And the raging storm she brav'd,/She pull'd away, 'mid the dashing spray,/And the crew she saved."

The Victorians took Grace Darling to their own English hearts, and for the remainder of her short life, modest Grace was the unwilling subject of countless poems, portraits, biographies, press reports, and visits from admirers who kept her from getting her work done. In 1842 she succumbed to tuberculosis and was interned at Bamburgh Churchyard, where an elaborate statue and epitaph were dedicated to her memory.

In 1885 a fund was raised to restore Grace Darling's tomb, and one of the contributors was her counterpart across the ocean: Ida Lewis, keeper of the Lime Rock Lighthouse in Newport, Rhode Island. She was born in 1842, the year Grace died, and helped her father, Captain Hosea Lewis, to tend the lighthouse until he was disabled by a stroke in 1858. At the age of sixteen she assumed all his duties, including rescuing the shipwrecked—which she was called upon to do almost immediately when four inexperienced young men capsized their boat in Newport harbor. Eight years later, a party of drunken soldiers made off in her brother's boat and kicked a hole in it. She

had to row out in the lighthouse craft and carry them all to safety. In both these instances, the rescued parties said as little as possible about their rescue. However, Ida Lewis was fully as modest as Grace Darling and expected no recognition for doing her job. Over the years, she made at least eighteen rescues before her last, which occurred when she was sixty-four years old.

By that time many grateful survivors had come forward to describe Ida's "dauntless courage and self-sacrifice" to the press, and she became widely known as "The Heroine of Lime Rock." Gifts and letters were sent to the lighthouse in profusion, and the *New York Herald Tribune* sent a reporter to Newport and published a glowing account on April 15, 1869, comparing Ida to Grace Darling. The Life Saving Benevolent Association sent a silver medal and a check for one hundred dollars, and Rhode Island's secretary of state introduced a resolution of commendation that was passed by the state legislature. Ida Lewis hats and ties appeared, and Frank Leslie's *Illustrated Newspaper* published a profile that described her as "of a very slight figure. [She] has never weighed more than 103 pounds, even when in the best condition, so that her endurance and strength are the more remarkable."

Fortunately for Ida Lewis, her notoriety was short-lived, as up to a hundred sightseers a day were interfering with her duties at the lighthouse by the summer of 1869. She lived to the age of sixty-nine and became the first woman to be awarded the Congressional Medal of Honor. Perhaps she was equally pleased when the local Lime Rock Yacht Club adopted her name: to this day it is known as the Ida Lewis Yacht Club.

Robin Langley Sommer

Opposite: Grace Darling during the Forfarshire *rescue*
Above: Ida Lewis looking over the harbor from Lime Rock Lighthouse

Mary MacKillop

One of Australia's best-loved heroines is Mary MacKillop, foundress of the teaching order of the Sisters of St. Joseph. She was born in Melbourne in what was then New South Wales, on January 15, 1842, the eldest child of Scottish emigrants who had met in Australia and married in 1840. Mary's father, Alexander, had studied for the Roman Catholic priesthood, and he educated all eight of his children much beyond the norm for a poor family. His employment history was erratic, and the MacKillops had to rely on relatives for much of their support, which created unhappiness at home. However, Flora MacKillop taught all her children to have faith in divine providence despite the many adversities of her life, which included the untimely deaths of four of Mary's brothers and sisters.

During Mary's girlhood, the population of the Australian colonies nearly tripled, from four hundred thousand to over one million people as a result of the gold rush of 1851 to 1860. Hardship was widespread, as Australians sought to develop a more diverse economy and to assimilate the burgeoning population, which was concentrated in and around the port cities of Sydney, New South Wales; Perth, Western Australia; Melbourne, in what is now Victoria; and Adelaide, South Australia.

In 1861 the nineteen-year-old Mary was working as a governess on her uncle's station (sheep ranch) at Penola, near Adelaide. There she became friends with the parish priest, Father Julian Woods, who shared her dream of providing Catholic schooling for the children of the outback—the arid interior of the island continent, which was as rough and lawless as the nineteenth-century frontier of the United States. Under Woods's spiritual direction, Mary prepared for her work as the future foundress of the Institute of the Sisters of St. Joseph, which she established in Adelaide in 1866. The order's rule of life, written by Father Woods, included a commitment to Franciscan poverty and centralized government

of the sisters by their own superior, rather than by the bishop of the local diocese. The Irish and European bishops serving in Australia were not accustomed to this arrangement, which soon caused problems for the fledgling order.

Unlike other religious institutions of its day, the Josephites welcomed novices from the poor, uneducated classes; some were illiterate when they presented themselves as candidates. Mary trained them as teachers while Father Woods undertook their spiritual formation. Unfortunately, the idealistic young priest was not an effective administrator, and the Mother House floundered and fell into debt after Mary led the first Josephite foundation to Queensland in 1869. Eventually, Bishop Sheil of Adelaide withdrew his support from the order on grounds that the Mother House was mismanaged and the Josephites too independent of the local clergy, who wanted to control their activities. When Mary returned to Adelaide in 1871, she was censured by Bishop Sheil and ordered to reform her order's rule of life. Unable to do so in good conscience, she refused, and the bishop, ill-advised and in poor health, took the drastic step of excommunicating her from the Church. The Sisters of St. Joseph were ordered to disband, but more than half of them stood by Mary, who conducted herself with exemplary dignity and discretion throughout the five-month period of her excommunication. Most people supported Mary and the sisters, whose good works had already extended beyond educating the poor into visiting hospitals and prisons, caring for orphans, and establishing Houses of Refuge for unmarried mothers and former prostitutes and Houses of Providence for the elderly poor and other women and children at risk. All of these activities were supported by asking for alms in money and kind and by school fees for those who could afford them.

The clergymen of Adelaide prevailed upon the bishop to send Father Woods into New South Wales "on business," and there was a painful breach between Mary and her spiritual mentor. Although Bishop Sheil withdrew the sentence of excommunication and restored the order on his deathbed, it was clear that Mary would have to go to Rome for approval of her order's rule of life, including their centralized government. New conflicts had already arisen with Bishops Matthew Quinn of the Brisbane diocese and James Quinn of the Bathurst diocese, who demanded direct control of the Josephites in Queensland. Mary persisted in her belief that autonomy was essential to her order's work in Australia, where small groups of sisters often had to travel to remote regions or live among the poor in the cities. They needed a Mother House where they could gather for mutual encouragement and support and make decisions affecting their ministry in many different locations and circumstances. Accordingly, Mary traveled to Rome in 1873 and petitioned for approval of the Josephite rule of life.

In her *Statement on the Rule and General Superior* (May/June 1873), she wrote that the sisters wished to retain their centralized government because many of them, "from personal experience in other places [had] reason to dread the dangers to unity and the preservation of the original intention of the rule which attend[ed] such communities as [had] no general superiors." She also explained that the Josephites' primary commitment, to the children of the poor, could be compromised by the jurisdiction of local bishops and clergy. Approval was granted, but Church authorities stipulated that the Josephites must give up their Franciscan rule of poverty and own at least some houses for their own security and protection. The sisters accepted this ruling, which widened the breach between Mary and Father Woods, who was bitterly disappointed and refused to see her until his final illness in 1888.

Mary's difficulties with bishops who resented opposition from a woman were not over yet. In 1880 the Josephites had to leave Queensland at the behest of the Bishops Quinn. Then the bishop of Adelaide withdrew his support after misunderstandings with Rome and expelled Mary from the diocese. Fortunately, Archbishop Roger Bede Vaughan, OSB (Order of St. Benedict), had befriended the order in 1880 and invited the sisters to staff Catholic schools in Sydney and its environs. As a member of the Benedictine order, rather than a diocesan clergymen, Vaughan sympathized with the Josephites' rule of life and welcomed their presence in Australia's largest city.

Mary established a House of Providence on Cumberland Street, in the Rocks area, and a novitiate on Mount Street that eventually became the new Mother House. She was widely respected for her steadfastness in the way of life to which she believed God had called her, in spite of opposition from the powerful bishops, whom she never criticized or flouted. From the new Mother House at Sydney, established in 1889, she oversaw the work of the Josephites in South Australia, New South Wales, Victoria, and New Zealand, founding many new schools and convents and visiting those already established. Her energy and confidence were undiminished by declining health, including partial paralysis in 1902, and her death, on August 8, 1909, was deeply mourned. It was Archbishop Michael Kelly of Sydney who initiated the cause of her canonization in 1929, and her beatification in 1995 was a long-deferred tribute to her labors on behalf of Australia's people.

Robin Langley Sommer

George Eliot

George Eliot was the pen name of Mary Ann (or Marian) Evans, author of some of the most powerful novels in the English language.

"George Eliot's" career began in 1853, the year in which Marian Evans, a thirty-four-year-old English-woman with unconventional opinions and an equally unconventional lifestyle, started to write stories. By then she was already well known as a distinguished translator and literary critic. She worked as an editor of the *Westminster Review,* a prestigious English magazine, and she numbered many of London's most prominent intellectuals among her friends and admirers. But Miss Evans was admired for her brilliant mind rather than for her looks. Her long, strong face and intense gray-blue eyes were not attractive by Victorian standards of feminine beauty. The philosopher Herbert Spencer bluntly told her that, although he enjoyed her company, he could never think of her as a potential wife. The popular Marian Evans was a lonely woman until, in 1851, she met a man named George Lewes.

Living in sin

George Lewes wrote reviews and articles for the *Westminster Review.* As a reviewer he got free tickets for operas and plays, and Miss Evans was often invited to join him on working "dates." Officially George Lewes was a married man, but three of his six children had been fathered by his wife's lover, who was yet another married man. Even if it had been possible for the Leweses to obtain a full legal divorce, in mid-Victorian England remarriage for either of them would have been out of the question. When Marian Evans and George Lewes fell in love they had no public way of showing their commitment to each other. Their only way forward, as a couple, was abroad.

In 1854 respectable society was horrified when Marian Evans and George Lewes left England and began to tour continental Europe under the names "Mr. and Mrs. Lewes." Since few people knew that the legitimate Mrs. Lewes was herself another man's wife in all but name, it appeared that Marian Evans and her new partner were sinful adulterers. Both of Marian Evans's parents were dead. She had argued bitterly with her father because she did not believe in the historical truth of the Bible. Now, because of her elopement, she also lost the affection of her only brother, Isaac Evans. As soon as he heard the disgraceful news, he refused to have anything more to do with his sister. Marian Evans risked isolation and condemnation because her new life offered huge compensations. She was completely in love with a man who loved her in the same way. For the next twenty-five years Marian Evans and George Lewes were a happy couple, and with success in love came success in art.

The birth of "George Eliot"

Books would be the children of this particular marriage. Marian Evans was in no doubt of her abilities as a thinker and a nonfiction writer, but George Lewes encouraged her to create fiction. She took the name "George Eliot" as a way of signaling her seriousness—women writers were looked down upon as the authors of silly, inconsequential stories rather than great literature.

Her first book, *Scenes from Clerical Life,* was a great critical success, and the novels that followed, *Adam Bede* (1859), *The Mill on the Floss* (1860), and *Silas Marner* (1861), were as popular with the general public as they were with critics. Then, in 1871, George Eliot's lengthy masterpiece, *Middlemarch,* was published. Its central female character, Dorothea, is a complicated woman who seeks intellectual distinction at the expense of emotional satisfaction. Dorothea's struggle for a complete life, as a woman and a serious-minded person, echoed the author's search for fulfillment.

As George Eliot, "Mrs. Lewes" became a wealthy woman. In many ways George Eliot and George Lewes's scandalous elopement helped their "marriage." Their lack of respectability gave them privacy: they were left in peace to do what they enjoyed most, reading and writing. Even so, celebrities from all around the world came to London to meet England's greatest novelist at her house near Regent's Park. The young American writer Henry James came to one of George Eliot's Sunday parties and immediately saw that there was something fascinating, even beautiful, about his hostess's "vast ugliness."

The second marriage

In spite of regular bouts of poor health, George Lewes was both as cheerful and positive as his partner was inclined to be depressed. He read all of George Eliot's reviews so that she only saw the most flattering ones, and whenever she was low he would find some way of lifting her spirits. When George Lewes died of cancer in 1878 George Eliot was devastated.

But in May 1880, less than two years after George Lewes's death, George Eliot married the tall, handsome and extremely nervous young man who for several years had acted as George Eliot and George Lewes's financial advisor, and who was regarded as a close family friend. At forty, John Cross was twenty years younger than his bride, but he worshipped her. Everyone close to George Eliot supported the marriage. She was given away by her favorite stepson, Charles Lewes, and after twenty-five years of silence, her brother Isaac offered her his sincere congratulations.

On the honeymoon in Venice John Cross suffered a nervous breakdown, which may have been brought on by a local fever. His wife hurried him back to England. But John Cross was destined to outlive his brilliant, sixty-year-old wife. In December 1880, less than six months after her second marriage, George Eliot died after a short illness. A hundred years later, in 1980, a memorial plaque was unveiled in the Poets' Corner of Westminster Abbey to the woman born Mary Ann Evans who, as the passionately intelligent George Eliot, brought the craft of the novelist to new heights of glory. Independent, clever, considerate, and tenacious, she created strong fictional heroines with these qualities which continue to inspire readers through the generations.

Margaret Mulvihill

Susan B. Anthony, Elizabeth Cady Stanton, & Abigail Scott Duniway

Two very different women, Susan B. Anthony and Elizabeth Cady Stanton, were lifelong friends and prime movers in the American women's suffrage movement. Inspired by their example, the pioneering Abigail Scott Duniway was a leader of the movement in the West. The individuality of these three women, as well as the similarities and differences among them, mirrors the great number of American woman who, for several generations, were active seekers of women's rights in the nineteenth century.

Not until 1920 did American women finally obtain the right to vote. Fifty years earlier the Nineteenth Amendment to the U. S. Constitution, which guaranteed that right, had been introduced to Congress at the personal behest of Susan B. Anthony. Twenty-two years before that, in Seneca Falls, New York, Elizabeth Cady Stanton called together the first convention to discuss equality before the law and voting rights for all American women. In the Far West, Abigail Scott Duniway had begun her journalistic career in the 1850s, promoting the campaigns that made several western states the first to grant full women's suffrage, decades before 1920.

Elizabeth Cady Stanton was born in 1815 to a prominent family in Johnstown, New York, northwest of Albany. Following the example of her high-spirited, independent mother, and encouraged by her affluent father—a lawyer and judge—to pursue education and physical independence, the young Elizabeth nevertheless grieved that she was denied college or the possibility of becoming a lawyer herself. Her parents' grief at the early deaths of all five of their sons made Elizabeth particularly sensitive to the social and legal disabilities of women.

When she married abolitionist Henry Stanton in 1840, their honeymoon included a trip to the World Anti-Slavery Convention in London. There, to Elizabeth's chagrin, all women, even official delegates, were relegated to a curtained balcony while the men deliberated. Elizabeth met Quaker leader Lucretia Mott in that balcony and they decided together to call a women's rights convention when they returned to America.

Eight years later, after several happy years in Boston and a move to the rural hinterlands of Seneca, New York, Elizabeth Stanton received a visit from Lucretia Mott. Within days, the women had planned, organized, and held the first American women's rights convention, drawing an enthusiastic audience of several hundred from many miles around. The most famous achievement of the session was Stanton's "Declaration of Rights and Sentiments," modeled upon Jefferson's great Declaration of Independence, specifying the accumulated legal grievances of women. The Convention unanimously adopted the resolutions, which became the foundation of America's women's rights movement.

For the rest of her life, Elizabeth Cady Stanton wrote many articles, lobbied legislators, and traveled throughout the country to lecture on women's issues, collaborating with other women to insist upon their rights. This was not an easy process. Mothering seven children limited her movements until later years. Her husband, a politician who frequently spent months away from home, disapproved of her campaign. A gifted and witty speaker, Stanton also stirred up opposition by her "radicalism"—demanding inheritance, property law, female health education, and divorce reform, along with political participation.

Susan B. Anthony (standing) and Elizabeth Cady Stanton

In 1895, at the age of eighty, Stanton published *The Woman's Bible*, a controversial translation and analysis which anticipated much modern feminist Biblical research. Though revered as a founding mother of the women's rights movement, she was repudiated for her unorthodox ideas by many younger suffragists; the Woman Suffrage Convention of 1895 censured her book. Elizabeth Cady Stanton died in 1902.

Susan Brownell Anthony was not at the Seneca Falls convention, but she heard about it with interest. Her friendship and collaboration with Elizabeth Cady Stanton began on the day they met in 1851. Susan died four years after Elizabeth.

Born in 1820, Anthony was five years younger than Elizabeth and never married. She was tall and angular in comparison to Stanton's increasingly ample figure, serious and reserved in comparison to Stanton's cheerful ebulliance. Daughter of a Quaker family in rural northwest Massachusetts, she never had Stanton's security of economic means and social status. Trained in moralistic piety, she could never "kick over the traces" with ease and good humor like Stanton's. But, like Stanton, she always followed her own advice, to "take your stand and hold it," never fearing to act according to what she believed was right.

For many years Susan visited the Stanton home, and while she helped with the children, Elizabeth provided the ideas, the theories, and the words of speeches. Then Susan traveled from place to place, circulating petitions, inspiring women's rights organizers, and delivering the speeches. As Henry Stanton put it, Elizabeth stirred up Susan while Susan was stirring the puddings, and then Susan "stirred up the world!" Or, as Elizabeth Stanton said, "I forged the thunderbolts, she fired them."

Together, Stanton and Anthony led the formation of the National Woman's Suffrage Association (NWSA) in 1869, focusing on all women's rights issues, such as divorce and health, as well as the vote. They traveled together not only in the east but to Chicago and Kansas, and even to California in 1871. In 1884 they worked together for months gathering information to produce the first volumes of *The History of Woman Suffrage,* an invaluable resource for all later historians.

In 1872, Susan B. Anthony was the most publicized of the many women who voted in the presidential election. Fourteen others accompanied Anthony in Rochester, New York, where she was arrested, brought to trial, convicted, and then fined. Anthony lectured the judge, saying he had "trampled under foot every vital principle of our government." She argued that women were both persons and citizens, therefore the Constitution already empowered them to vote.

The judge instructed Anthony to be quiet, but she continued to argue. Finally she refused to pay the $100 fine, expecting to be sent to jail, from which she would be able to appeal for justice to the Supreme Court. But the judge insisted she must pay the fine before she went to jail. She refused to pay, and he did not jail her—a hollow victory which grieved her for the rest of her life.

The NWSA merged in 1890 with the American Woman Suffrage Association, a group much more closely connected to the temperance movement, one of Anthony's earliest concerns. By this time Stanton was a widow and had resigned her presidency to make an extended visit to her daughter in England. She continued to write impassioned speeches for her friend to deliver. But when the new suffrage association repudiated Stanton's *Woman's Bible* in 1895,

Opposite: Elizabeth Cady Stanton   Above: Caricature of Susan B. Anthony

Anthony did not defend her; this iconoclasm was too much even for Anthony.

The cause of woman suffrage was Susan B. Anthony's lifelong calling. Throughout most of her career, she had taken the brunt of antisuffrage sentiment from both women and men, enduring spoken and published insults about her "old maid" status, her plain looks, and her unconventional lack of "femininity." But in her old age, the woman suffrage movement had become a force to be reckoned with among both politicians and large numbers of middle-class ladies.

By 1899 Susan B. Anthony was the acknowledged symbol of women's rights at the International Council of Women held in London. And at her eightieth birthday the next year, Susan remarked, "Once I was the most hated and reviled of women, now, it seems as if everybody loves me."

Anthony died in 1905, shortly before the scheduled National-American Woman Suffrage Convention in Portland, Oregon, which became a public tribute to the suffragists' beloved "Auntie Susan."

It was in Portland that the redoubtable Abigail Scott Duniway first met Anthony in 1871. In May of that year Duniway began publishing the *New Northwest*, a weekly newspaper dedicated to the cause of women's rights. When Anthony and Stanton visited California, Duniway invited them to Oregon too.

Susan B. Anthony accompanied Abigail Duniway on a two-month, two-thousand-mile lecture tour by river steamer, canoe, stagecoach, and farm wagon throughout the frontier Pacific Northwest during its legendary mud-and-rainy season. She hoped to make enough money from her lectures to pay some of her many debts. But the women faced unfriendly audiences and scathing press denunciations of their "licentious social theories." Anthony explained to the Washington Territory legislature that women as U.S. citizens already had the constitutional right to vote, and the legislators promptly passed a law forbidding woman suffrage. Anthony experienced at times a "mortal agony," and headed home "as single-handed and penniless as usual."

Duniway, however, considered the trip a great success. She shared none of Anthony's meticulous eastern sensibilities or personal reticence. She had gathered many new subscribers, discovered her own love of extemporaneous lecture platforms, and expanded the passionate commitment to women's rights that she had felt ever since childhood.

Abigail Jane Scott Duniway was born in a log cabin in Groveland, Illinois, in 1834, one of twelve children. Her father was a farmer and postmaster, and her "invalid" mother died suddenly of cholera on the overland trail as the Scott family traveled westward in 1852.

Abigail, then seventeen, became Mrs. Benjamin Duniway one year later. On an isolated Oregon ranch she almost died in childbirth with the second of her six sons. Bedridden temporarily, she began writing for the local newspaper as she recovered, and soon published the first novel printed in Oregon, based on her overland trail experiences.

Ben Duniway lost "their" farm in 1861 because of a mortgage which he alone had signed, making Duniway acutely aware of unjust property laws. Ben's serious back injury shortly afterwards left his wife the family breadwinner. Running a boarding school and then a millinery shop for the next decade gave Abigail even more insight into the legal inequities most women endured. By the time she started the *New Northwest*, her brother was already the eminent and powerful editor of the Portland *Oregonian*. For years she counted on this relationship for support, until she discovered that Harvey Scott was "betraying" her by behind-the-scenes opposition to women's rights.

Abigail Scott Duniway's accounts of her myriad frontier lecture tours in the 1870s and 1880s make vivid reading. She also crossed the country to attend the national association conferences, and in 1884 was elected one of its vice-presidents, along with Susan B. Anthony, under the presidency of Elizabeth Cady Stanton.

After 1890, however, Duniway had a falling out with the national leadership, especially the newer generation of eastern-bred middle-class prohibitionists. Because of her own opposition to "making woman suffrage a tail to the prohibitionist kite," she was widely slandered by Women's Christian Temperance Union supporters for supposedly having "sold out to whiskey." Like Elizabeth Cady Stanton, Abigail Duniway fought for woman suffrage as a matter of equal rights for all, not merely as a means to middle-class social control.

In 1910, Washington finally approved votes for women, followed by California in 1911 and then Oregon in 1912. (Wyoming, Colorado, and Idaho had previously done so in 1870, 1893, and 1896 respectively.) Abigail Scott Duniway became Oregon's first registered woman voter. She also helped found the National Council of Women in the Pacific Northwest, which was later replaced by the National League of Women Voters in 1920. At eighty-one, Duniway died in 1915.

The long campaign for women's right to equality of property ownership, job opportunity, and political participation—from 1848 to 1920 and on into our own time—was made possible by the labor and commitment of thousands of ordinary and extraordinary women throughout our country. So that these other leaders and followers might also have voices and live freely, heroines like Elizabeth Cady Stanton, Susan B. Anthony, and Abigail Scott Duniway gave their voices, their examples, and their lives.

Ruth B. Moynihan

Opposite: Abigail Scott Duniway   Below: Commemorative Susan B. Anthony US silver dollar issued in 1979

Sarah Winnemucca

"*I* was born somewhere near 1844," in the great Nevada desert basin, said Sarah Winnemucca at the beginning of the autobiography which she published in 1883. This entire region was known as the Paiute country (spelled Piute then), where her people had lived and thrived for centuries. She described how as a small child she saw the first white people cross those deserts on the way to California in their "movable houses," and never forgot the terror she felt when "our mothers told us that the whites were killing everybody and eating them." On one occasion their mothers buried Sarah and her cousin in sand with sagebrushes to shelter their faces, in order to hide them from hostile Gold Rush immigrants who were pouring over the land, destroying Indian food supplies, and mistreating any Indians they met.

But Sarah's grandfather, Chief Truckee of the Paiutes, had befriended the first white settlers in California and was convinced that a cooperative future held great opportunities. He took a large group of fearfully reluctant Paiutes with him to live and work in California. There Sarah learned English and was even enrolled in a mission school for three weeks, until white Californians enraged at the presence of Indian pupils among their daughters demanded her removal.

After Chief Truckee's death, Sarah and her family returned to Nevada Territory. But from 1860 on, the Paiute people were restricted to the Pyramid Lake Reservation, with the promise of regular "government issue"— clothes, blankets, food, and tools, which were to be doled out in exchange for the rest of their land. As Sarah later wrote about that treaty arrangement, "though there were thirteen agents there in the course of twenty-three years, I never knew of any issue after that first year."

Because of her knowledge of English and her position as daughter of the ailing Chief Winnemucca, Sarah herself soon became the recognized chief of the Paiutes. Furthermore, her reputation for intelligence and honesty gave her credibility with agents sent by the Bureau of Indian Affairs and also with army officers sent by the U.S. government to establish control over western Indian tribes and their land. Mediating patiently between her people and the whites in regard to innumerable broken promises or incomprehensible new requirements, she managed to retain the trust of both throughout most of her life. Some of her tribespeople blamed her for government deceptions, but most of them could see that her heroic efforts were just not sufficient to the magnitude of the forces against them.

Fairmindedness was one of Sarah's outstanding characteristics. She was glad to credit every good white person she had known, even as she chronicled others' betrayals. There was the young housewife who had lovingly treated her when she was a terrified sick child in California. There was Mrs. Parrish and her agent husband at the Malheur Agency in Oregon, who paid her forty dollars a month in 1875 to be his interpreter. "The dear, lovely lady," Mrs. Parrish, made Sarah her assistant to open a school for over four hundred Indians, a work which both women loved.

But within weeks a perfidious new agent arrived, closed the school, forced the Indians to work on "government land" which was rightly theirs, and charged them for government supplies. Sarah expressed her frustration in a lecture: "If I possessed the wealth…I would place all the Indians of Nevada on ships in our harbor, take them to New York and land them there as immigrants, that they might be received with open arms, blessed with universal suffrage…out of the reach of Indian agents."

By 1878 the nearby Bannocks had gone on the warpath, along with some Paiutes. This included Sarah's father and brother, who appeared to have joined them, though they were actually prisoners. The army paid Sarah to persuade the Bannocks to surrender even as it prepared to fight them.

Sarah Winnemucca chose to save her own people by warning them in secrecy to leave the Bannock camp and then making a desperate ride back to the army to get help. "That was the hardest work I ever did for the government in all my life," she later remembered. For two days non-stop at full speed "having been in the saddle night and day,…about two hundred and twenty three miles…. I, only an Indian woman, went and saved my father and his people."

Nevertheless, the eventual result for the Paiutes was as tragic as for all other Indians. The army recognized Sarah's bravery throughout the Bannock War, but when it ended they confiscated the Paiute reservation too. Officials insisted that her people, innocent as they were of war participation, should march through the dead of winter over the Cascade Mountains from southern Oregon to an alien reservation in Yakima, Washington. Old men and women, children, invalids, and others died in misery along the way. Sarah's beloved sister died soon after, and the Paiutes themselves were victimized and robbed on the Yakima reservation both by government agents and by other reservation Indians, who saw them as interlopers.

In 1880 Sarah Winnemucca and a few friends made an extraordinary journey across the country to Washington, D.C., where they had been promised an interview with the president, "the great white Father." Only Secretary of the Interior Carl Schurz finally, after much delay, talked to them. He made a number of promises for justice which turned out to be empty, for which Sarah's people eventually blamed her.

But Sarah Winnemucca did make the acquaintance of several white women reformers. They took up her cause, facilitated a lecture tour for her in many cities from Washington to Boston, and then arranged to publish her book, *Life Among the Piutes*, in 1883. Boston matron Mrs. Horace Mann, wife of the renowned educator, helped to ensure attention by serving as the book's "editor" and writing the introduction.

Appearing at the same time as Helen Hunt Jackson's carefully researched *Century of Dishonor*, which exposed the long history of U.S. government treaty-making and betrayal, Winnemucca's continued lecturing and her book were crucial factors in the gradual reform of American Indian policies. She herself married a white man named Hopkins in 1882 and finally retreated from public life to establish an Indian school.

Sarah Winnemucca contracted tuberculosis and died in poverty in Montana in 1891.

Ruth B. Moynihan

Aletta Jacobs

"I am convinced that our lives were not in vain. We fulfilled our task and can depart the world in the belief that we leave it behind in a better condition than when we first encountered it."

—ALETTA JACOBS, LETTER TO CARRIE CHAPMAN CATT, 1928

letta Jacobs was a leading figure in the international women's suffrage movement early this century. The right to vote was only one of the many issues in Aletta's crusade to fight discrimination against women. Known as Holland's first feminist, she achieved significant advances in both health care and labor conditions for women.

The eighth of eleven children, Aletta was born in 1854 and grew up in a liberal family in the countryside of Groningen, the northernmost province of The Netherlands. From the start, her extraordinary determination and independence were apparent. When she was only six, she already knew what she wanted to be: a doctor, just like her father and two of her brothers. That she persisted in her wish—and ultimately succeeded in fulfilling it—was remarkable in a time and place in which girls weren't even allowed to enroll in high school. Aletta set many precedents for Dutch women: she was the first girl to attend high school, the first woman to study at university and to be accepted as a student pharmacist, the first to take her doctoral degree, and, by the age of twenty-five, the first woman to have a medical practice. She accomplished all this largely through her own initiative, discipline, and tenacity.

As a student, Aletta was motivated by her desire to become a doctor—an ambition she considered only natural—rather than by an interest in political or social issues. What made her so different from her female contemporaries? In the first place, her personality and intelligence. Nonintellectual activities quickly bored her, and once she had decided upon something, she was unstoppable. Secondly, her father encouraged her academic ambitions, allowing her to take lessons in Greek and Latin, and instilling in her the belief that boys *and* girls should have a profession. Aletta was later to call him "an ideal dad."

By the time she opened her medical practice in Amsterdam, the hostility and ridicule Aletta encountered during her studies had opened her eyes to the reality of discrimination against women. Her work in an Amsterdam hospital also brought her into contact with social problems she never knew existed: the poverty and wretched living conditions of the working class. She decided to do her best to counter these problems and opened a free twice-weekly clinic for the poor (another first in Dutch history), continuing the practice for fourteen years. Her experiences led her to believe that many of the difficulties facing working-class women derived from their high number of pregnancies. She designed a contraceptive diaphragm (very similar to those available today) and handed it out free of charge. Inevitably, a storm of protest followed. "The hypocrisy I encounter these days!" she wrote in her diary at the time. But, no stranger to protest, she was undaunted. She herself protested poor working conditions for almost fifteen years, eventually winning salesgirls the right to have a chair behind the counter; she also campaigned on behalf of the city's prostitutes, among other causes.

But of all her trailblazing activities, she won the most recognition for her activism for women's suffrage. In 1883, pointing out that the Dutch constitution did not explicitly exclude women from the right to vote, she wrote to the Amsterdam council requesting that her name be added to the register of voters. Her request was met with derision. Undeterred, she fought on, appealing through the courts. In 1902, she

figure in women's equality movements internationally. She traveled the world attending the congresses of the World Union for Women's Suffrage. While at home, she corresponded with other like-minded women she had met, including prominent American suffragette Carrie Chapman Catt, with whom she traveled for sixteen months (1911-12) through Africa and Asia to study the position of women there. During their trip, the two women met Mahatma Gandhi in Johannesburg, inspiring Aletta with yet another cause: peace. At the beginning of the First World War, she organized a women's peace conference in The Hague, which led to the founding of the Women's International League for Peace and Freedom (WILPF), with Jane Addams of Chicago as its president.

Regarding the whole world as her domain, Aletta continued to travel throughout her life. She was involved in women's and peace issues from China to the United States, where she met presidents Woodrow Wilson and Calvin Coolidge—albeit with cool receptions. Returning to the United States in March 1925 to give a lecture at the International Congress of Birth Control, she was welcomed to the White House with much warmth and enthusiasm by Mrs. Coolidge.

By this time, Aletta's health often made it difficult for her to work as hard as she wanted. "But I cannot possibly live like a little old woman and do nothing," she wrote to a friend, and until her death she continued to deliver lectures, write articles, attend peace conferences, and sign petitions.

Short and not physically strong, Aletta nevertheless exuded enormous strength and power. Hers was not a friendly face, and often her expression was rather surly. "She was a remarkable woman of a fiery, passionate temperament, and courageous, but she could also be very tender to those she loved," a friend remembered. In the words of another friend, "She walked like a general and was continually involved in improving the world." The reverse side of her perseverance and tenacity was a tendency to be obstinate, always convinced that she was right. But she commanded enormous respect, and few could deny that she was a truly remarkable person: extremely intelligent, with enormous vitality and a talent for helping, giving, and making things better for others.

Carla van Splunteren

became president of the Organization for Women's Suffrage in The Netherlands.

During the following years, she received much support from her husband, Carol Victor Gerritsen, who was a radical council member. He was extremely progressive in many areas, appreciating Aletta's courage and following the progress of her career before they ever met. He agreed with Aletta that the existing marriage laws were unacceptable to women—they only married (in 1892) because they did not want their child to suffer the social disadvantages of being born to unmarried parents. Tragically, when the couple did have a child some years later, it only lived for one day.

Aletta persevered with her campaigns. Finally, in 1919, Dutch women acquired the right to vote through a law known as "Jacobs-law." She was also a leading

Mary Kingsley

I n August 1893 a thirty-one-year-old English lady named Mary Kingsley boarded the ship that was to take her to West Africa. Before setting out on this momentous voyage she had seldom ventured beyond the confines of her parents' house. But within the next five years Mary Kingsley was to become famous as one of the most intrepid, and least likely, explorers the world has ever known.

A scientist's odd-job woman

When she was growing up Mary Kingsley was more familiar with the "Dark Continent" of Africa than most Victorian young ladies. Her childhood home in Highgate, north London, was full of books about African culture. Her father, Dr. George Kingsley, a scientist, relied on his daughter to help him arrange and record the specimens of plant and animal life he collected on his tropical expeditions. While he was a dedicated if somewhat absentminded scientist, she was efficient and capable. She was also full of practical energy—if a tool or machine broke down she would try to fix it herself. As a European traveler in Africa Mary Kingsley would survive many dangers because of her cheerful, on-the-spot resourcefulness.

When her brother, Charles, went to university, the family moved to Cambridge to be near him. It must have irritated Mary to be so near a university, though as a woman, so far from enjoying its facilities. Her father paid for German lessons for Mary because that language was essential for her work as his assistant, but she received no other formal education. Although as Dr. Kingsley's secretary and odd-job-woman, Mary was exposed to the biological, geological, and anthropological ideas of the day.

The lure of Africa

In 1892 both of Mary's parents died within six weeks of each other. She offered to stay on as housekeeper for her brother, but he was going abroad and did not need her services. At thirty Mary Kingsley faced a future in which she had neither a family nor a career. Instead of feeling free, she felt depressed. She decided to go to Africa because she felt duty-bound to complete some of her father's tropical research. The newly orphaned Mary Kingsley also did not mind the fact that the trip to Africa might likely claim her life.

Mary Kingsley disregarded the conventions of polite society, which would have sent her to Africa as a Christian missionary rather than a scientist. With the help of her father's colleagues, Mary assembled an expeditionary scientist's kit: preserving liquor, bottles, and collecting cases. She also ignored advice about the clothes that might be suitable for a single lady scientist in Africa. Instead of packing men's trousers Mary packed a number of strong black traveling skirts. Even paddling an African canoe through raging rapids Mary Kingsley was more comfortable in a skirt. On one occasion her impractical outfit saved her life: when she fell into a game trap only her tough skirt prevented her from falling onto lethally sharpened stakes.

Six months later, in spring 1894, a triumphant Mary Kingsley returned to England. She brought beetle and fish specimens from the Congo to the British Museum of Natural History. One hitherto unknown species of freshwater fish, *Ctenopoma kingsleyae*, was named for its finder. The traders with whom she had sailed along the West African coast had showed her how to communicate with the inland villagers of Angola without an interpreter, and she even made a profit for herself by dealing in small quantities of rubber and ivory.

After the thrilling sights and sounds of her travels, Mary found England gray and dreary. Late in 1894, less than a year after her return, she set off again for her beloved West Africa.

Canoes, crocodiles and cannibals

African religion and laws fascinated Mary even more than African animals and plants. Now she wanted to meet true Africans, people who were uncontaminated by what she called "rubbishy white culture." She aimed to sail up the River Ogooué (in modern Gabon) by steamboat, continuing by canoe when she reached the rapids, then returning to the coast by an overland route. This journey would take her into the heart of the Fan (or Fang) tribe, a people notorious among coastal Africans as well as Christian missionaries for their cannibalism.

Among the Fan, women were held in high regard, and this unusual woman fascinated them. When Mary cured the sick mother of a powerful chieftain her safety in the land of these "uncommonly fine people" was guaranteed. When she was sailing back to England Mary was inspired by the sight of Mount Cameroon. She simply had to land and climb this 13,760-foot (4070-m.) peak, and from a direction not previously attempted by a European of either sex.

A best-selling celebrity

Back in England, Mary Kingsley wrote a best-selling book about her experiences. Her *Travels in West Africa*, published in 1897, was as entertaining as it was informative, and its author was extremely popular as a lecturer. In Victorian England Mary Kingsley was a daringly original thinker. She demanded greater respect and understanding of black African culture. Polygamy, for example, was attacked by missionaries as an example of African "savagery" but Mary Kingsley defended this custom. She explained that,

for African women, more wives meant less back-breaking work. Mary also campaigned against British colonial taxation schemes that failed to take account of African communal landowning traditions.

Back to Africa

In spite of her success as a writer and lecturer, Mary longed to return to Africa. In 1899, when war broke out in South Africa between the Boers and the British colonial authorities, she volunteered to serve as a nurse. Working as a nurse in a military hospital she was in her element. She was a brave and resolute nurse, but in the summer of 1900 she died of the fever that was ravaging her patients. She asked for a simple burial at sea, but a gun carriage carried her coffin to the pier and a torpedo boat committed it to the ocean. It was an unusual burial, but in eight hectic years Mary Kingsley had proved herself as a most unusual person. In 1901 the African Society (later the Royal African Society), an organization dedicated to greater understanding between white Europeans and black Africans, was founded in her honor.

Margaret Mulvihill

Marie Curie

 arie Curie was the first woman scientist to achieve world acclaim for her contribution to the science of radioactivity. She was born in Warsaw, Poland, on November 7, 1867, the fifth child of professional parents. Her early life was struck by misfortune: two years after a sister's death when Marie was nine, her mother died of tuberculosis. Many impoverished years followed. At the age of eighteen she began working as a governess and helped finance her sister Bronia's medical studies in Paris. Her sister was to return the kindness; in 1891 Marie joined her there. In Paris she attended lectures and studied late into the night in her student garret. She graduated from the Sorbonne in the University of Paris with honors in mathematics and physical science.

In the spring of 1894 she met Pierre Curie, and the following year they were married. The couple had two daughters, Irène in 1897 and Eve in 1904. Soon after her marriage Marie decided that the subject for her doctoral thesis would be the mysterious radiation emitted by uranium, which had been discovered by Henri Becquerel in 1896. Fascinated by Becquerel's findings, she decided to investigate whether other elements were capable of emitting radiation. In 1898 she found that the ore of uranium, pitchblende, was more radioactive than uranium, indicating that it contained a much more "radioactive" element.

Despite all the potential difficulties, she and Pierre set out to extract the active substance from several tons of pitchblende residue, which was cheaper than the ore. It was a long and laborious task, and they worked unaware of the dangers of exposure to high levels of radioactivity. Few scientists could have worked in greater discomfort: they worked in an old store shed, and their research was often hindered by lack of money. However, they persevered, and after repeated chemical treatments of pitchblende they isolated a compound that was one thousand times more radioactive than uranium. This compound consisted of two new elements: polonium, named in honor of Marie's native country, and radium.

In 1903 Marie obtained her doctorate for her thesis on radioactive substances. International recognition for her work followed: she and Pierre shared the Davy Medal awarded by the Royal Society of Great Britain. In 1903 they were awarded the Nobel Prize for Physics jointly with Henri Becquerel for the discovery of radioactivity. Many other honors followed, but recognition and fame overwhelmed both Marie and her husband. They shunned the limelight and turned down many lucrative offers. Even when industrialists saw a future for medical and industrial applications of radium, the Curies claimed no royalties and refused to take out any patents. They chose to

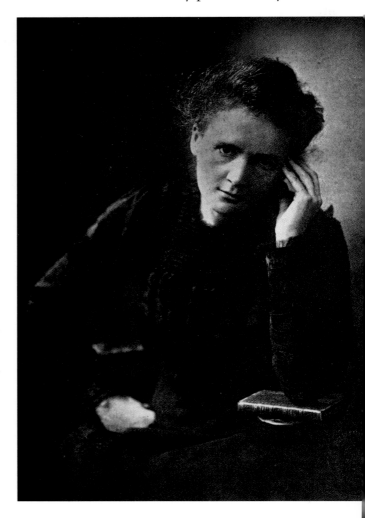

remain in France and gave free advice to anyone who asked for it.

The accidental death of her husband in 1906 in a road accident affected Marie Curie deeply. She coped by putting all her energy into the scientific work that they had begun together. The Sorbonne offered her the lecture post that Pierre had held, which made her the first female lecturer at the Sorbonne; in 1908 she was appointed professor of physics. Her achievements did not end there. In 1911, only eight years after she had first won it, she was again awarded the Nobel Prize, this time for chemistry for the isolation of pure radium. It was the first time that a scientist had received the award twice.

When World War I broke out she developed, with her daughter Irène's help, the medical use of X rays in military hospitals; she also organized courses in radiology for the military medical staff. The Red Cross made her the head of its radiological service and she equipped the ambulances that she accompanied to the front lines with portable X ray apparatus.

Her next achievement was to become head of the research department of the Radium Institute established by the University of Paris; she and her husband had planned the institute years earlier. One of Marie Curie's major achievements was to recognize the importance of a stockpile of radioactive substances for medical and scientific use. American women were so moved by Madame Curie's talent and generosity that they opened a national subscription to offer a gram of radium, and in 1921 she visited the United States with her daughters to receive a gold key from President Warren G. Harding to the case holding the precious substance.

In the years that followed, she labored to establish safety standards for workers handling radioactive substances and as vice president of the International Commission for Intellectual Cooperation, to increase the number of available international postgraduate scholarships. In addition to all this she found time to lecture and continue her research on the chemistry of radioactive materials and their medical applications.

Due to a decline in her health, her work was disrupted. She never mentioned her illness and only complained about the interruptions in her work imposed by doctors. Her health deteriorated further; in 1932 she suffered lesions on her finger as a result of handling radium. She spent the final months of her life in a sanitarium in the French Alps, where she died of leukemia on June 29, 1934, the disease undoubtedly caused by her prolonged exposure to radiation.

Eleni Stylianou

"Mother" Jones

 Mary Harris Jones, known affectionately as "Mother" by the union miners she called her "boys," was one of the most wildly popular labor leaders of the turn of the century. Once called the "most dangerous woman in America" by a West Virginia prosecutor trying her for the death of a mine guard, Mother Jones looked like a sweet grandmotherly woman, with twinkling blue eyes and a dark dress and bonnet. But her fiery tongue and stinging wit revealed a devoted unionist, an eloquent rabble-rouser who defied categorization.

As an organizer for the United Mine Workers, and later for the more militant Western Federation of Mine Workers, Mother Jones was involved both on the periphery and at the center of some of the most significant labor battles of twentieth-century America: the railroad strike of 1877, the 1886 Haymarket Square bombing, the 1894 Pullman strike, the Colorado mining strike of 1913-14 and its bloody aftermath, and the 1919 steel strike.

The very qualities which charmed her followers — her inflammatory rhetoric, her intense individualism, her political inconsistency, and her fierce anti-institutional nature — have for the most part kept Mother Jones out of the history books.

While a socialist at heart, she rejected the Socialist Party. Though she dedicated her life to social justice, she opposed the suffrage movement. While she let no man tell her what to do—from company bosses to American presidents—she believed that a woman's place was in the home, supporting her husband and raising her children. When referred to as a "great humanitarian" in a public meeting, she objected: "Get it right. I'm not a humanitarian. I'm a hell-raiser."

Mother Jones, for all her passion and activism on behalf of working people, was a late-blooming hell-raiser. Born Mary Harris on May 1, 1830, near Cork, Ireland, she came from a long line of Irish Catholic tenant farmers. Her father, forced to leave the country for agitating, brought his wife and their three children to settle in Toronto, Canada, in 1838.

Young Mary Harris attended Toronto public schools and graduated from high school, a rare opportunity for a woman of her time. Trained as a teacher and a seamstress, she taught in Canada, New England, and Michigan before eventually taking a position in Memphis, Tennessee, where she met and married George E. Jones, an iron molder, in 1861.

Her early union education began with her husband, a devout member of the Iron Molders' Union. The couple had four children and lived a contented life until the summer of 1867 when a raging yellow fever epidemic swept through Memphis, taking with it George Jones and all four children.

The thirty-seven-year-old widow moved to Chicago to set up shop as a seamstress, living in the midst of a bustling hive of factories and workshops, a hub of the nation's expanding industrialization. Sewing fancy dresses for the newly affluent capitalist class while passing the abject poor in the street, Mary Harris Jones witnessed the country's growing class gulf.

In 1871, the great Chicago fire destroyed Jones's home and livelihood, leaving her with nothing but the clothes on her back. She attended the early meetings of the idealistic Knights of Labor—the first American union to try to organize both skilled and unskilled workers, and the first to admit women—and soon became a dedicated unionist, without property or a home, and the most adored labor leader of her time.

Specializing in organizing miners in their fight for decent wages and working conditions, Mother Jones experienced firsthand the poverty and tyrannical control that so many large companies of the day exercised over their workers. She lived with miners and their families during strike campaigns, sleeping on a different floor night after night, organizing soup kitchens and women's auxiliary groups, heaving a drink or two with the miners, speaking with them in their own—often profane—vernacular, and urging them on to fight for union recognition.

Mother Jones organized strikes across the nation

throughout her long career, and participated in the formation of the most influential labor unions of the time, including the radical Industrial Workers of the World, known as the Wobblies. But it was in the coal fields and in the workers' tent colonies of West Virginia and Colorado that Mother Jones did her best and most effective work.

In 1908 she traveled to a mine strike in Paint Creek, West Virginia, where there had been weeks of violence. She marched a thousand strikers to Charleston where she demanded that the governor send in the state militia to help negotiate a settlement. Instead, the militia imposed military law, so she set out on a lecture tour of the northeast, using her best talent, her powerful rhetoric, to spread word of the plight of the West Virginia miners. The media coverage won her and her cause further notice in the halls of power in Washington, but the violence continued.

Company thugs attacked a mining camp before Mother Jones returned from her speaking tour, machine-gunning miners, women, and children. When a company guard was killed in revenge, Mother Jones and several others were arrested and kept in solitary confinement for several weeks without knowledge of the charges against them and without access to a lawyer. The seventy-eight-year-old Mother Jones refused to be tried in a military court on the grounds that it was unconstitutional, but was nonetheless denied a civil court hearing, convicted, and sentenced to twenty years. Public protest over her subsequent five-week incarceration in a military guardhouse led to a senatorial investigation of the West Virginia labor situation. She and her fellow prisoners were released and martial law lifted. Soon after, the company recognized the coal miners' union and granted most of their original demands.

In 1913 Mother Jones went to Colorado. She had been deported a decade earlier by the governor's militia for "agitating" for an eight-hour day and fair wages for miners. In true hell-raiser form, she had hopped off the train in Denver, penned a scolding letter to the governor, and returned to the fray.

Ten years later, the miners in the south who had never achieved union recognition struck again. The governor, with the state militia standing ready, threatened to jail any outside agitators, specifically, he said, troublemakers like Mother Jones. She headed for the strike zone where she was arrested and imprisoned for nine weeks. When the governor offered her freedom in exchange for leaving the state, the eighty-three-year-old refused. Released nonetheless, she returned to the strike zone and was again jailed for a month, where she wrote in her autobiography she had to "fight sewer rats with an empty bottle."

Eventually she returned to the strike zone and witnessed the aftermath of the Ludlow Massacre, a bloody confrontation in which sixty-five were killed. National guard troops attacked a tent colony, machine-gunned the camp, and burned it to the ground. The bloody confrontation again brought labor's struggle to the nation's attention, but despite federal attempts to resolve the strike, the company prevailed.

Active almost to the end of her one hundred years, Mother Jones tirelessly organized and lectured on the right of workers to a decent life. She closed her 1925 autobiography with these words:

"In spite of oppressors, in spite of false leaders…the cause of the workers continues onward. Slowly his hours are shortened… slowly his standards of living rise to include some of the good and beautiful things of life…. Slowly, those who create the wealth of the world are permitted to share it…. The future is in labor's strong, rough hands…."

When she did finally succumb to age on November 30, 1930, she was buried in the United Mine Workers cemetery in Mount Olive, Illinois, among the graves of her "boys." Over twenty thousand admirers attended her funeral.

Holly Lloyd

The Pankhursts

Late in 1903, in the northern English city of Manchester, a resourceful, forty-five-year-old widow by the name of Emmeline Pankhurst founded the Women's Social and Political Union. Mrs. Pankhurst's husband had been a radical lawyer, and when he was alive the Pankhurst household had campaigned for every progressive political cause. Mrs. Pankhurst supported herself and her four children by working as Manchester's registrar of births and deaths. In spite of her economic independence, she was acutely conscious of her political powerlessness as a woman. This new organization, the WSPU, was dedicated to one issue: Votes for Women!

Ladies versus women

There was nothing new about the idea of votes for women. Many British people were critical of a parliamentary political system that denied the vote to poor men as well as all women. But before Mrs. Pankhurst's campaign, supporters of votes for women, who were called "suffragists," tended, in practice, to be supporters of votes for *ladies* rather than all women. This was because most of the suffragists, like Millicent Garrett Fawcett, were wealthy and highly educated ladies. Naturally enough, radical working women were suspicious of female suffragists and more inclined to put their faith in general campaigns for real democracy based on universal suffrage, or votes for all adults.

Mrs. Pankhurst's WSPU changed all that. The WSPU insisted that it didn't matter if only a minority of women won the vote, to start with: "Our main concern was not with the numbers of women to be enfranchised but with the removal of the stigma upon womanhood as such. Even if the vote were to be given only to women with black hair or to women of a certain height, it would mean that the barrier against women had been broken." Mrs. Pankhurst's eldest daughter, Christabel, was studying law. In spite of her brilliance, Christabel could not practice as a lawyer because of her sex. But the WSPU would benefit from Christabel's eye for fresh political strategies and legal loopholes.

Late in 1905 the WSPU hit the headlines with an action that was designed to rouse women as they had never been roused before. Christabel Pankhurst and Annie Kenney deliberately disrupted a large political meeting in

Emmeline Pankhurst (above and opposite, below) Christabel Pankhurst (opposite, top)

traditionally the day on which the British government outlines its schedule for the forthcoming year.

Right from the start the WSPU leadership understood the importance of publicity. When they organized a demonstration they made sure that the newspapers knew about it in advance. With an eye to striking photographs, marching suffragettes would be asked to wear white clothes, or, if they were nurses or university graduates, their uniforms or academic gowns. Often, catchy WSPU slogans would become newspaper headlines. For the new popular newspapers, with their bold headlines and large pictures, the dynamic Pankhursts were a gift. While Emmeline and Christabel made speeches and gave interviews, Sylvia, Emmeline's second daughter, worked on the suffragettes' brilliant banners and posters. But it was not all color and glory. When the government realized how serious the suffragettes were, there were serious consequences.

Manchester by continually shouting "will you give votes to women?" at a prominent Liberal politician. As they were being forcibly removed from the hall, the two young women spat at a policeman to make sure that they would be arrested and charged with an offense. Then, rather than pay a fine, they chose to go to prison. When, after a week in jail, Britain's first female political prisoners were released, they were national heroines, and "the Cause" of votes for women gained national recognition.

The suffragettes

Within weeks of Christabel's release, Emmeline Pankhurst moved the WSPU's headquarters to London. Unlike previous female suffragists, WSPU supporters were not content to sit on committees and organize petitions. The *Daily Mail* called these militant women "suffragettes," and they were never out of the news. Taking advantage of an ancient right, the right of the common people to make a direct appeal to the king, the WSPU organized a massive "rush" to Parliament on the day of the King's Speech—

In 1912 Christabel Pankhurst had fled to France to avoid arrest. Through the WSPU newspaper she continued to direct WSPU strategy, having even more charisma as an outlaw in exile. It was at this stage in the WSPU's campaign that Sylvia Pankhurst broke with her mother and elder sister. While the elegant Emmeline and Christabel Pankhurst were being feted by high society, the much messier Sylvia was making her base in London's working-class East End. She was involved with working women, and trade union and socialist struggles, as well as the WSPU "cause." Christabel disapproved of Sylvia's support for striking dockers, miners, and railwaymen, and Sylvia disapproved of some of Christabel's wilder tactics. As Christabel gradually moved to the political right, Sylvia was moving into the world of revolutionary international socialism.

Cat and mouse

In 1908 Mrs. Pankhurst herself was arrested for the first time. Faced with a hostile government, the WSPU had moved from mass demonstrations into more controversially militant tactics. The WSPU was run like an underground army. Suffragettes disrupted public events and harassed prominent antifeminist politicians. Groups of women smashed windows in London's large stores, while others set mailboxes on fire. When they were arrested, usually for damaging property or breaching the peace, suffragettes were treated as common criminals rather than political prisoners. In protest against this many went on hunger strikes.

To deal with hunger strikers the government authorized a dangerous method of forced feeding in which liquid food was poured into a hunger striker's stomach through a rubber tube clamped to the nose or mouth. But the public was outraged by this torture. The government then introduced the Prisoners Act of 1913, called the "Cat and Mouse Act," by which hunger strikers were released and then, as soon as their lives were no longer at risk, re-arrested. Mrs. Pankhurst was released and re-arrested twelve times. On one occasion she arrived at a meeting on a stretcher. In the same period Sylvia Pankhurst suffered forced feeding, only to be released from prison as a haggard skeleton.

War and victory

In September 1914 Britain joined in World War I. Immediately, in return for the suffragettes' help with the war effort, suffragette prisoners were released. Emmeline and Christabel were enthusiastic patriots. Christabel urged able-bodied men to join the army, and Mrs. Pankhurst toured the United States, using her skill as an orator to help persuade Americans to join the Allies. In 1918 British suffragettes were rewarded when the vote was given to women over thirty. The age restriction was introduced because it was feared that female voters over the age of twenty-one would outnumber male voters. By then the Pankhursts had diverged into new campaigns and causes. Mrs. Pankhurst was less concerned with political rights and more concerned with morality, or "social hygiene." But she did live to celebrate the Equal Franchise Act of 1928, which finally granted the vote to women on the same terms as men.

Like her mother, Christabel was increasingly concerned with the sexual rather than the political oppression of women. Instead of retiring as a brilliant veteran of the suffragette cause, she put her energy into evangelical Christianity. She turned down an offer to star as herself in a movie about the triumph of militant suffragettes. Eventually, Christabel settled in California, where she died in 1959 as a champion of Second Adventism.

Sylvia Pankhurst actively opposed World War I, which she saw as a dispute between superpowers that were equally to blame for social evils. She spent the war running a pacifist campaign, as well as a Montessori school and a clinic in London's East End. Inspired by the Russian Bolshevik revolution of 1917, Sylvia hoped for a similar revolution in Britain, and she became a founding member of the British Communist Party. In the 1930s Sylvia Pankhurst was active in the antifascist movement, and the father of her child was a prominent Italian socialist, Silvio Orto. She became involved with Ethopia's struggle against its Italian fascist invaders and eventually settled in that African country. When she died, in 1956, she was the editor of Ethiopia's main English-language newspaper.

Mrs. Pankhurst's youngest daughter, Adela, never took to the limelight like her older sisters. In her personality and sympathies Adela was more like Sylvia than Christabel. Sylvia and Adela believed that they represented the radical principles of their father, Richard Pankhurst. During the most militant phase of the WSPU's campaign, just before World War I, Adela became ill with the strain of her political work. Partly because of her health, and partly because of political disagreements with her mother and Christabel, she emigrated to Australia in 1914. There she became involved with socialist and pacifist movements, as well as feminist campaigns. Before World War II Adela Pankhurst was active in the Australia First campaign, arguing for an alliance with Japan rather than the imperial British motherland. Later she worked as a nurse for handicapped children and she died, in 1961, as a convert to Catholicism.

In their phenomenal careers, each of the Pankhurst women displayed the one thing they had in common—a passionate and unswerving dedication to the ideals that inspired them.

Margaret Mulvihill

Sylvia Pankhurst, opposite, and leaving suffragette headquarters for Buckingham Palace in 1914, above

Rosa Luxemburg

 osa Luxemburg spent her entire adult life, much of it in prison and most of it in political exile, organizing the resistance in Europe to war and exploitation. Passionately dedicated to permanent revolution and workers' power, she had a horror of bloodshed. She was one of the most important and original thinkers of the European socialist movement, and also one of its most trenchant critics.

Born of middle-class Jewish parents in the small Polish town of Zamosc, Luxemburg was captivated as a child by the poetry of Polish socialism, which promised deliverance to oppressed peoples, including the despised Jews. At the age of sixteen she joined Poland's illegal revolutionary party. Two years later she escaped arrest by fleeing to the Swiss town of Zurich. There she entered the university to study natural sciences, mathematics, and economics. She immersed herself in the works of Karl Marx and was active in Zurich's revolutionary emigre circles.

In 1898 she moved to Germany, which was then the center of the international socialist movement. Already recognized as the intellectual leader of the Polish revolutionary movement and one of the major contributors to Marxist thought since Marx himself, she wrote articles and addressed mass meetings urging workers to strike for better conditions and topple the established order. Twenty-eight years old, a Jew in her native Poland, a foreigner in her adopted Germany, a woman, and a cripple since childhood, Rosa Luxemburg fearlessly attacked German socialist leaders for flinching from revolution and the "immediate class consciousness of the working masses," in favor of more gradual reforms.

In 1904 her views landed her in prison for "insulting the Kaiser." When revolution swept Russia the following year, she wrote pamphlets for the Polish party dismissing the "policeman's theory" of a revolution propagated by conspiratorial groups of agitators. The leadership's role in revolution is limited, she wrote; it is the workers who in these upheavals achieve the unity which gives a historical dimension to revolutionary consciousness and enables it to triumph.

At the end of 1905, as Russian revolutionaries were rounded up and arrested, Rosa Luxemburg smuggled herself into Russian Poland, where she was imprisoned for four months, released on health grounds, then imprisoned for a further two months in Berlin. It was from her Berlin prison cell that she wrote her most original work, *The Accumulation of Capital*, an analysis of the problems of expanded capitalist reproduction, which predicted that the cause of its undoing would be its exploitation of the backward countries.

One of the few socialists at the time to recognize that capitalism's new imperialist phase carried with it the imminent threat of world war, she still hoped that socialism could defend Europe from war. On the outbreak of the 1914 war, when socialists in the German parliament voted to support war credits for the Kaiser's government, Rosa Luxemburg, Karl Liebknecht, and Klara Zetkin led the struggle against militarism. Insisting that only workers' power could bring peace, Luxemburg was arrested for inciting soldiers at the front into mutiny. After defending herself in the dock in a damning indictment of imperialism, she left the courtroom to deliver her antiwar message to mass meetings around Berlin. In 1916 she wrote from prison her "Junius Pamphlet," in which she described war as a reversion to barbarism, and posed the choice between "imperialism, the destruction of culture, desolation, degeneration, a vast cemetery. Or the victory of socialism, the conscious struggle of the international proletariat against imperialism and its method: war."

When revolution swept Russia in February 1917, Luxemburg called on German workers to support their Russian comrades by overthrowing the Kaiser's army. Greeting the Bolshevik revolution eight months later as the spark which could ignite world revolution, she also criticized Lenin's centralist leadership for imposing on people "a passive obedience to duty."

"shoulder to shoulder against capitalism."

As German government forces mobilized against the revolution, socialist leaders threw in their lot with the state and the revolution was smashed. Thousands of workers were murdered, and on January 15 soldiers smashed Rosa Luxemburg's skull with their rifle butts and dumped her body in the canal.

This woman of passionate faith, whose motto was "doubt all," longed throughout her life for both a family and a political life at a time when men were expected to be leaders and women were expected to support them. Yet despite writing articles for Germany's socialist women's newspapers and speaking at women's meetings, she always denied that women were any more prone than men to the conflicts between passion and politics. Her life's struggle was for women to be accepted in the front line of socialist theory and leadership. Soaring above the contradictions of her nature and of the present, Rosa Luxemburg inspires us

When revolution broke out in Germany in November 1918, Rosa Luxemburg was released from prison. Throwing herself into an endless round of public meetings, she called for workers' and soldiers' councils to take over power and for the masses to fight still with her vision of a "life worth living," which would give everyone the right to "love with a clear conscience."

Cathy Porter

Charlotte Despard

harlotte Despard, British feminist and social reformer, packed three intertwined careers into her ninety-five hectic years. The first of these began in 1890, the year she took to charitable work to get over her grief at her husband's death. As a wife Mrs. Despard had written long and sentimental novels laced with indignation about social injustice; as an independent widow she resolved to do something about human suffering.

Charity and politics

Charlotte Despard's chosen area was a slum called Nine Elms in Battersea, south London. Instead of condemning alcoholic fathers, careless mothers, and delinquent teenagers, she tried to improve the demoralizing conditions in which these families lived. She set up a health clinic and a youth club, campaigned for free school meals and medical inspections for poor children, and, most important, she actually lived in Nine Elms, in a flat above the shop that served as the headquarters of her mini welfare state. The people of Nine Elms were overwhelmingly Irish and Catholic, and they regarded Mrs. Despard as a kind of saint.

From charity Charlotte Despard moved into politics. As an elected Poor Law Guardian, a member of the committee that managed local workhouses, she did her best to represent the people who depended on public welfare. It seemed clear to her that there would be no real improvement in the lives of the poor until the common people had a say in government, locally and nationally. Now the saintly Mrs. Despard of Nine Elms became the socialist Mrs. Despard who gave rousing speeches at socialist mass meetings.

The "Fighting *Temeraire*"

When the Women's Social and Political Union, founded by Emmeline Pankhurst, moved from Manchester to London in 1906, Charlotte Despard joined the suffragette struggle in the same spirit as she had joined the socialist movement. Charity was not enough—she believed that women as well as working men had to have political power before social injustice could be overcome. She was soon recognized as one of the leaders, along with Millicent Fawcett and Emmeline Pankhurst, of the struggle for votes for women. Younger suffragettes were encouraged by her presence and the newspapers nicknamed her "the fighting *Temeraire*," after an old battleship.

In 1907, the suffragette movement split, and Mrs. Despard left the WSPU to become the leader of another organization, the Women's Freedom League. The WFL favored propaganda work and passive resistance over campaigns against property. The famous grille protest, in which suffragettes chained themselves to the offensive rail that screened off the Ladies Gallery in the House of Commons, was organized by the WFL. Eventually, the rail had to be removed with the women still attached to it, but it never returned to Parliament. (It is now an exhibit in a London museum.) Mrs. Despard justified WFL actions by saying: "There are times and seasons in human history when civil disobedience is the highest duty we can offer to our generations."

Militant pacifism and international socialism

Like other suffragettes, Charlotte Despard joined in the war effort on the outbreak of World War I. Since her beloved only brother, Sir John French, was Inspector-General of the British Army, she might have been expected to take a patriotic line on Britain's part in the war, but she didn't. While Emmeline and Christabel Pankhurst were scorning conscientious objectors and condemning Britain's "enemies," Charlotte Despard was primarily concerned with the relief of families on the home front.

When the war ended, late in 1918, she supported a new charity, Save the Children, which tried to help young victims of war, whether they were "enemies" or not. In the spring of 1918, soon after the vote was granted to women over thirty, she resigned from the WFL presidency. While other prominent suffragettes were "retiring" and writing their memoirs, Charlotte Despard started a new political career in Ireland.

The call to Ireland

Charlotte Despard regarded herself as an honorary Irishwoman and was often described as "Irish-born" in the British press. She was fond of her Irish in-laws, her Irish friends in Nine Elms, and proud of her father's Irish ancestors. Her sympathy for the Irish republican movement brought her into conflict with her brother. In 1918 he had been sworn in at Dublin Castle as Lord Lieutenant, or Viceroy, of Ireland. While he set about crushing Irish "rebels," his sister was supporting them.

Soon after the Anglo-Irish Treaty was signed in 1921 Charlotte Despard moved to Ireland. She had hoped to play a part in the setting up of a

proud new state, but, as Ireland collapsed into a bitter civil war, she found herself back at work as a campaigner for civil rights and the relief of distress. She lived outside Dublin with the celebrated Irishwoman, Maud Gonne MacBride, and their household was at the center of radical Irish campaigns in the 1920s. Although she was nearly eighty years old, Charlotte Despard was still active enough to be classified as a dangerous subversive under the terms of the Irish Free State's Public Safety Act.

At the celebrations to mark the Equal Franchise Act of 1928, when women were granted the vote on the same terms as men, she was fêted as an honored veteran of the suffragette cause.

In 1939, Charlotte Despard died after a fall. She was buried, with full Republic honors, at the Glasnevin cemetery in Dublin. At the funeral Maud Gonne MacBride called her a "white light in defense of prisoners and the oppressed." Although votes for women was probably the only clear "victory" on Charlotte Despard's long list of struggles, many of the causes that her more conventional political comrades found eccentric—her vegetarianism, her pacifism, her concern for the environment—are at the top of today's political agenda.

Margaret Mulvihill

Helen Keller

elen Keller's struggle to acquire language and her subsequent academic and literary achievements have served as inspiration for the education of the learning disabled throughout the world. The extraordinary story of her emergence from her solitary "phantom world" to international fame as a writer and tireless campaigner for the disabled is well documented, and she is respected as a testament to the human capacity for strength, determination, and compassion.

Helen was born in Tuscumbia, Alabama, in 1880. At nineteen months she suffered an undiagnosed illness which left her deaf and blind. Plunged into darkness and silence, her initial grasp of language soon faded and she became mute, unable to communicate with her family apart from using a small number of signs.

Helen remained trapped in this autistic existence for more than five years. She later described it as a

period of mental drought during which she experienced nothing but unchanging blankness. When Helen was six years old, Alexander Graham Bell advised her mother (who had read Charles Dickens's account of the education of another deaf-blind girl, Laura Bridgman) to contact the Perkins Institute for the Blind in Boston. Bell was very much involved with the education of the deaf, as both his wife and mother were deaf. The head of the Perkins Institute responded to Helen's case with great interest and recommended a recent graduate from the Institute, Annie Sullivan, as Helen's tutor.

Annie Sullivan was herself a remarkable woman. Born into appalling poverty, Annie and her younger brother, Jimmie, were abandoned by their father to a Massachusetts poorhouse after the death of their mother. Annie's sight was deteriorating rapidly as a result of an untreated trachoma in early childhood, and Jimmie suffered from a tubercular hip. Jimmie died shortly after the two arrived at the poorhouse, and Annie lived there in circumstances of extreme emotional and material deprivation. At fourteen, she begged a visiting commission of the State Board of Charities to allow her to attend a school for the blind, and in October 1880 she enrolled at the Perkins Institute. Despite her unhappiness at the school, Annie enjoyed academic success and graduated valedictorian of her class in 1886.

Annie arrived in Tuscumbia as Helen's tutor at the age of twenty. Although she had studied the account of Laura Bridgman's education and had learned the manual alphabet to communicate with Laura (who was still a resident at the Institute during Annie's education), Annie had only six years of formal education and no teaching experience. She relied heavily on the experience of her blindness (now partially relieved by an operation) and the isolation of her childhood to guide her in Helen's education.

Before meeting Annie, Helen had lived in a chaotic world, lacking any form of discipline. She existed with no concept of the impact of her actions on her sur-

her own curiosity and enthusiasm. Their joint labor and success brought them international fame through Michael Anagnos, the head of the Perkins Institute, who published reports widely of Helen's case.

Having learned to communicate, Helen longed to learn the oral language and to graduate through college. To her regret her speech did not improve dramatically, and Helen always considered this her greatest handicap. She did, however, realize her ambition to attend college, enrolling at Radcliffe in 1900. She persisted despite a punishing entrance schedule and a battle to be accepted as a student. She completed the requirements to graduate with a bachelor of arts degree in 1904—a feat quite astonishing considering that most of the reading material was not provided in raised print. Annie had to spell the texts (as well as the lectures) laboriously into Helen's hand. During her studies at Radcliffe, Helen developed a passion for writing, and her first autobiography, *The Story of My Life*, was published in 1902 to enormous acclaim.

After graduation Helen continued to write, but began to direct more of her energy and enthusiasm into politics and campaigning for the disabled. In 1906 she was appointed to the State Commission for the Blind, leading a highly successful campaign against ophthalmia neonatorum, an eye disease in infants. She published a collection of socialist essays, *Out of the Dark* (1913), and became an ardent supporter of militant suffragism. During this period, frequent accusations were launched by a public who had adored her poignant and charming image as a child battling against her afflictions but now viewed her as hijacked to leftist politics. Ignoring these blows to her maturity and independence, Helen continued to devote her life to her political convictions, lecturing and fundraising around the world for the education of the deaf-blind and lobbying for changes in legislation to provide support services with the American Foundation for the Blind.

It is difficult to encapsulate Helen Keller's individual accomplishments and her commitment to others, something perhaps best stated in her own words: "When we do the best we can, we never know what miracle is wrought in our life, or in the life of another."

Rachel Hunt

roundings. She suffered deep frustration, evidenced by frequent violent outbursts. Described by most who knew her as wild and destructive, it was widely assumed—although not by her parents—that her illness had left her significantly brain-damaged.

Annie's attempts to introduce order and meaning into Helen's life were at first met with violence and rage. So upsetting was this to Helen's family that Annie insisted that she and Helen should live in a separate annex, where Annie could physically restrain Helen without the intervention of her parents. Determined to liberate Helen from her isolation, Annie stayed with her day and night, spelling continuously into her hand. After just four weeks, Helen made the vital connection between the finger spelling and her surroundings. She understood that everything she touched and smelled had a name and that the finger spelling was the code for discovering these names. Annie's perseverance had offered Helen the key to human thought and communication. Reintroduced to language, the outside world slowly revealed itself to her.

Annie recognized Helen's potential, and worked hard and long, encouraging Helen to learn through

Alexandra Mikhailovna Kollontai

*I*n *Autobiography of a Sexually Emancipated Woman*, Alexandra Kollontai writes of women's "eternal defensive war against men's encroachment on our individuality, a struggle revolving around the problem: work or love." It was in her search for a synthesis between the two that Kollontai built her vision of happier, freer relations between men and women, and of a society in which women could control their own lives and bodies.

She was a solitary child, immersing herself in her parents' libraries and writing stories. As a young woman, she rebelled against her parents' plan to bring her out into the St. Petersburg marriage market. At the age of eighteen, she married her cousin, Vladimir Kollontai, a factory inspector. Not long after the marriage and the birth of their son, Misha, she began to chafe against what she called "love's tyranny," and to question whether patterns of sexual domination and dependence could ever truly be transformed within marriage. The "turning point" in her life came in 1896, when she and Vladimir visited a large textile factory near St. Petersburg, and she first witnessed the horrifying realities of Russian workers' lives. In that year the capital was swept by a wave of strikes, in which large numbers of women joined for the first time. Kollontai left her husband, taking her son with her, in order to study the works of Karl Marx and play her part in the growing strike movement.

In 1902 she joined the Bolshevik party, writing articles on workers' lives in Finland and working to keep the Finnish and Russian workers' movements in touch with each other. When revolution broke out in Russia in 1905 and strikes and demonstrations swept the country, she urged women workers to overcome their diffidence and lack of education and to join the strikes. In 1908, as the revolution was smashed and strikers were rounded up, Kollontai avoided arrest by fleeing St. Petersburg for Berlin. For the next nine years she lived in exile in Europe and America. There she addressed public meetings and wrote her fist articles on women's sexuality, "Love and the New Morality," and "Sexual Morality and the Social Struggle," and her detailed sociological study *Women and Motherhood*.

After the outbreak of the First World War, Alexandra Kollontai was organizing antiwar meetings and writing her pamphlet "Who Needs War?" for frontline soldiers in Europe. In March 1917 she returned to Petrograd (the new name for St. Petersburg) bearing Lenin's "Letters from Afar," which called on Russia's workers to turn the imperialist war into a revolutionary class war. It was at the Kronstadt navel base near Petrograd, bastion of Bolshevik support in the tsarist Fleet, that she met and fell in love with Pavel Dybenko, president of the Baltic Fleet Party committee. Many Bolsheviks were shocked by the startlingly open sexuality of the aristocratic Kollontai's relationship with this sailor and former stevedore sixteen years her junior, and perhaps her subsequent writings on sexuality were partly based on the affair and its repercussions.

On October 25, 1917, the Bolsheviks took power and Alexandra Kollontai became Commissar of Social Welfare. The only woman in the new government, she had to help some of the most pitiable victims of war-torn Russia: the orphans and soldiers' widows, the unemployed and the disabled. Although many of the Bolsheviks' earliest laws were clearly shaped by her ideas, Kollontai realized that liberalizing marriage, easing women's working lives, and simplifying divorce would be worth no more than the paper it was written on without women's grassroots participation in these political issues.

Throughout 1918 and 1919, as the capitalist armies attacked Bolshevik Russia and civil war raged,

Kollontai toured the battle fronts. The makeshift canteens, creches, and crowded living conditions of the civil war years, although hopelessly squalid and inadequate, provided Kollontai with a rough-and-ready model of a genuinely collective society. But she was determined that the Bolsheviks do more for women, and that each party organization have its own women's commission so that women could raise before the party some of the desperate problems facing them.

Alexandra Kollontai is chiefly remembered now in Russia for her diplomatic achievements. Her ideas on sexual liberation and workers' control were before their time, and certainly suggested more complexity and diversity than was acceptable, or perhaps possible, in postrevolutionary Russia. Yet her descriptions of the tragic and universal conflicts between the personal and the political touch on sensitive nerves still, and her writings about more joyous sexual relationships, widely read in Russia during her lifetime, have made her a heroine to women in the West today.

Cathy Porter

Käthe Kollwitz

C elebrated in Germany as one of the greatest draughtswomen and printers of all times, Käthe Kollwitz knew that her upbringing and her temperament would lead her to an art that was critical of the social conditions that surrounded her.

She was born in 1867 into a family of politically committed nonconformists—her father was a Social Democrat, and her maternal grandfather, Julius Rupp, was the founder of a nonconformist Evangelical church. Despite the fact that women were not admitted to any kind of higher education in Germany until 1908 (and even then most art academies refused to admit female students), her father encouraged her to study art.

Käthe studied with private tutors, as well as at a Berlin art school for women. In 1888 she was studying in Munich where she encountered the work of Max Klinger. One of the greatest German etchers, Klinger believed that painting was best suited to "glorifying" the triumphs of the world while the graphic arts were better for attacking and criticizing the realities of life. Käthe was greatly influenced by Klinger, not only in her decision to concentrate on graphic art rather than painting, but also in her choice of subjects. It was in Munich that she first translated her interest in working-class life into art, as in *Zweikampf im Wirtshaus* (*Duel in the Inn*) which depicts a scene from Emile Zola's novel *Germinal*.

Since the age of seventeen Käthe Schmidt had been engaged to a medical student, Karl Kollwitz, and as soon as he qualified in 1891, the couple married. They moved to a working-class district in northeast Berlin where Dr. Kollwitz started his practice as a panel doctor sponsored by the tailors' union. Eleven months later their son Hans was born, followed four years later by a second child, Peter. Käthe worked at home in a studio below their apartment and next door to her husband's surgery, but she often felt torn between the demands of her family and her art. Consequently, throughout her life she had extended periods of artistic inactivity. She was always conscious of the problems she faced as an artist who happened to be a woman, and when she was celebrated as the leading female artist in Germany, she was unhappy being the "woman's representative in artistic matters."

Despite her domestic obligations, Käthe Kollwitz did produce a great deal of work. Her first graphic cycle, *Ein Weberaufstand* (*A Weavers' Uprising*) (1893) took its theme from Gerhart Hauptman's play *Die Weber* (*The Weavers*) about the plight and revolt of Silesian weavers, which she had seen in a private production in 1893. This cycle was first exhibited at the Berlin salon, where it was proposed that the work be honored with a gold medal. The Kaiser, who disliked modern art and realism in particular, refused to sanction the award. In 1899 the medal denied her in Berlin was awarded in Dresden, and *A Weaver's Uprising* was acquired by the Dresden Print Cabinet.

Two years later, and now firmly in the eye of the public, Kollwitz began work on her next graphic cycle, *The Peasant War* (completed in 1908), which is based loosely on historical events and has a similar revolutionary message to *A Weavers' Uprising*. These two print series with their obvious social message were to reinforce the widespread view of Kollwitz as a politically committed, left-wing artist. Kollwitz went to great lengths to point out that she did not have clearly defined political views and to argue that there was more to her art than propaganda. She found the motifs in the lives of workers beautiful and interesting, and she wanted her art to affect the way ordi-

nary people thought. Through her husband's work in the poor section of Berlin where they lived, Kollwitz became aware of the realities of existence for the working poor. She began to draw portraits of some of her husband's patients; *Pictures of Misery* reflected an angry and frustrated sympathy and was drawn for the Munich journal *Simplicissimus*, a popular satirical magazine.

Kollwitz herself suffered great personal tragedy. Her son Peter perished in battle in 1914; his death affected her profoundly. A central theme in her works thereafter was the mother protecting her child, or the mother with a dead child. In 1919 she began making woodcuts. One of the first, dedicated to the memory of Karl Liebknecht, was based on drawings of the revolutionary leader done in the morgue and show his corpse surrounded by mourners.

During the years of the Weimar Republic, Kollwitz produced a further major graphic cycle *War* (1922-23). In 1932 the sculpture *The Parents* was erected in the cemetary where her son Peter was buried, as a memorial to youth of all nations killed in the war. While these works are no longer restricted to working class subjects, they still depict tragedy and melancholy, but as part of the universal human condition.

Her exhibited works were removed from display with the Nazi victory in 1933. The deaths of her husband and her cherished grandson, who was killed in action in 1942, were followed by the bombing of her studio. She died on April 22, 1945, only days before the end of World War II.

Maria Costantino

Above: Self Portrait, *sculpture by Käthe Kollwitz*

Larissa Mikhailovna Reisner

ighter, writer, and first Bolshevik woman commissar, Larissa Reisner was a legendary figure in postrevolutionary Russia, a woman whose strength and beauty embodied for many people all the heroism of the October Revolution.

She was born in Lublin, Poland, of cultured, socialist parents who fully supported women's equality. In 1903 her father's sympathy for his revolutionary students cost him his job as law professor at St. Petersburg University, and the family fled to Berlin to avoid arrest. They returned to St. Petersburg in 1907, in the bloody aftermath of the 1905 revolution, and for the next ten years Larissa dedicated herself to writing poetry.

In 1915 she and her father launched an antiwar poetry magazine, which was closed down the following year by the censors, and after the revolution of February 1917, as leading Bolsheviks flooded back to Russia from exile, she started teaching literacy and literature at workers' clubs around the capital. Thrown from poetry into revolution, she made contact with sailors at the Kronstadt naval base, a stronghold of Bolshevik support, where she met and fell in love with Bolshevik organizer Fyodor Raskolnikov.

After the Bolsheviks took power in October 1917, she worked for the new government cataloging the art treasures of the old regime. The following summer she married Raskolnikov, joined the Bolshevik party, and left Moscow with sailors of the Volga Naval Flotilla to defend the revolution against White guards and the invading armies of the West.

Larissa Reisner sailed for three years on the great warships of the Red Navy as scout, political commissar, and cavalry instructor, fighting on the front line of the Civil War from Kazan to the Caspian Sea. Thousands of young women, most of them without children, left home in those heady days to fight with the Reds and make a new life for themselves. As the daughter of Alexandra Kollontai's generation of socialist feminists, Larissa Reisner felt able to take for granted much of what they had struggled for. Unlike Kollontai, she was never primarily involved in addressing the inequalities which woman continued to suffer after the revolution, nor, unlike Kollontai, did she have the political prestige to do so had she wanted to. Larissa Reisner came of age at a time when it finally seemed possible for women to overstep the conventional female boundaries of family and marriage. Her writings vibrate with the power and challenge of women's life in the Revolution, and of the limitless possibilities, uncertainties, and dangers opening up for them. She believed that only by fighting for the revolution as men's equals could women take their place in the reorganization of power.

Larissa Reisner was one of the first to write about the Civil War, describing all the horror and the heroism of those days in her book, *The Front* (1924). Sailors who fought with her describe her reckless courage in battle, and the wit and warmth of the talks on literature and revolution which she delivered to them on board ship before battle. Like most who fought at the front then, she talked more of heroism than of personal feelings, and her writings make light of the difficulties she experienced as a woman. Beneath the surface of *The Front* we can read how women's confidence was continually eroded by men desperate to cling to their power, and her friends recall her struggle to win men's trust, and the trials to which they subjected her.

When Raskolnikov was appointed first Soviet ambassador in Afghanistan in 1921, Larissa accompanied him to Kabul to infiltrate the harem and persuade the emir's wives to support the Bolsheviks. Leaving Raskolnikov two years later, she returned to Moscow where she attended writers' meetings, worked

Northern Siberia, and the textile towns outside Moscow, where she adopted a twelve-year-old orphan named Alyosha Makarov. Although weakened by frequent attacks of malaria, which she contracted during the Persia campaign, she evoked the lives of those she met on her travels in her book, *Coal, Iron and Living People*, and she continued working as a journalist until 1926. Early in that year she contracted typhus, and on February 9, shortly before her thirty-first birthday, she died.

Larissa Reisner's writings span just a decade, but they evoke a whole epoch, and her short life was such a dramatic one, even in those dramatic times, that it is often hard to see her clearly through the halo of legends that surround her. Almost immediately after her death, popular Bolshevik writers wrote plays about her, poets such as Boris Pasternak invoked the extraordinary appeal of her life, and in the years to come scores of friends, fellow writers, and fighters brought her vividly to life, recalling her endless wanderings, her thirst for experience, her courage in battle, and her poetic— some say "virile"—mind. Strong, proud, and liberated, a model for the future and of the "new Soviet woman," Larissa Reisner has inspired generations of women in Russia.

Cathy Porter

as a journalist, and published *Afghanistan*, her lushly exotic account of her Kabul years. In 1925 she traveled to Germany as *Izvestiya* correspondent and clandestine Comintern officer, witnessing with her lover, Karl Radek, the aborted revolutions in Berlin, Hamburg, and the Ruhr, and describing them in her book, *Hamburg at the Barricades*.

In the year before her death she traveled as a special *Izvestiya* correspondent through Byelorussia,

Radclyffe Hall

I t is unlikely that Radclyffe Hall would have warmed to the role of heroine, but whatever aspects of this role are assigned to her in the worlds of literature and sexual liberation, they are obscured by the rather different rank of champion that is thrust upon her. Born in 1883 in Bournemouth on the southern English coast and christened Marguerite (though in later life calling herself John), Radclyffe Hall belonged to a privileged sector of English society. Educated at King's College, London, and in Europe, she became independently wealthy at the age of twenty-three when her father died. The following year she met Mrs. Mabel Batten, a society lady, with whom she lived for ten years and under whose influence she converted to Catholicism. When Mrs. Batten died in 1916, Radclyffe consolidated a relationship with Una Troubridge which was to continue for the rest of her life.

Radclyffe Hall wrote prolifically, publishing volumes of poetry and seven novels, one of which, *Adam's Breed*, won the *Prix Femina Vie Heureuse* and the James Tait Black Memorial Prize. However, it was her fifth novel, *The Well of Loneliness*, which explores the tragic and unfulfilled life of a woman born with masculine qualities and affections, that was to precipitate her into scandal and confer upon her, deservedly or not, the role of lesbian champion for decades to come.

The book was successfully prosecuted in 1928 under the Obscenities Act, although only one line within it ("…and that night they were not divided…") gives any hint of the consummation of a homosexual relationship. There was a huge public outcry, and *The Well of Loneliness* was banned for the following twenty years. It is interesting to note that it was the book, not its author, that was on trial and as such the publication could not call upon those worthies ranked to defend it (whose numbers included Virginia Woolf and Vera Brittain). The irony of the scandal was, unsurprisingly, that far from suppressing female homosexuality, the word "lesbian" was vaunted publicly for the first time (most of the nation was unaware of the possibility of such a relationship). Also for the first time, homosexual women who had been previously beleaguered in their sexuality felt that they were no longer alone. As Alison Hennigan states in her admirable introduction to the novel, "the critics [ensured] that the Well would never be quite so lonely again."

Important social repercussions notwithstanding, the book has been vaunted, in my view unfairly, as the Bible of Lesbianism, and a crown it never invited topples precariously on its head. The simple truth of the matter is that Radclyffe Hall penned, very courageously, a novel of the 1920s that expressed aspects of her sexuality about which she must have felt, for all the buffering of her wealth and social standing, very isolated. Gothic, melodramatic, didactic, and presumptuous though the book may seem to our modern literary appetites, it must be perceived within the context of its time. Radclyffe Hall was, after all, principally a writer and not an advocate of lesbianism.

However, much as one would like to evaluate Radclyffe Hall on her merits and achievements alone, one cannot be too disingenuous about the powerful social effects of her book. *The Well of Loneliness*, while jejeune in many of its evaluations of lesbians (it refers to them as "inverts" and is prescriptive about their height, their physiology, and their affinities) has nonetheless proved to be an immeasurably powerful focus around which others can express and thus come to understand their own selves and sexuality, if only through contention. A contemporary of Radclyffe Hall, the American lesbian Djuna Barnes, penned and published a scathing pastiche on the privileged Hall and her social cohorts, allowing an expression in herself which may otherwise have remained dormant.

In our current times, lesbianism has, for many, become very closely associated with feminism. Much of the criticism of *The Well of Loneliness* is therefore on the grounds that it affronts the political aspects of modern-day feminism. In describing a lesbian who both identifies with masculine traits and feels herself an "invert," Radclyffe Hall's personal and individual sexuality cannot represent lesbianism in general, while her insecurity and feelings of "otherness" are unsurprising when seen in context. We live in a society greatly liberated from the restrictions which prevailed seventy years ago, and freedom to think notwithstanding, who knows how our contemporary evaluations of sexuality will be judged in another context?

It is unfair to judge Radclyffe Hall on the basis of her having failed to perceive the commonplaces that would prevail fifty years after her death. Her achievement was to speak with the voice of her time, and to do so courageously. Ultimately a heroine must be judged to be such by the strength of her convictions and the extent to which she is prepared to uphold her truth, rather than the extent to which subsequent circumstances foist a championship status upon her.

What is undoubtedly true is that for many lesbians of the 1920s the book represented a reassuring and timely acknowledgment of their sexuality, and for subsequent generations the work has proved sufficiently resonant to be a substantial focus of discussion, exploration, and revelation. Radclyffe Hall, although remembered chiefly for her sexuality

and the trial of her book, was a woman of considerable literary talent who had the courage to live openly by her convictions. The heroic status of *The Well of Loneliness*, as that of its author, is an accident of circumstance. The achievement of Radclyffe Hall within the context of her generation and her particular talents and scope is not.

Catherine Mooney

Margaret Mead

lthough she traveled to New Guinea to test her hypothesis that women's self-image comes from cultural messages rather than their biological destiny (nurture versus nature), anthropologist Margaret Mead had already learned the answer closer to home. She wrote in her autobiography, *Blackberry Winter* (1972), "I was always glad that I was a girl. I cannot remember ever wanting to be a boy. It seems to me this was because of the way I was treated by my parents."

Born in 1901, the second of five children, Margaret Mead grew up in a progressive household in Philadelphia. Her father was an economics professor at the Wharton School of Business. Her mother, Emily Fogg Mead, took her daughter along while she was studying Italian immigrants for her doctoral dissertation in sociology. Margaret began honing her observation skills early. Under her grandmother's tutelage, she observed the behavior and speech of her two younger sisters, keeping detailed notebooks like the ones her mother had kept about her.

When business reverses made her father reluctant to send Margaret to college, her mother convinced him to let their daughter attend his alma mater, DePauw University in Indiana. The midwestern fraternity- and sorority-dominated university was the wrong place for Margaret, but she transferred to Barnard College in New York City after one year. There she became a member of a close-knit group, the "Ash Can Cats," who lived off campus in an apartment. She explained how liberating that friendship was in *Blackberry Winter*. "We belonged to a generation of young women who felt extraordinarily free-free from the demand to marry unless we chose to do so, free to postpone marriage while we did other things, free from the need to bargain and hedge that had burdened and restricted women of earlier generations."

She took her first anthropology course in her senior year. Anthropology was a relatively new field, headed by Franz Boas, her professor at Columbia, and Branislaw Malinowski, at the London School of Economics. Instead of doing ethnography (studying an entire primitive culture), Boas encouraged his students to develop a hypothesis to study a particular aspect of a culture. Mead was drawn to Boas and his shy but brilliant teaching assistant, Ruth Benedict, who told her over lunch one day, "Professor Boas and I have nothing to offer but an opportunity to do work that matters."

While earning her master's degree in psychology, Mead took as many courses as she could with Boas, a mentor for many women, including Zora Neale Hurston. Boas suggested that she study adolescence, but Mead decided to go Samoa despite his objections that it was too dangerous. She enlisted her father's financial support to force Boas to agree, getting additional funding from the Committee for the Biological Sciences of the National Research Council. However, Boas offered very little practical advice about doing field work, as she recalled in *Blackberry Winter*: "When I agreed to study the adolescent girl, I had a half hour's instruction."

In 1925 the twenty-four-year-old Mead set out for Samoa, while her husband of two years, Luther Cressman, went to Europe to continue his divinity studies. She was equipped with half a dozen cotton dresses, a camera, several large notebooks, and the good wishes of Boas and Benedict. She had to find her own site for field work (the island of Tau), her own living quarters (the back room of the British medical dispensary), and her own way of winning the trust of the villagers.

It was lonely work, with many doubts that went along with the joy of discovery. "But nobody really asked what were the young fieldworker's skills and aptitudes—whether he had, for instance, the ability to observe and record accurately or the intellectual discipline to keep at the job, day after day, when there was no one to supervise, no one to compare notes with, to confess delinquencies to, or to even boast to on an especially successful day," she wrote in *Blackberry Winter*.

Although lacking in practical training, her education proved invaluable for communicating with the villagers (despite limited knowledge of their language). "Our training equipped us with a sense of respect for the people we would study. They were full human beings with a way of life that could be compared with our own and with the culture of any other people. No one spoke of the Kwakiutl or the Zuni—or any other people—as savages or barbarians."

This attitude permeates *Coming of Age in Samoa* (1928), which can also be described as the coming of age of anthropology in America. In her study she proved that in a culture more relaxed about sexuality, adolescence was not the stressful time it was in America. Her book was accessible to the general public, which would be the hallmark of much of her writing, including ten major works between 1928 and 1977.

The field trip also led to her being hired in 1926 as an associate curator at the American Museum of Natural History where she was to remain for over forty years. Divorcing Luther Cressman in 1928 to

marry New Zealand anthropologist Reo Fortune, she went to New Guinea to study sexual mores among three primitive tribes. The couple met and joined forces with British anthropologist Gregory Bateson, who would become Mead's third husband and the father of her daughter, Mary Catherine Bateson, born in 1939.

Her conclusion that culture determined male and female roles was published in *Sex and Temperament in Three Primitive Societies* (1933). According to Mead, in the Arapesh tribe both men and women were expected to be nurturing, while among the Mundugumor both sexes were hostile to children—which interestingly made Mead determined to have a child of her own.

For much of her life Mead was a popular, if sometimes controversial figure. She was generous in her support of younger anthropologists, founding the Institute for Intercultural Studies (1944). She taught at Columbia University and at Fordham University, where she chaired the social services division from 1968 to 1971.

In an era when anthropologists were still defining their field, she reached out to the general public, appearing on radio and television and writing a monthly column for *Redbook* women's magazine. She acknowledged the mixed blessings of her celebrity in *Blackberry Winter*, "I have been publicly discussed, lambasted and lampooned, lionized and mythologized, called an institution and a stormy petrel, and cartooned as a candidate for the presidency, wearing a human skull around my neck as an ornament." However, she also played on her eminence, carrying a tall tribal staff with her as she walked through the halls of the museum.

After her death in 1978, Australian anthropologist Derek Freeman attacked her methodology in her first Samoan field trip, igniting a controversy that has not yet been resolved. Margaret had her own answer for such criticism: "Field work is a very difficult thing to do. To do it well, one has to sweep one's mind clear of every presupposition, even those about other cultures in the same part of the world in which one is working." She remained to the end very clear minded and free from cultural prejudices.

Sydney Johnson

Amelia Earhart

melia Earhart, aviation pioneer and early feminist, was adventurous and bold from an early age; she said of herself in a magazine interview in 1928:

"Whether it was considered the thing to do or not was irrelevant. As a little girl I had ridden my buggy in the stable; I had once climbed up on a delivery horse; I had explored the fearsome caves in the cliffs over-looking the Missouri; I had invented a trap and caught a chicken. I had jumped over a fence that no boy my age had dared to jump; and I knew there was more fun and excitement in life than I would have time to enjoy."

This talented tomboy was born into a comfortable middle-class family in Atchison, Kansas, in 1897. Her first experience with real difficulty came with the realization, at about fourteen, that her father was an alcoholic. Her parents separated several times; Amelia and her mother, Amy, and sister, Muriel, stayed with friends in Chicago while the girls were in high school.

During World War I, Amelia left college to serve as a lab assistant and sweeper-upper at Spadina Military Hospital in Toronto. When the war was over, she enrolled in medical school at Columbia University, but left to rejoin her parents in California. She was twenty-three years old, a tall slender young woman with a boyish grin and no particular plans for the future.

When Frank Hawks took her for an airplane ride, she knew that she had found her life. She had to fly—she had to learn to fly and she wanted to compete and set records. She took lessons from Neta Snooks, and she flew with Mabel Boll and Elinor Smith, two other pioneer aviators. They all competed against each other. They were young in a young industry and it was to be expected that they would crash land from time to time or do ground loops upon landing. With financial help from her mother, Amelia bought her first plane from Bert Kinner. It was a rebuilt plane Kinner called an Airster. Amelia had it painted yel-

low and called it the *Canary*. In this plane she set a women's altitude record of fourteen thousand feet.

Amelia met George Putnam, a publisher and promoter, in 1928, just as her career was beginning to take off. Much has been said about their relationship; there is nothing to support the contention of some that this was not a lovematch. They were both bright, loving people with adventurous spirits; both loved to laugh and play practical jokes; each found the other very amusing. However, it is true that George Putnam was good for her career: his connections were prodigious and he was able to put a universe of opportunity into her hands. With his help, the legend of Amelia Earhart grew. George Putnam wholeheartedly supported her career and ambition to be a great pilot. George, in fact, was immediately struck by her physical resemblance to Charles Lindbergh, who had already crossed the ocean in 1927. George saw the possibilities for Amelia to excel as a pilot and as a woman pilot, and Amelia, for her part, was just as committed to building the "property" as he was. Together they planned and executed her solo crossing of the Atlantic five years after Lindbergh; Amelia did a record-breaking transcontinental crossing in 1932. Amelia wrote *The Fun of It* about her flying and was a long-term success on the lecture tours that George arranged for her. They visited the Roosevelts in the White House (Eleanor Roosevelt became a close friend to Amelia); she became the first person to fly solo across the Pacific from Honolulu to Oakland; then she was off on her trip around the world's equator, a flight she said would be her last record-breaking attempt. She was thirty-nine.

Her disappearance near Howland Island in the Pacific was truly a tragic end to her life. She once wrote a note to her husband, George Putnam: "Please know, I am quite aware of all the hazards.... I want to do it because I want to do it. Women must try to do things as men have tried. When they fail, their failure must be but a challenge to others."

Amelia and her co-pilot, Fred Noonan, had flown fifteen of the eighteen legs of the journey, stopping at exotic places such as Natal, Dakar, and Keopang. Their plane, an Electra, had gone twenty-two thousand miles and now had seven thousand to go, all of it over the Pacific. They took off from Lae on the last

leg at 10 a.m. local time. The flight from Lae to Howland was supposed to take some eighteen hours; obviously something went badly wrong. Amelia's last message said: "We'll repeat this message. We'll repeat this message on 6210 kilocycles. Wait listening..."

Her fame and reputation live on. Her legacy to us is her valor, gallantry, and heroism, and above all her courage, the courage of her hopes and dreams. In my office is a picture of Amelia, standing on the tire of the Lockheed in which she flew to Ireland. She stands there in her flying clothes, looking chivalrous and capable, and I go back to work.

Jane Anderson

Margaret Bourke-White

For forty years one of America's best known journalists, Margaret Bourke-White defied the contemporary stereotypes of women: she competed in business on the same terms as men and on the basis of merit.

From 1928 until 1936 Bourke-White's work consisted largely of photographing the practices and products of industry, beginning with the Otis Steel Mills in Cleveland, Ohio. Among photographers of industry Bourke-White was unique in capturing not only the beauty of her subjects but also the age in which she lived.

Her work with *Fortune* magazine began in 1929 and gave her national exposure and the opportunity to cover a wider variety of industries and travel more extensively. Her *Fortune* assignments at this time included photographing shoemaking in Massachusetts, the Chicago stockyards, the Corning Glass factory, and behind-the-scenes life in an industrial city, South Bend, Indiana.

In content and form, the aim of Bourke-White's photographs was to convey the power of the industrial age, and while her work was recognized as art—frequently exhibited in museums and receiving medals at salons—it must be remembered that her work was primarily commercial. Her photographs functioned as advertising and promotion for the business and industry of America. For Bourke-White, photographing anything was an artistic endeavor. She often went to potentially dangerous extremes in order to get a single shot; her professional code was based on her belief in being able to produce a picture under any conditions and in any circumstances.

Bourke-White was invited to the Soviet Union to photograph the First Five-Year Plan. Following the 1917 Revolution, no foreigner had been permitted to take photographs in the country and no photographs of any significance emerged until Bourke-White returned in 1930 with eight hundred pictures taken on her journey to the new centers of Russian industry. She made two more trips to the Soviet Union.

Advertising work kept her occupied continuously through the spring of 1934 but the work was becoming less satisfying: her instinctive desire to convey something of the meaning of the times in which she lived was drawing her increasingly towards news photography. Ultimately she decided to quit advertising work and in December 1934 she began her association with the NEA News Syndicate. She also accepted a commission from Trans World (whose routes covered the western and southwestern United States), to photograph the Dust Bowl in Texas.

Her observations of the sufferings in the region brought Bourke-White into the growing circle of artists who were vocal critics of the American social condition. From 1936 onwards when advertising work was excluded completely, she committed herself to photo assignments that she believed could be undertaken in a creative and constructive way.

By coincidence she heard that Erskine Caldwell, author of *Tobacco Road*, was interested in collaborating on a project that would show that the southern world of *Tobacco Road* with its poverty and racism was not a far-fetched fiction. Their collaboration resulted in two things: the book *You Have Seen Their Faces* and their marriage in 1939.

In October 1936 Bourke-White became one of the first staff photographers for *Life*. Her first assignment was to photograph the chain of dams on the Columbia River; her photograph of Fort Peck Dam became the magazine's first cover. While the majority of her early assignments were news stories, among her notable photo essays of American life is her series on Muncie, Indiana, illustrating the daily habits of the town that had been the focus of a landmark 1920s sociological study.

Bourke-White covered World War II for *Life*. She and Caldwell also collaborated again for *North of the Danube*, published in 1939. She pursued independent projects because she felt *Life*'s policy was too restrictive: she wanted to present images that would provoke social debate.

In 1939 *Life* assigned Bourke-White to Europe where in London she photographed Winston Churchill and Emperor Haille Selassie of Ethiopia before traveling on to Romania, Turkey, Egypt, and Syria. Still dissatisfied with *Life* as an artistic outlet, she quit the magazine to begin work on a new daily afternoon newspaper, *PM*. The newspaper did not last long; an anonymous document claiming that *PM*'s staff were either Communist Party members or communist sympathizers was circulated among New York newspapers. The FBI followed up, and for the next fifteen years Bourke-White was the subject of FBI investigation.

Bourke-White returned to *Life* as a freelancer. *Life* was for the remainder of her career the primary source of her photographic assignments, including a cross-country trip with Caldwell resulting in their book *Say, Is this America?* (1941). After this, they stopped collaborating on book projects, although Caldwell's *All Out on the Road to Smolensk* and Bourke-White's *Shooting the Russian War* emerged from their 1941 trip to the Soviet Union. Traveling via China, Bourke-White had photographed Chiang Kai-shek and his wife and the "warphanages," homes for Chinese war orphans, before arriving in Moscow. She photographed the siege of that city when the nonaggression pact between Germany and the USSR broke down. She photographed the bombardment from the balcony of her hotel near the Kremlin, using light from the flares.

When the United States entered the war Bourke-White was eager to become a war correspondent. In addition to surviving a torpedo attack on the convey in which she was traveling to cover the campaign in North Africa, in 1943 she became the first woman to accompany an Air Force crew on a bombing raid.

Frequently one of the first correspondents to follow the conquering Allied forces into newly liberated sites, Bourke-White toured and photographed all along the Western Front until she entered Buchenwald and the Erla prison camp near Leipzig. The haunting images of these camps shocked the world.

She continued to tour Germany for *Life* until the end of the war but stayed until October 1945 in order to write *Dear Fatherland, Rest Quietly* (1946). She traveled to India to photograph Mahatma Gandhi in 1946 and in 1947 returned to cover the religious

violence there. She photographed Mahatma Gandhi again. Only hours after she had interviewed him, Gandhi was assassinated.

In 1949 *Halfway to Freedom: A Report on New India* was published, and although Bourke-White continued to lecture and write newspaper and magazine articles, she did not publish a book again until 1963 when her autobiography, *A Portrait of Myself*, was published. She had begun working on the book in 1952; she was now suffering from Parkinson's disease. Despite two cranial operations her ability to move and speak gradually diminished, but not before she helped to focus nationwide attention on the plight of fellow sufferers. In June 1959 *Life* ran a feature with photographs by Alfred Eisenstaedt on her struggle.

Before she became completely disabled Bourke-White continued to work as vigorously as ever and traveled extensively: to South Africa in 1949, Japan and Korea in 1952.

After 1952 she was too ill to photograph at a professional level and concentrated on her autobiography. While the scenes that had passed before her lenses were always changing, Bourke-White's photographs and writings reveal her constant concern for the issues behind the surface of the news, and despite a critical eye, her thinking never turned into cynicism.

Maria Costantino

Frida Kahlo

I n April 1953, less than a year before her death at forty-seven, Frida Kahlo held her first major exhibition in her native Mexico. She was very ill by this time, and no one expected her to attend the opening. But in characteristic dramatic style, she was carried on a stretcher into Mexico City's Gallery of Contemporary Art and brought to a four-poster bed decorated for the occasion. This event exemplified the qualities that marked Kahlo as a person and as an artist: her courageous spirit in the face of physical suffering and her love of spectacle (particularly as a mask to preserve her privacy and dignity). It also reinforced the central theme of most of her paintings—herself: in her short career, most of the two hundred paintings she produced were self-portraits.

The daughter of a German immigrant, Wilhelm Kahlo, and his second wife, Mathilde Calderon, Frida had a largely traditional upbringing for a Mexican girl—devout and domestic. When she was six years old the mischievous child she recalled in her diary was replaced by a more serious, withdrawn child. Illness elicited this change: she was stricken with polio and spent nine months confined to her sickbed. Kahlo's rehabilitation program comprised a rigorous physical regimen supervised by her father. Unusual for girls a the time, the activties included boxing, soccer, swimming, and wrestling.

Her father encouraged her interest in art: Wilhelm was a photographer by trade and taught his daughter to use a camera and to develop, retouch, and color photographs. At school, Frida was a voracious reader but not a dedicated student. Although she was interested in art and literature, people fascinated her more.

In 1925 Frida was traveling on a bus that collided with a tram. Her injuries were severe, and her life from then on was a continuous battle with slow decay. During her rehabilitation following the accident Kahlo began painting. Her first subjects were portraits of friends, family, and herself.

In late 1927 she had recovered sufficiently to lead an almost normal life. She rejoined her school companions, most of whom were by now students at the university and active in protest demonstrations. Through these friendships she was drawn into the bohemian world of artists and communists. She joined the Communist Party and met Diego Rivera.

Like Rivera, Kahlo was easily bored; they were both delighted to have a companion who viewed life with the same mix of irony and black humor. During their courtship, Frida began to paint more extensively. In August 1929 Kahlo and Rivera were married. Kahlo painted little during their first months of marriage: being married to Rivera appeared to be a full-time job. She learned to cater to his tastes from Lupe Marin, Rivera's second wife, who taught Kahlo to cook his favorite meals. In return Kahlo painted Lupe's portrait.

It was not until a belated honeymoon that Kahlo began painting regularly again. In November 1930 Rivera and Kahlo traveled to San Francisco where Rivera was to paint two murals for the city. During their six-month stay, Frida painted several portraits. As always, the subjects of these portraits were her friends, and the link between artist and model affected the look and meaning of her work.

Rivera was increasingly feted by the wealthy art patrons of America. Kahlo accompanied Rivera on his travels to New York to attend the opening of the retrospective of his work at the Museum of Modern Art. Kahlo's initial shyness in New York society gave way over the years to an active and glamorous life: among the couple's friends were Henry Ford, Nelson Rockefeller, Dolores del Rio, and Paulette Goddard. In Mexico their home became a mecca for an international circle of friends that included Leon Trotsky, André Breton, and Sergei Eisenstein. In Paris, Kahlo's hosts were Marcel Duchamp, her lover Isamu Noguchi; Miró, Tanguy, and Kandinsky were admirers.

During a stay in Detroit in 1932 Kahlo became pregnant for the second time and lost the child again (her first pregnancy, in 1930, had to be terminated). Her painting *Henry Ford Hospital*, dated simply July

1932, depicts the first of a series of bloody and shocking self-portraits that were to mark Kahlo as one of the most original painters of her time. In this portrait, Kahlo lies naked on her hospital bed holding six veinlike ribbons attached to floating objects symbolizing her miscarriage. Three more times Kahlo was to try to have a child and fail. In place of her own children Kahlo transferred her maternal affections to her nieces and nephews, her collection of dolls, and numerous pets.

When the Riveras returned to Mexico from the United States Frida's hopes for a harmonious family life were shattered: Rivera began an affair with Kahlo's younger sister Christina. Furthermore, Kahlo was hospitalized at least three times in 1934. While Kahlo may later have dismissed her husband's affair she did not forget it: testimony to its lingering impact are *Memory* (1937) and *Remembrance of an Open Wound* (1938). In these two paintings Kahlo used physical wounds as symbols for her mental pain. She is also no longer the passive female submitting to her fate — instead she appears staring at the viewer as if conscious of her personal suffering.

In 1938 Kahlo exhibited her work for the first time in New York and had her first major sales. The same year she came to the attention of the surrealist André Breton who offered to organize an exhibition for her in Paris. Kahlo was now recognized as independent from her husband: she was a painter in her own right.

On her return to Mexico, Kahlo and Rivera separated and then divorced. Yet even after their divorce Kahlo and Rivera's lives remained intertwined: Kahlo continued to handle Rivera's correspondence and business affairs, and the couple frequently made public appearances and often entertained guests together.

In December of 1940 they were remarried in a brief ceremony in San Francisco. Immediately afterwards Rivera went off to work on a mural and Kahlo returned to Mexico. Their new marriage settled into a pattern whereby they lived more or less independently of each other.

In the 1940s, as a result of her exhibitions abroad

and her participation in the International Exhibition of surrealism in Mexico City, Kahlo's career took on greater momentum. But from 1944 onward her health deteriorated slowly. Though in public she made light of her illness, in private she was obsessed by her suffering and her wounded self-portraits were a form of silent weeping.

In August 1953 Kahlo's right leg had to be amputated. After the operation she refused at first to wear an artificial leg—she found it distasteful and painful—but after three months she had learned to walk short distances. Despite the surgery Kahlo did not recover completely: her behavior was unpredictable and she became increasingly dependent on large doses of prescription drugs. Not having painted for almost a year, Kahlo forced herself out of bed and into her studio, where she would paint for as long as she could stand the pain.

In July 1954 Frida Kahlo made her last public appearance, at a communist demonstration. In a crowd of more then ten thousand people, Rivera pushed Kahlo in her wheelchair through the streets of Mexico City. Photographs of her taken during the march show her holding a banner emblazoned with the doves of peace in her left hand, clenching her right hand in a tight fist. Unfortunately Kahlo was suffering from pneumonia at the time; the infection deepened and she died on July 13, 1954.

Maria Costantino

Lise Meitner

Austrian nuclear physicist Lise Meitner was a pioneer in her field, both as a scientist and as a woman. She was born in Vienna on November 7, 1878, the third of eight children of Hedwig Skovran and Philipp Meitner, an attorney. Both her parents were of Jewish origins and her father was a freethinker, but all the children were baptized and raised as Protestants.

Meitner showed a precocious interest in physics, but her parents encouraged her to study for the state examination in French so she could support herself as a teacher if necessary. She passed the examination then studied privately for the entrance test for the University of Vienna, where she was enrolled in 1901. At first she was treated rudely, but her diligence impressed both classmates and teachers, and she became the second woman to receive a doctorate in science from the university.

For several years Meitner remained in Vienna, doing experiments in the new field of radioactivity with Stephan Meyer. She designed and performed one of the first experiments to demonstrate that alpha rays are slightly deflected in passing through matter. Then an interest in theoretical physics took her to Berlin to study with Max Planck, originator of the quantum theory. Soon afterward she became his assistant. She had some difficulty in finding a place to do experimental work until she met Otto Hahn, who was in need of a physicist to help him in his work on the chemistry of radioactivity. Hahn himself was working at the Chemical Institute under Emil Fischer, who did not allow women in his laboratory. So Hahn and Meitner fitted up a carpenter's workshop for radiation measurement and began the long collaboration that would be so important to the development of atomic energy. (Two years later, Fischer welcomed Meitner into his laboratory—after women's education had been regularized in Berlin.) As a chemist, Hahn was interested mainly in the discovery of new elements and the examination of their properties, while Meitner was more concerned with understanding their radiations.

In 1912 Meitner joined the Kaiser-Wilhelm Institute for Chemistry, recently opened in Berlin. Her work was interrupted by World War I, when Hahn was called to military service and she volunteered as a roentgenographic (X-ray) nurse with the Austrian army. Occasionally she and Hahn obtained leave at the same time and returned to their laboratory work in Berlin. The study of radioactive substances lent itself to this episodic approach, since measurements made at fairly long intervals allowed some activities to build up and others to decay. By 1918 they were able to announce that they had found the unknown precursor of actinium, a new element they named protactinium.

That same year Meitner was appointed head of the physics department at the Kaiser-Wilhelm Institute while maintaining her ties to the University of Berlin.

Her inaugural lecture there, given in 1922, was on cosmic physics (reported in the press as "cosmetic physics"). In 1926 she was appointed extraordinary professor, contributing to the weekly physics colloquia with Planck, Albert Einstein, Gustav Hertz, and others of their stature.

Throughout the 1920s Meitner continued her studies on the relationships between beta and gamma rays. She believed that primary electrons emitted in beta decay and studied by photography must form a group of well-defined energy. This was in the spirit of the quantum theory then being applied to nuclei. She and Wilhelm Orthmann published an influential paper on this subject in 1929, which led to a correspondence with Wolfgang Pauli in which he proposed the existence of a new neutral particle (the neutrino) too elusive to be detected by means then available. (Not until 1956 would this hypothesis be confirmed.)

During the early 1930s nuclear physics made dramatic advances with the successive discoveries of the neutron, the positron, and artificial radioactivity. In 1934 Meitner resumed her work with Hahn to follow up experimental results obtained by Enrico Fermi. After Austria was occupied by Nazi Germany, Meitner had to leave the country because of her Jewish origin, which she had always acknowledged. She went briefly to Holland, then to Denmark, where she was welcomed by physicist Niels Bohr and his wife. She was invited to work at the new Nobel Institute in Stockholm, where a cyclotron was being constructed, and accepted eagerly. At the age of sixty, she went to Sweden, acquired a good command of the language, and built up a small research group.

In 1938 Otto Hahn and another German chemist, Fritz Strassmann, split the uranium atom when they bombarded uranium with neutrons and produced barium. The following year Meitner and her nephew, physicist Otto Frisch, published their interpretation of the work of Hahn and Strassmann. Meitner developed a mathematical theory to explain the splitting of the uranium atom into two fragments and calculated the energy released in nuclear fission. It was her major contribution to science.

Meitner was vehemently opposed to the use of her discoveries for purposes of destruction. During World War II, she was invited to join the team at work on the development of the nuclear-fission bomb. She refused categorically. Indeed, she hoped until the very end that the project would prove impossible.

In 1946 Meitner spent half a year in Washington, D.C. as a visiting professor at Catholic University. In 1947 she retired from the Nobel Institute and went to work in the laboratory established for her by the Swedish Atomic Energy Commission at the Royal Institute of Technology. She continued to travel, lecture, and attend concerts (she had a lifelong love for music) during her remaining years in Sweden. In 1960 she retired to Cambridge, England, where she died on October 27, 1968, a few days short of her ninetieth birthday. After the development of the atomic bomb, she did no further work in nuclear fission.

Robin Langley Sommer

Simone de Beauvoir

A dominant literary figure in postwar France, Simone de Beauvoir was the most celebrated woman in a coterie of left-wing writers and intellectuals. Her work encompasses novels, articles, essays, interviews, and philosophical and theoretical texts. She achieved renown as an advocate of women's emancipation and a leading existentialist thinker. However, she is undoubtedly best known for her groundbreaking work *The Second Sex* (1949), which has become a standard feminist classic.

Simone de Beauvoir was born into a bourgeois Parisian family on January 9, 1908. Her happy, sheltered childhood growing up near the Luxembourg Gardens on Boulevard Raspall is recounted with startling honesty in the first volume of her autobiographical trilogy, *Mémoires d'une jeune fille rangée* (1958). It also relates her school days at the Institute Sainte Marie in Neuilly, as well as her later studies at the Sorbonne and the École Supérieure Normale preparing for a degree in philosophy, which she received in 1929. It is as a student that de Beauvoir first began to develop the sense of political awareness that led her to the idea of *engagement* (commitment) that is central to her thinking. Her concept of engagement expressed a deeply held conviction that writers and intellectuals must be politically committed—or *engagé*—and must strive to change the world through the influence of their ideas.

At the Sorbonne in 1926, away from the influence of her conservative and conventional family, de Beauvoir was introduced to a circle of acquaintances radically different from the milieu in which she grew up. She met politically active students such as Pierre Nodin and other members of student Marxist groups who initiated her conversion to the political Left. Later, at the École Nationale Supérieure she befriended René Maheu, who gave her the nickname "Castor" (a pun on her name, "castor" being French for "beaver") which stayed with her for the rest of her life. Through him she was drawn into a clan of friends—an elitist foursome which succeeded in outraging and alienating the rest of the students. The others in the group were Paul Nizan, who would become a harsh critic of the ineffectiveness of intellectuals, and Jean-Paul Sartre, whose name is synonymous with Existentialism, and who had a profound effect on her intellectual development.

Like Sartre, who became her lifelong companion, de Beauvoir attempted to develop a philosophy that recognized the responsibilities of being a conscious individual, an ideology reflected throughout her writing, especially in such early works as *Pyrrhus et Cineas* (1944) and *Pour une morale de l'ambiguïté* (1947). The couple shared as well, as she said, a hatred "of the Right, conventional thinking and religion." Her criticism of bourgeois morality, tantamount to a rejection of her own background, led to an estrangement from her beloved father, a staunch supporter of the Right, which perhaps confirmed her commitment to the Left.

In the spring of 1939, with the spread of fascism and the increasing inevitability of war, she further developed her idea of political engagement. She committed herself to writing, and in 1943 she ceased her brief career teaching philosophy with the success of her first published novel, *L'invitée*. But it is *The Second Sex*, translated into no less than fifteen languages, that established Simone de Beauvoir as a major figure of French literature. *The Second Sex*, which has been called a beacon lit by de Beauvoir to guide women of the second half of this century, is a rejection of the notion of woman's "natural" inferiority to man. Drawing on history, sociology, and psychoanalysis, de Beauvoir examines female servitude to her biology, laying out the historical facts and myths that have relegated women, throughout three centuries and throughout the world, to a social and economic position subsidiary to that of men because of the confinements of her biological functions. Describing how women have been positioned as the "other," or the second sex, she follows the development of the female

from birth to adolescence, sexual initiation, and into adulthood, insisting that "one is not born a woman, one becomes a woman."

In 1954 she once again received recognition when she was awarded the Goncourt prize for *The Mandarins*, a novel which describes the uneasy relationship between the individual intellectual and structures of political opposition, such as the communist party. De Beauvoir's own influence as a writer and her notion of engagement were tested by that very same tension. Considered suspect by the revolutionary left for her bourgeois origins, she also was never fully able to identify with the proletariat who she championed. Negotiating the gap between theory and practice, she maintained the view that an intellectual's responsibility could manifest itself as an ethic and not necessarily as physical intervention. In her later years, however, de Beauvoir's own engagement did entail practical activism as she assumed a leading role in the women's movement of the 1970s, joining the fight for reproductive rights and becoming president of the League for Women's Rights in 1974. She was also interested in the issues of aging and the treatment of the elderly, and she addressed this in two books: *Une Mort très douce* (1964), an account of her mother's death in a hospital, and *La Vieillesse* (1970).

Simone de Beauvoir died on April 14, 1986. Her career can be read as a chronicle of feminism and existentialism.

Catsou Roberts

Anne Frank

"In spite of everything, I still believe that people are really good at heart."

—ANNE FRANK, *DIARY OF A YOUNG GIRL*

When I first read those words I was roughly the same age as the author who wrote them—about thirteen. Like her, I kept a diary and dreamed of being a writer. We were both Jewish.

But it was impossible not to be painfully aware of the differences in our situations. I was reading her diary on a sunny summer afternoon on my family's backyard porch; I was American; and I and my family could live and worship openly as Jews. But Anne Frank, a Jew in Nazi-occupied Amsterdam, was compelled to dream her dreams while hidden in an attic where she, her family, and a handful of others attempted to escape detection and deportation to a Nazi concentration camp—simply because they were Jewish.

By my age, Anne Frank had seen and experienced so much suffering and persecution because of her religion that I could only wonder at the extraordinary resilience and faith she expressed in her diary.

Anne was born in 1929 in Frankfurt, Germany. In 1933, Adolf Hitler came to power, and Anne's father, Otto Frank, moved the family to Amsterdam, where he thought they would be safe from the Nazi's increasingly harsh restrictions against the Jews. But in 1940, Germany invaded and occupied the Netherlands. The new Nazi regime lost little time in decreeing anti-Jewish laws. These harsh and humiliating injustices included closing stores owned by Jews, forcing Jews to wear yellow stars, and expelling Jewish students from most schools. Worst of all, the Nazi government began rounding up Holland's Jews for deportation to so-called "work camps" that, in reality, were death camps designed to carry out the systematic extermination of the Jewish people—final destinations named Auschwitz, Bergen-Belsen, and their like.

Once again, Otto Frank tried to save his family, this time by arranging to hide them in a secret annex carefully hidden in the same building as Frank's former business. Anne, her sister Margot, and their par-

ents took up their new "residence" on July 9, 1942, sharing their tiny attic space with four other Jews: Mr. and Mrs. Van Daan and their son Peter, and a dentist named Albert Dussel.

These eight people were to spend the next two years confined at such close quarters that it was less surprising that they had their occasional quarrels than that they managed to retain so much mutual good will. Completely housebound by necessity, they also became strangers to natural daylight. They lived an inverted schedule—moving quietly or sleeping during the business hours of the offices located on the floors below, and only talking, stirring, and making noise at night.

In her diary, Anne Frank recorded the trials and hopes of those days and nights of confinement. Her observations reveal clarity and maturity well beyond that of a typical adolescent—except one who was blessed with a gift for poetic insight and at the same time cursed by the tragedy of history. She writes with objective lucidity about herself, her family, her budding romance with the adolescent Peter Van Daan.

Below: Anne's diary entry next to the photo said "This is a photo as I would like to look all the time. Then I would maybe have a chance to come to Hollywood."

Dit is een foto, zoals
ik me zou wensen,
altijd zo te zijn.
Dan had ik nog wel
een kans om naar
Holywood te komen.
AnneFrank.
10 Oct. 1942

There is hope, despair, irritation, hurt, wistful yearning and even humor and optimism, especially after news reached the group of the Allied landing in Normandy in June, 1944.

Then, with the war drawing to a close, on August 4, 1944 the Nazi Gestapo, acting on a tip from an informer whose identity was never uncovered, raided the secret annex. The Franks, Van Daans, and Dussel were arrested and deported to concentration camps. Mrs. Frank died at Auschwitz; Anne and Margot perished at Bergen-Belsen. Of the eight, only Otto Frank survived.

Throughout the Franks's time in hiding, one of Otto Frank's most trusted former employees, Miep Gies, and her husband, Henk, risked their own lives by providing the chief link between the hidden group and the outside world, supplying food, gossip, news, and moral support. It was also Miep who, after the Gestapo raid, returned to the abandoned hiding place and rescued virtually the only thing she could—the scattered pages of Anne's diary. These papers she carefully preserved and gave to Otto Frank upon his return from his ordeal at Auschwitz some months after the war. In 1947, as a memorial to his daughter, he consented to the publication of her diary.

Since then, Anne Frank's *Diary of a Young Girl* has been published throughout the world, having been translated into more than thirty languages. It has been dramatized for stage, screen, and television. Anne Frank was one of far too many ordinary adolescents who died in the extreme conditions of the Nazi Holocaust. But Anne Frank left an extraordinary legacy in her diary—a voice that remained filled with hope and light, despite the darkness that surrounded her.

Diane Cole

Rosa Parks

 hen Rosa Parks refused to give up her seat on a bus on December 1, 1955, it was a spontaneous and individual act in defiance of bus segregation. She did not think at the time of the possible long-term effect of her action. But in many ways, her experiences prepared her for such an action, and the people around her had long supported a sense of justice and hope for civil rights.

First there was the inspiration of Rosa Parks' mother, Leona McCauley, a former school teacher, who had benefited from the NAACP's struggle to secure equal pay for black teachers in the 1940s. A staunch believer in freedom and equality, Leona McCauley felt that change for oppressed people was possible in this country, an optimism she passed on to her daughter.

Then came the loving support of her husand, Raymond, a lifelong advocate for civil rights.

There was also the backing of church and community, and support from friends at Highlander, an educational center in Tennessee where adults stud-

ied resolutions for social, political, and economic change. There Rosa Parks encountered numerous activists, including Martin Luther King Jr., Ralph Abernathy, and Pete Seeger.

Rosa Louise was born in Tuskegee, Alabama, on February 13, 1913, to James and Leona McCauley. Her mother, after separating from her father, moved to Montgomery with Rosa and her brother, Sylvester, and they lived with Leona's parents as an extended family. As a young girl, Rosa attended Montgomery Industrial School, where she developed a love for learning and mastered the craft of sewing.

A child of the segregated South, Rosa witnessed the humiliation of her mother and grandparents not being accorded the respect due adults, and watched them work for inadequate and unfair salaries. As she came of age, she too would experience the second-class treatment of blacks in the South. Parents tried to shield their children from the harsh realities of segregation, but it was not possible to hide the ugliness and shame that black people experienced on a daily basis.

Daunted though Rosa's spirit may have been growing up with such degradation, it was rekindled through church and community. For in this circle—neighbors congregating on porches, in Sunday morning services where there were lessons on faith and endurance—Rosa Louise was ever reminded of her worthiness. These circumstances were the proving ground for the person who would become the "Mother of the Civil Rights Movement."

Rosa married Raymond Parks, a barber, in 1932. Both were members of the Montgomergy branch of the NAACP, where Mrs. Parks served as secretary in the 1950s. Mrs. Parks' decision to make hers a test case was one she came to with her husband and mother. They discussed whether or not she should challenge the law of segregation on public transportation and agreed that it was the right thing to do.

"When people made up their minds that they wanted to be free and take action, then there was a change," Mrs. Parks has said of the response to her courageous act. "People just stayed off the buses because I was arrested, not because I asked them. If everybody else had been happy and doing well, my arrest wouldn't have made any difference at all."

Rosa Parks' refusal to give up her seat and subsequent arrest led to a bus boycott that lasted for 381 days and ended with the victory of desegregation of the city bus system in Montgomery.

She and her husband were unable to continue working and living in Alabama. They moved to Detroit, along with her mother, where Mrs. Parks worked in the office of congressman John Conyers.

Prior to refusing to give up her seat on the bus, Mrs. Parks had attended Highlander at the invitation of E.D. Nixon, president of the Alabama branch of the NAACP, and Virginia Durr, a white woman from Montgomery who worked against segregation in the South.

Myles Horton, founder of Highlander, recalls in his autobiography, *The Long Haul*, that Rosa Parks didn't know what she could do to fight segregation "in the cradle of the confederacy." He adds that in a later workshop, she spoke passionately about her first workshop experience:

> "At Highlander, I found out for the first time in my adult life that this could be a unified society—that there was such a thing as people of different races and backgrounds meeting together in workshops and living together in peace and harmony… I gained there the strength to persevere in my work for freedom—not just for blacks, but for all people."

Mrs. Parks speaks in *I Dream a World: Portraits of Black Women who Changed America* of how her display of courage affected not only blacks but whites as well. "Many whites, even white southerners, told me that even though it may have seemed like the blacks were being freed, they felt more free."

In 1987 she and her husband founded The Rosa and Raymond Parks Institute of Self-development to provide career training for black youth. Rosa Parks has co-authored two books, and has received numerous awards and honorary degrees. Her insurmountable courage and gentle spirit continue to make her one of the most admired women in the world.

Brenda Wilkinson

Above: Rosa entering the courthouse in 1956

Golda Meir

Growing up, I always thought of Golda Meir as the quintessential Israeli—a woman who dedicated her life to founding and building the new country which she would one day lead, the State of Israel.

It wasn't until I was older that I discovered that she was born in the old world, in Kiev, Ukraine, in 1898. (She was not reborn as "Golda Meir" until 1956, when she hebraized her name at the suggestion of Ben Gurion, another of Israel's founders.)

Goldie Mabovitch, as she was called at birth, did not live long in the Soviet Union; she and her impoverished family moved to the United States when she was eight. Yet in those few years she saw enough of czarist Russia's harsh persecution of the Jewish people to carry a lifelong imprint of the memory.

Even in her seventies, Golda Meir could recall how, as a bewildered four-year-old, she had watched her father, a poor carpenter, barricade their meager home to protect the family against an expected pogrom against the Jews. Although this particular pogrom never came to pass, the emotions of fear and rage at the possibility of such an outbreak never quite left her.

I have always been struck by the fact that these feelings were so intense that she chose to recount them on the very first page of her autobiography, *My Life*, (1975): "I remember how scared I was and how angry that all my father could do to protect me was to nail a few planks together while we waited for the hooligans to come," the seventy-seven-year-old Golda wrote. "And, above all, I remember being aware that this was happening to me because I was Jewish, which made me different from most of the other children in the yard. It was a feeling that I was to know again many times during my life—the fear, the frustration, the consciousness of being different and the profound instinctive belief that if one wanted to survive, one had to take effective action about it personally."

But then, action characterized her life, and I have also felt that a good part of her strength resided in her sheer tenacity. Perhaps most tenacious of all was her belief that her dreams—even one so far-fetched as the creation of a modern independent Jewish state—could become reality.

Golda had turned seventy and was officially retired from public life when she was elected prime minister. But in her story there are models for the young as well as old. As a young girl in Milwaukee, where her family settled after leaving the Soviet Union, eleven-year-old Goldie displayed a sense of social consciousness—along with a precocious feel for political activism—when she successfully organized a group called the American Young Sisters Society to raise money to pay for poor children's textbooks. Three years later, when her parents objected to her continuing her studies (a high school education was considered a luxury in those days for the daughters of poor families), rather than yield, the determined fourteen-year-old ran away.

The story unfurls like a novel, except that it really happened. Goldie fled to Denver where, in the home of her progressive-thinking older sister Sheyna, the teenaged Goldie received a different kind of education. As she listened to the household visitors' non-stop political talk, a new world seemed to open to her. By the time Goldie returned to Milwaukee two years later—her parents finally having agreed to let her complete her studies—the nascent nation builder had become deeply drawn to the Zionist movement and its dream of founding a Jewish state in the land called Palestine.

While in Denver, the young woman had also met the man whom she would eventually marry, Morris Meyerson. They wed in 1917, the same year that British Foreign Minister Alfred Balfour issued his famous declaration promising his government's support for a Jewish homeland in British-ruled Palestine. Increasingly politically active, Goldie became ever more determined to settle in Palestine to help make this promise a reality.

In 1921, the couple set sail for Palestine. For three years they lived on a farming kibbutz, an experience

II, she did what she could to bring world attention to the plight of Europe's Jews, but her forceful pleas garnered little response. Afterwards, when the full tragedy of the Holocaust became known, she remonstrated with the British to allow those who had survived Hitler's concentration camps to emigrate and start life anew in Palestine. When the British, no longer willing or eager to fulfill the Balfour Declaration, intercepted and refused entry to ship after ship filled with hopeful Jewish refugees, Jewish resistance to British rule intensified.

Goldie, newly appointed to head the Jewish Agency's Political Department, devoted herself in public to negotiating with the British to lift immigration restrictions. Privately she worked to help make Palestine an independent state. In one famous episode, she disguised herself in Arab robes to meet secretly with King Abdullah of Jordan in an unsuccessful attempt to dissuade him from joining the Arab attack against Israel. And when, on May 14, 1948, Israel's independence was proclaimed, she was one of the proud signatories of the new state's Declaration of Independence.

That same year Goldie became Israel's first ambassador to the Soviet Union. She was elected to the Knesset (the Israeli parliament), served as minister of labor from 1949 to 1956, as foreign minister from 1956 until 1966, and was instrumental in the formation of the Israeli Labor Party. Then in 1969,

that tested physical as well as emotional resources. But when they moved to Jerusalem, where their two children were born, the dynamic new mother attempted the one role she could not master—that of nonworking housewife. Tensions between husband and wife grew, and slowly their marriage began to dissolve. It speaks well of both that they maintained a mutually respectful and amicable relationship for the remainder of their lives.

Perhaps predictably, Goldie soon became active in various political groups, serving in increasingly responsible positions. Before and during World War

Three women Prime Ministers in 1971: Golda, Indira Ghandi of India, and Sirimavo Bandaranaika of Ceylon (now Sri Lanka)

advancing age and poor health convinced her that it was time to depart from the political arena.

Character is difficult to overcome, however, and for Golda, always the woman of action, retirement was not yet in the cards. When her party drafted her to run for prime minister, she not only was elected but quickly became an international symbol of the archetypal Jewish mother: not simply a strong leader, but an unassuming maternal figure who often invited her cabinet ministers to her kitchen to discuss important issues over tea and cake.

Political pundits had predicted Golda would be an interim leader, but her leadership skills proved so successful that her "temporary" government lasted five years, a time buoyed, for the most part, by economic prosperity as well as by her personal popularity. But her administration was to end with one of the great tragedies of Israeli history. On October 6, 1973—on Yom Kippur, the holiest day of the Jewish calendar—Egypt and Syria mounted a surprise attack on Israel. The war left two thousand seven hundred Israelis dead, shook public confidence in the government for not having foreseen the war, and left Golda with an unrelenting sense of guilt. "The awful knowledge that I might perhaps have prevented this war will stay with me until the day I die," she wrote. In April 1974, Golda resigned; this time she remained in retirement.

Golda had her critics. She could be rigid in her political stances; some argue that her refusal to seriously consider peace overtures by Egyptian President Anwar Sadat in the early 1970s contributed to the 1973 war. But during the war that same steadfastness of character also helped see the country through adversity and pain.

Intensely private about her personal life, Golda's public persona remained one of warmth and dignity until the end. And it was in keeping with her character, too, that it was not until her death in 1978 that it became known that she had waged a fifteen-year battle against leukemia, secretly undergoing radiation treatments even during the time she was prime minister.

In a way it was only appropriate that one of the world's last glimpses of Golda Meir came in November 1977, when Anwar Sadat made his historic visit to Israel. Television cameras captured the old adversaries sitting beside each other, laughing as Golda reproached the Egyptian leader for having at one time called his former enemy "the Old Lady."

No, her laughter seemed to say, she had not been an "Old Lady" when she first dreamed the dream of an independent Israel so many years before, even if she had grown into old age as she strove to make that dream a reality. She had presided over and mourned a tragic war; yet here she was, laughing, celebrating the possibility of peace. As I watched on, half a world away, I could not help but laugh with her and admire anew the spirited toughness that lives on as the hallmark of Golda Meir.

Diane Cole

Georgia O'Keeffe

idely considered one of the most important American artists of the twentieth century, Georgia O'Keeffe began her painting career in the 1910s and continued into the late 1970s. The paintings she is best known for, however, are those completed in the 1920s through the 1940s, which are characterized by the subject matter that has become associated with O'Keeffe: flowers, bones, and the landscape of New Mexico.

O'Keeffe received early training in drawing and painting as a child in Wisconsin; after graduating from high school in 1905 she enrolled at the school of the Art Institute of Chicago where she spent a year. In 1907 O'Keeffe headed east to New York to study at the Art Students League.

It was during her study at the League that O'Keeffe first came into contact with the photographer Alfred Stieglitz. O'Keeffe and a group of student friends visited the gallery, called "291," that Stieglitz had opened to exhibit the works he preferred. Some students deliberately provoked Stieglitz into delivering one of his famous passionate speeches in defense of modern art. O'Keeffe recalled that she felt intimidated by Stieglitz and unimpressed by the work displayed, drawings by French sculptor Auguste Rodin.

Stieglitz had studied photography in Berlin in the 1880s and had achieved technical feats such as taking the first photographs in the rain, during a snowstorm, and at night. On his return to America he struggled to elevate the craft of photography to an art form and to introduce avant-garde art from Europe to the United States.

When it became apparent the following year that her family was no longer able to finance her studies in New York, O'Keeffe returned to Chicago where she found work as a commercial artist in the youthful advertising industry. Around 1910 she returned to Wisconsin where her mother was ill with tuberculosis.

In 1912 the twenty-five-year-old O'Keeffe heard of a vacancy for a drawing supervisor in Amarillo, Texas,

and she headed west for the first time. Texas was then still cattle country—oil and gas had yet to be pumped—and Amarillo was a rowdy frontier town boasting more bars than churches. Texas also had its fair share of natural dangers: tornadoes, dirt storms, prairie fires, in addition to the constant wind that drove up the dust unceasingly. Nevertheless, the vast sparsely populated land, wilder than the Wisconsin prairies of her youth, made her euphoric: "That was my country—terrible winds and wonderful emptiness."

After a year of study at Teachers College in New York, O'Keeffe once again had to find work and was finally offered a teaching position at a teacher's college for women in Columbia, South Carolina. Characteristically aloof from the atmosphere of "southern belle" femininity, she spent much of her free time outdoors, walking in the foothills of the Appalachians and gradually becoming more absorbed in her own paintings. In January of 1916 she sent a roll of charcoal drawings to her friend Anita Pollitzer in New York. Instead of showing them to the instructors at Teacher's College as O'Keeffe requested, Pollitzer took them to Alfred Stieglitz. He is said to have declared, "At last, a woman on paper," and offered to exhibit the drawings in his gallery. From this point O'Keeffe's association with Stieglitz and her reputation as one of America's leading artists began.

In August 1916 O'Keeffe took up a new job as head of the art department at West Texas State Normal College in Canyon, Texas. She would often send Stieglitz a selection of watercolors in addition to the long stream of letters with which they kept in touch.

In November 1916 Stieglitz included O'Keeffe's work in a show of established "regulars" at 291, including Arthur Dove, John Marin, Marsden Hartley and Abraham Walkowistz. Stieglitz had correctly predicted that her work would cause a sensation and word soon spread among the cognoscenti and the curious. Many were shocked by the sexuality they saw. Indeed, the explicit sexual imagery which many

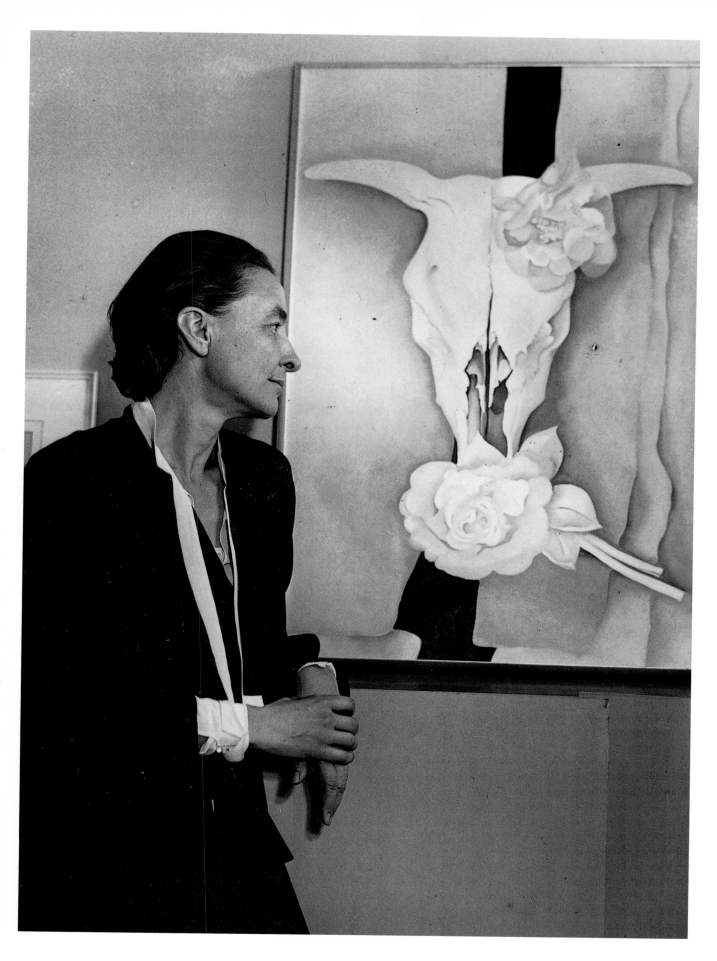

believed could be found in O'Keeffe's work was an interpretation that Stieglitz himself helped to foster.

After a brief visit to New York in 1917 to see her first solo show at 291 before it was dismantled, O'Keeffe returned to the southwest. After teaching the summer school session she had a month free and planned a trip to the Colorado Rockies. Bad weather closed the route to Denver, so she traveled via Albuquerque, New Mexico, where she first glimpsed the landscape

of the Sangre de Cristo Mountains. En route she painted what she saw and stopped at Santa Fe, one of the oldest towns in America and a thriving artists' colony. "I loved it immediately," she later recalled, "from then on I was always trying to get back." Her journey back to New Mexico would take, in fact, another twelve years.

In the winter of 1918 O'Keeffe became ill with influenza. Stieglitz, worried that she might have tuberculosis and concerned that she was not painting, sent a friend to take her back to New York. A month after her arrival in the city, she and Stieglitz became lovers and were sharing a small apartment. They spent time at his family's summer home at Lake George in the Adirondack Mountains, where O'Keeffe enjoyed long

periods of solitude in which to paint.

In 1924, when his divorce from his first wife became final, Stieglitz began to insist that they marry. Since the couple had already weathered the scandalous gossip about them, O'Keeffe saw no reason to get married. While Stieglitz sincerely wanted her to inherit his estate, it is also likely that he wanted to maintain his influence on O'Keeffe, who was twenty-four years his junior. In December 1924 they were married. No wedding rings were exchanged and, bowing to O'Keeffe's feminist beliefs, the words "love, honor, and obey" were omitted from her vows.

In 1924 she completed her first painting in a series that would contribute further to her already considerable fame. She had always enjoyed painting flowers, but her canvasses now showed blooms of gigantic proportions and, in addition, these flowers were never wholly realistic. They were more than botanical studies: she maintained that the paintings expressed her personal feelings about the flowers. Her flower paintings were interpreted as veiled representations of male and female genitalia—interpretations that she felt trivialized her work, but which nevertheless encouraged great numbers of the public to go to her shows.

A second theme emerged in O'Keeffe's paintings in New York in 1925 when the couple moved into the Shelton Hotel, one of New York's first true skyscrapers. Surrounded by the growing city, she began to paint it—in spite of objections from Stieglitz, who contended that nature was the more feminine sphere and that even male artists had difficulty depicting the architectural structures of the metropolis. Stieglitz was later forced to admit that he was wrong: O'Keeffe's first cityscape painting sold immediately, and in the next five years she painted approximately twenty cityscape and skyscraper scenes.

Stieglitz's failing health put increasing pressure on their relationship. At one point he refused to let her visit her family in Wisconsin, although he finally relented and O'Keeffe departed for a month-long visit. She was becoming acutely aware of her need to travel to find new subjects and that this urge was at odds with Stieglitz's own lifestyle and working methods. In May of 1929 O'Keeffe left New York for Taos, New Mexico, where she used the proceeds from the sale of two paintings to buy a Model A Ford to tour the state.

In April 1930 O'Keeffe spent a week painting in

Maine before traveling to Lake George where she began the series of seven paintings based on the jack-in-the-pulpit theme. Realizing that Lake George was no longer her world, she returned to New Mexico where she became fascinated with the dry, sun bleached bones scattered over the desert floor. Her exhibition at the end of 1931 gave the art establishment a few more shocks. Some critics found her skull-and-flower paintings morbid. O'Keeffe said she did not see them that way and said that she was excited about the wideness and wonder of the world in which she lived and was also excited about America when she painted *Cow's Skull—Red, White and Blue*, with its patriotic colors.

O'Keeffe returned to New Mexico in June 1934. The following year while her show contained only nine new works, they were among some of her best: *Blue River, Red Hills and Pedernal* reflected the love of the land she painted. Like O'Keeffe's later painting of an elk's skull and antlers floating over the New Mexico mountains, *From the Faraway, Nearby* (1937), *Ram's Head* was interpreted by many as the symbolic representations of the opposing forces of life and death, or of man and woman. Always at pains to dismiss psychological interpretations of her work, O'Keeffe insisted that the compositions "just sort of grew together." By this stage O'Keeffe had established a pattern of work that would rarely be broken until Stieglitz's death: each spring she set off for New Mexico and in the fall returned to New York, the back seat of her car full of new paintings. Each fall Stieglitz would organize her annual exhibition. In 1941 she was awarded an honorary doctorate from the University of Wisconsin and in 1942 the Art Institute of Chicago staged the first retrospective of her work, with sixty-one works dating from 1915 to 1941.

Now in her late fifties, O'Keeffe was aware of her own advancing age and realized that she would have to prepare for a life without Stieglitz, who was now in his eighties. After Stieglitz died in July 1946, O'Keeffe spent the next three winters settling his estate and trying to find a suitable place for his collection of over eight hundred works of modern art, photographs, and letters. The bulk of his collection went to the Metropolitan Museum of Art in New York.

Without financial reason to show her work, O'Keeffe decided to return to New Mexico to live. Once there, she retreated into isolation. While shunning human contact, she was nonetheless devoted to a succession of fierce little Chinese chow dogs, the first of which she had received as a Christmas present in 1952.

Although O'Keeffe enjoyed being out of the limelight, many of her old admirers wondered if she was still painting, while a whole new generation of young artists was not even familiar with her work. In 1960 O'Keeffe was persuaded to hold a major show—the first since Stieglitz's death—at the Worcester Art Museum in Massachusetts. The show was a success; it contained many new works, more than third of which had been executed since 1946 and many that had been completed the previous year. The Worcester exhibition put O'Keeffe firmly back in the public eye: *Newsweek* heralded her as the "grand old lady of painting."

During the 1960s bestowal of awards and honors became frequent events for O'Keeffe, but the most prestigious came in 1962, when she elected to a seat on the fifty-member American Academy of Arts and Letters. O'Keeffe was in exclusive company: only five of the members were women, and she was the only painter among them.

At the encouragement of Juan Hamilton, a young man who had become her assistant, O'Keeffe overcame her reluctance to write about herself and agreed to publish her autobiography. In the fall of 1976 Studio Books published *Georgia O'Keeffe*. It featured over one hundred color reproductions, many of which had never been seen by the public prior to the publication.

O'Keeffe liked to say that she would live to be one hundred years old. When she passed her ninetieth birthday, she upped the figure to one hundred twenty-five. She said, "When I think of death, I only regret that I will not be able to see this beautiful country anymore, unless the Indians are right and my spirit will walk here after I'm gone." On the morning of March 6, 1986, Georgia O'Keeffe was admitted to Saint Vincent's Hospital in Santa Fe where she died a few hours later. Her ashes were scattered, at her request, over the landscape she so loved and with which her work will always be identified.

Maria Costantino

Audrey Hepburn

Audrey Hepburn, the gifted actress who became known for her work on behalf of impoverished children for the United Nations Children's Fund (UNICEF), was born into a wealthy Belgian family on May 4, 1929, and christened Edda Kathleen Van Heemstra Hepburn-Ruston. Four years after her parents separated, the ten-year-old Hepburn was sent to boarding school near London. There she studied ballet and began to dream of a career as a dancer.

In September 1939, when Britain declared war on Germany, Hepburn's mother returned to Holland with her daughter because she feared that England would be invaded. Unfortunately, the city of Arnheim, close to the German border, was occupied by German forces. Fear pervaded the Low Countries, especially among families like the Hepburns who were of Jewish blood. Hepburn's schooling and ballet lessons gave way to participation in her mother's work for the Resistance. The child often carried messages hidden in the soles of her shoes, and her fluent English made it possible for her to convey information to British paratroopers who were hiding in the forests around the city.

During these dangerous years, an uncle and a cousin were arrested and executed. Her older brother was deported to a labor camp in Germany for refusing to join a Nazi Youth organization, and the family was stripped of all its assets. When word of the Allied advance filtered through in 1944, the Germans began pulling people off the streets at random to make up for the labor shortfall in German institutions. The fifteen-year-old Hepburn was picked up, but when the officer in charge turned his back for a moment, she fled and hid in a cellar where she stayed for three weeks, suffering from malnutrition and hepatitis.

When the war finally ended in 1945 and her brother returned from internment in Germany, the family moved to Amsterdam. Although she was still frail from the ordeal of the war years, Hepburn's love for dancing was undiminished. She continued her ballet studies in London, and in addition to full time class work, she took on other jobs, from holding up placards to announcing nightclub acts to the occasional modeling assignment, which increased her awareness of fashion.

In spite of growing misgivings about a career in ballet because of her short stature, the need for money encouraged her to audition for a part in the London production of *High Button Shoes*. To her amazement, Hepburn was one of ten girls selected for the chorus. When this production closed, she appeared in two Cecil Landau revues, a series of late-night cabaret acts, and was eventually cast as the female lead in *Laughter in Paradise*. Hepburn turned the role down in favor of touring, but when bookings failed to materialize, she went back to the director. The role had been recast, so she accepted a day's film work as a cigarette girl. Although she had only two lines, Pinewood Studios was buzzing with talk of the gamine new ingénue, and she was offered a seven-year contract. Her first featured part was in the comedy *Young Wives Tales*, and

in 1951 she finally got to dance en pointe in *Secret People*, in which John Field was her partner.

In 1953 Hepburn made her American film debut in *Roman Holiday* opposite Gregory Peck. Almost unknown, and with little film experience, she received the Academy Award for best actress at the age of twenty-four. Paramount then cast her in *Sabrina*, opposite Humphrey Bogart.

During the London premiere of *Roman Holiday* (1953) Hepburn met actor Mel Ferrer; the attraction between them was immediate, and they married in September of that year. The following spring she suffered a miscarriage.

Hepburn's next film, *Funny Face* was the last in which she was featured as a dancer and the first in which she sang. A series of unsuccessful films with her husband Mel Ferrer followed.

Hepburn's performance in *The Nun's Story* (1959), based on a true story of a devout Catholic nun who breaks her vows to work with the Belgian Resistance against the Nazis, rang true. The film was nominated for six Academy Awards. During the shooting of her next film, *The Unforgiven*, Hepburn was thrown from a horse and broke four vertebrae in her back, resulting in another miscarriage. She refused further film work and in July 1960 gave birth to her son, Sean.

The 1960s brought some of Hepburn's most popular films, including *Breakfast at Tiffany's*. "Moon River," the theme song, won an Academy Award, and the film's memorable images became part of the iconography of the decade. Another major success was *Charade* (1963) in which she starred with Cary Grant. It was closely followed by *My Fair Lady*, which garnered twelve Academy Award nominations. Hepburn was paid one million dollars for her portrayal of Eliza Doolittle, still another Cinderella. Only Elizabeth Taylor had ever received so large a fee, for her celebrated role in *Cleopatra*.

In 1971 Audrey Hepburn began her second career when she agreed to appear on a television special for UNICEF. This led to a one-year commitment as a special goodwill ambassador for the United Nations' relief work on behalf of impoverished children. She visited places and people in need of help, including refugee camps, Third World cities, and remote rural areas. When her year was up, Hepburn renewed her commitment to UNICEF and traveled to India, Southeast Asia, and Africa. Undoubtedly, her own years as a refugee in war-torn Europe gave her a deep empathy for others in this situation. During her later years she settled with her family in Switzerland—a country, she said, where there could never be a war.

Hepburn's last trip on behalf of UNICEF was in September 1992, to Somalia. She was already suffering from the colon cancer that would take her life on January 20, 1993. A month before she died, she was awarded the Presidential Medal of Freedom, America's highest civilian honor, and the Screen Actors' Guild Award for Lifetime Achievement.

Appropriately, her last encomium from Hollywood, received posthumously in April 1993, was the Jean Hersholt Humanitarian Award, which she shared with Elizabeth Taylor.

Maria Costantino

Clara Hale

"**I**'m not an American hero," declared Clara Hale. "I'm a person that loves children." This was her modest explanation for her dedication to hundreds of children for more than four decades. Lauded by President Ronald Reagan in his 1985 state of the union address and recipient of two prestigious awards from the Salvation Army, what mattered most to Clara Hale was giving love to children in need of it.

Born in Philadelphia, Pennsylvania, in 1904, Clara McBride was one of four children. Her father was murdered when she was a child and her mother died when she was only fourteen. Clara Hale expressed fond memories of her mother, recalling that there were always many children around, a practice she would continue in her own household.

Another characteristic she inherited from her mother was an understanding of the importance of building self-respect in children. "I want you to hold your head up and be proud of yourself," she says her mother admonished her. It was a directive Clara Hale passed on to her own children, Lorraine, Nathan, and Kenneth, as well as the many foster children she mothered.

Clara McBride married Thomas Hale after high school. Thomas ran a floor-waxing business in New York and attended business classes at City College in the evening. The couple had high expectations for their children; but Thomas Hale died at the young age of twenty-seven, leaving his wife to work toward fulfilling the dreams they had. Domestic work was all that was available to Clara Hale, so she cleaned office buildings to provide for her family.

Growing concerned about having to leave her children at home alone so much, Clara Hale decided to become a foster parent. She began taking children in daily, weekly, and finally permanently as a licensed foster parent. Clara Hale, or "Mother Hale" as everyone began to call her, saw numerous children from birth through high school, with many going on to college. New York City teachers, lawyers, and doctors attest to early years in her care.

At age sixty-five Mother Hale was contemplating retirement as a foster parent when a young woman arrived at her door with an infant in her arms. The woman was addicted to drugs, and she carried a note indicating that Mrs. Hale's daughter, Lorraine, had instructed her to bring the child to be cared for by Mrs. Hale.

The story is that Lorraine had observed the young woman on the street, nodding on a milk crate with the child. Not only did Clara Hale accept the baby, but within days she had taken in the woman's other children as well. Word quickly spread that this was a place where drug-addicted babies could receive love and shelter. "My decision to stop didn't mean any-

thing," Mother Hale said of what began to happen. "God kept sending them. He kept opening a way for me to make it."

As the AIDS epidemic spread in New York, Mother Hale began to take in babies who were diagnosed with HIV infection. When asked her method of caring for sick children, she responded, "We hold them and rock them. They love you to tell them how great they are, how good they are. Somehow even at a young age, they understand that."

The Hale House Center for the Promotion of Human Potential was officially founded in 1970. Under the direction of Lorraine Hale, who has a Ph.D. in child development, the center receives public and private funding.

Mrs. Hale's program has had its obstacles. She fought government bureaucrats who argued that children are better off in private homes than in group settings like the one provided by Hale House. But when such criticism mounted, the public always rallied to her cause. Celebrities held benefits; individuals volunteered time, increased their financial contributions, and lobbied government officials to be supportive of her work.

Mother Hale died on December 19, 1992. Her memorial service at Riverside Church was attended by dignitaries from around the world. Clara Hale had said that she would remain in service to her people until the end, and indeed she did, exemplifying the very best in human nature.

Brenda Wilkinson

Above: Mother Hale and Vietnamese refugee Jean Nguyen, honored as heroines at the White House in 1985

Wilma Rudolph

etween the starter's gun and the finish line tape, a sprinter's life is seconds long, a single breath. For Wilma Glodean Rudolph, the most revered woman sprinter in Olympic history, life was much more like a marathon—arduous, full of twists and turns, a true test of endurance. That Wilma Rudolph had staying power was clear from a very early age.

The twentieth of her railroad-porter father's twenty-two children from two marriages, Wilma weighed only 4.5 pounds when she was born on June 23, 1940, in Clarksville, Tennessee, and she grew up a frail and sickly child. At the age of four she was stricken with double pneumonia and scarlet fever; a short time later she was diagnosed with a mild form of polio. When Wilma's mother, Blanche, overheard the doc-

tor say of her young daughter that she might never walk again, her response was firm and clear: "Wilma will walk again. I'll see to that!"

She did. At home, Wilma's crippled right leg was massaged three times a day with various members of the family taking a turn. Forced to wear a cumbersome metal brace and a special high-top orthopedic shoe until she was a teenager, Wilma desperately wanted just to fit in. "Some people learn how to fake a limp," she said, "I learned how to fake a normal walk."

Normal was all Wilma Rudolph ever wanted to be. "To be average," she once said. "To be able to run, jump, play and do all the things the other kids did…that's what I always wanted." Normal, however, was the one thing Rudolph could never be, because

when the brace came off for good at age twelve, she started to run and never stopped.

Her first love was basketball. In high school she was six feet tall, and though she still weighed less than one hundred pounds, her energy running up and down the court was so indefatigable she earned the nickname "Skeeter," short for mosquito. As a high school junior Rudolph scored 803 points in only twenty-five games, setting a Tennessee Negro girls' record. After one of her games that year Rudolph was approached by Ed Temple, the track coach at Tennessee A&I University. "You could be a great

runner," Temple said. "Won't you let me coach you?" Rudolph spent that summer in Nashville being coached by Temple to be a sprinter. Success followed quickly. In 1956, at the age of only sixteen, Rudolph earned a place on the U.S. Olympic team and won a bronze medal as a member of the 4 x 100-meter relay team.

Four years later, though, Rudolph was clearly in a class by herself. In July 1960, at a track meet in Los Angeles, Rudolph set a world record in the 200 meters with a time of 22.9 seconds, becoming the first woman to break 23 seconds for that distance. Two months later, at the Rome Olympics, with her elegant but powerful style of running—arms pumping right out of the blocks, long legs striding hugely toward the finish line—Rudolph humbled her competition. She won all of her heats in the 100 meters, and then ran a blistering 11.0 seconds in the final. The time would have been a world record except that it was determined to be wind-aided.

In her second event in Rome, the 200 meters, Rudolph was forced to run heats twice within 90 minutes, but to no ill effect—she simply smashed the Olympic record (23.20) in the semifinal on her way to a second gold. Days later, Rudolph anchored the U.S. women's 4 x 100-meter relay team for her third gold.

One of the most enduring images of these 1960 Olympics was of Rudolph and another young Olympic hero, Cassius Clay, flush with youth, confidence, and promise, riding together around Rome in a pink Cadillac convertible.

As gifted a runner as Wilma Rudolph truly was, she was also gifted with people. Mae Faggs-Starr, a three-time Olympian and mentor to Rudolph, said of her fellow Tennessean at the time of Rudolph's death of brain cancer in November 1994, "Thirty-four years after she won her three golds, people still adored her. When she smiled and looked at you she was awesome."

And yet as awesome as Rudolph was as an athlete and a person, she saw her own gift in much simpler terms. "When I was running," Rudolph once said, "I had always had this sense of freedom, of running in the wind. I never forgot all the years when I was a little girl and not able to be involved. When I ran, I felt like a butterfly."

Amy Nutt

Valentina Tereshkova

The phrase "launching a new career" is particularly appropriate when describing the life of Valentina Vladimirovna Tereshkova, a Russian factory worker and recreational parachute jumper who on June 16, 1963, at the age of twenty-six, became the first woman in space. Consider the timing.

It was the height of the Cold War and the heat of the space race between the Soviet Union and the United States. The Russians had already launched four manned space flights—two *before* John Glenn became the first U.S. astronaut to orbit the Earth in 1962, and two after. The first cosmonauts and astronauts were married men with children—it was believed that they were the most psychologically stable. But Valentina proved that women could endure the rigors and challenges of space equally well—fifteen years before the United States even announced the names of its first six female astronauts. Sally Ride would not become the first American woman in space until 1983.

Valentina was born March 6, 1937, in the small Russian village of Maslennikovo, near the city of Yaroslavl. Her father, Vladimir, a tractor driver, was killed in action during the Russian-Finnish War, leaving her mother, Elena, to raise their three children. The family moved to Yaroslavl, where Valentina attended school until she was sixteen. She then worked first in a tire factory and later in a textile factory, simultaneously earning a technical school diploma through correspondence courses. Valentina also joined a local air club, making her first parachute jump in May 1959. As she explained in her autobiography, "I loved everything to do with machinery . . . but my hopes flew higher than life on the ground."

After the historic 1961 flight of Russian cosmonaut Yuri Gagarin, the first man in space, she wrote a letter to the Soviet Space Commission applying for cosmonaut training. In February 1962, after being approved by a special medical commission, Valentina and four other Soviet women were chosen to undergo the same intense physical and mental training as the male cosmonauts. All were expected to be in perfect health and master mechanics, rocketry, astronomy, space navigation, space medicine, and radio communication. Together, the cosmonauts ran, exercised, cycled, skiied, and made consecutive flights at high altitudes. To test their bodies' responses to simulated space conditions, they each spent time strapped to the centrifuge (to experience sudden speed accelerations), on the swing (which turned them upside down), on the squirrel (a sphere that changed orientation and weight), and on the the vibration table (simulating the propulsion phase of a rocket engine in flight). The cosmonauts spent anywhere from two hours to two weeks training alone in a soundless, motionless isolation chamber; they also logged hours in the hot room, enduring high temperatures. Mental preparation was key: atmospheric friction during launch and re-entry would cause flames to surround the capsule that would be visible through the porthole, and the pressure on their bodies would reach 9gs, causing tightening in the chest and difficulty breathing.

During training, biologists and doctors determined that menstruation in space would be a problem, explained Valentina, so the women were not required to train on the centrifuge at that time of the month. "My flight took place between periods," she added. It was always believed, she said, that "a woman could become a cosmonaut if she had the same physical and mental capabilities as a man, and the courage."

The men, all professional, licensed pilots, helped train the women to pilot a plane; the women, all expert parachutists, helped train the men who were not parachutists on jump techniques and conditions. Parachuting skills were essential for re-entry to the Earth's atmosphere in a Vostok craft. The cosmonauts all automatically ejected in their seats at twenty-two thousand feet, then separated and opened a parachute at eight thousand feet in high winds, and landed in a heavy space suit with life-support equipment.

wedding ceremony, which was broadcast nationwide. The birth of their daughter, Alyona, in June 1964 was then said to signify that space travel had no deleterious effect on reproductive function. Today Alyona is an orthopedic surgeon. Valentina's marriage ended in 1977.

Expanding her formal academic training, Valentina graduated from the Zhukovsky Air Force Engineering Academy with a degree in technical sciences in 1969, then earned a doctorate in engineering in 1976. Since her flight she has continued to play an active role in the Soviet space program. Valentina is currently working with scientists from seven nations on a manned Mars landing, anticipated by the end of the century. She is also an instructor in cosmonautics in Star City, the cosmonaut training center.

Named a hero of the Soviet Union shortly after her flight, Valentina embarked on her own personal mission of international shuttle diplomacy. "As I saw the planet from space, I realized how small Earth is, and how fragile, and that it could be destroyed very quickly," she explained. Valentina resolved to set forth a peace plan to establish ecological harmony and end armed hostilities. Over three decades, she has visited world leaders and spoken at international conferences on the topics of women's rights, world peace, and international space exploration. Also active in Russian politics as an advocate of women's rights, Valentina said, "I have dedicated the best years of my life to working to help women achieve their potential."

Andrea Feld

Valentina was launched in *Vostok 6* forty-five hours after *Vostok 5*, on the second "twin" Russian mission. The two crafts passed each other at a distance of about three miles and were in frequent radio contact. Valentina sent back films and still photos of the Earth's atmosphere, conducted biological seed and insect experiments, and carried out psychological tests to learn about the effects of weightlessness on humans. Medical sensors hooked to her body sent back valuable medical data. Although her flight was supposed to last twenty-four hours, she received permission to stay in orbit for a total of two days and twenty-two hours. When *Vostok 6* landed in a farm field on June 19, 1963, she had traveled 1.2 million miles and made forty-eight orbits around the Earth, a solo endurance record still unequaled by another woman.

Five months after her flight, Valentina married Adrian Nikolayev, pilot of *Vostok 3* and the only unmarried male cosmonaut to train with her. Nikita Krushchev presided over their November 3, 1963,

Mother Teresa

"I am nothing. God is all."

— MOTHER TERESA

he small, frail woman who has come to be revered as a saint in her own lifetime reached the slums of Calcutta by a circuitous route. She was born Agnes Gonxha Bojaxhiu to a working-class family in Skopje, Albania, on August 27, 1910. With her brother and sister she attended government schools and her parish church, where she first learned of the work of missionaries to India, notably the Sisters of Loreto. At the age of eighteen, Agnes had a profound spiritual experience in which she felt called to serve God and others as a missionary nun. She joined the Sisters of Loreto as a postulant—one who aspires to take vows in a Roman Catholic order after a period of train-

ing—and studied English so that she could teach in convent schools in India.

Her first assignment was in Darjeeling, where the Sisters of Loreto had a school for the children of wealthy British tea planters and Indians of the higher castes. It was here, in 1929, that she took her first vows and adopted the name Mary Teresa in honor of the Blessed Virgin and St. Thérèse of Lisieux, the nineteenth-century French Carmelite. Two years later, the twenty-one-year-old missionary was transferred to St. Mary High School in Calcutta to teach geography.

Just beyond the school's green lawns and white walls were the slums of the section known as Moti Jhil, where people lived and died in unrelieved poverty. Their suffering distressed Sister Teresa, who obtained permission to visit the poor after school and on Saturdays with leftover food, bandages, and whatever supplies she could garner from the convent. She continued this work for nine years after she took her final vows in 1937. Then she traveled to Darjeeling for a retreat and received what she described as "a call within a call." She knew she must find a way to live and work among Calcutta's poor.

It took two years to obtain a dispensation from her vows as a Sister of Loreto, but finally word came from Rome that she could leave her convent. She traveled to Patna to learn basic nursing skills and returned to Calcutta alone at the age of thirty-six. In place of the black and white nun's habit she adopted a cheap white cotton sari trimmed in blue, found a second-floor room with friends, and began begging food and medical supplies for the street people. Her first act was to give away four of the five rupees she had in her pocket.

Calcutta had even more than its usual quota of displaced peasants and homeless refugees in 1948, the year after India won its independence from British rule. Many residents of the newly created state of East Pakistan flooded into nearby Calcutta to swell the numbers of rural people who had been driven from the land by famine and strife. Open sewers bred dis-

ease, and people slept on sidewalks and traffic islands. The sick were turned away from overcrowded hospitals; elderly people were dying in the streets.

Within a few months, a nineteen-year-old Hindu girl named Subashini Das, a former student at St. Mary, came to the door and announced, "Mother, I have come to join you." A few years later, eleven others had followed, most of them former students from the convent, some of them from wealthy Hindu families. Permission was granted by Rome to form an order to be called the Missionaries of Charity, which would minister to the poor while living among them in poverty.

Practical and clear-sighted, Mother Teresa insisted that applicants to the Missionaries of Charity be healthy, sensible, and cheerful: the work was grueling, and would-be mystics had to have both feet on the ground. A young woman could not take her final vows until she had spent eight years with the order, after which she took the customary vows of poverty, chastity, and obedience, along with a binding promise of "whole-hearted free service to the poorest of the poor."

From the outset, Mother Teresa and her followers were involved with caring for and educating orphans, nursing the sick, begging food for the hungry, and sheltering the dying for whom nothing else could be done. Mother Teresa constantly reminded her sisters that God had disguised himself in the poor: when they took care of the poor, they touched the body of God. To those who supported the work, she explained that her sisters were not social workers, nurses, or teachers. They were in the business of doing "something beautiful for God."

As news of the order's work spread beyond India, many lay people banded together as the Co-Workers of Mother Teresa. By the early 1960s, they numbered more than three million men and women from seventy countries and many different faiths; some of them came to India, others worked with the poor in their own communities. Requests for help came from abroad, and Mother Teresa traveled widely to see if the Missionaries of Charity could help in a given situation. By the early 1960s, there were new houses in Ceylon, Tanzania, Australia, Venezuela, and Italy. In 1963 an Australian priest who had worked in Calcutta for years started the Brothers of Charity. Later, a mission to the homeless and victims of AIDS was established in New York City.

All of the work was financed by donations or gifts in kind, which were turned to good account. When the pope gave Mother Teresa his white Cadillac, she promptly auctioned it off, and when she was awarded the Nobel Peace Prize in 1979, she used the cash part of the award to start a new home for lepers.

Despite advancing age and a painful heart condition, Mother Teresa continued her work and her travels throughout the 1980s. Unobtrusive and seemingly tireless, she appeared in Northern Ireland, Israel, and Lebanon, where her visit to rescue thirty-seven endangered Beirut children resulted in the first cease-fire in months of fighting.

Like her namesake, St. Thérèse of Lisieux, she had emphasized the importance of "doing little things with great love." Her faith remains unwavering in the face of several heart attacks and increasing debility. She is confident that the Missionaries of Charity will continue their work under new leadership in the years to come and says serenely, "We will act the way He leads us." Many of those who come to India to meet her, write about her, or observe the work remain to help and go home profoundly changed. They have learned the truth she has expressed so often: "Loneliness and the feeling of being unwanted is the most terrible poverty."

Robin Langley Sommer

Nien Cheng

When Mao Zedong's Cultural Revolution broke upon the People's Republic of China in 1966, Nien Cheng, who would spend seven years as a prisoner of conscience, was an immediate target for denunciation: she was a Christian and a wealthy intellectual with close ties to people in foreign countries. Born in 1915 to a cultured landowning family, she was among the first generation of Chinese women to study abroad. She met her husband, Kang-chi Cheng, at the London School of Economics, where they were inspired by the ideals of the *Communist Manifesto*. When they returned to China, Kang-chi Cheng became a diplomat and was appointed to the Chinese embassy at Canberra, Australia, where their daughter, Meiping, was born.

The Chengs traveled widely and made many friends abroad. When they settled in Shanghai, Nien Cheng's husband continued to work for the Nationalist government until it was driven from mainland China to Taiwan in 1949. The Chengs did not leave the country because they believed it would be possible to cooperate with the new Communist government to improve conditions for all Chinese. However, two of Nien Cheng's sisters moved to the United States after the Communist takeover, which made Nien Cheng especially vulnerable to charges of being a "running dog" of foreign oppressors. When she was widowed in 1957, Nien Cheng accepted a position with the British-owned Shell Oil Company, where her husband had served as general manager for some years.

During the early 1960s Meiping joined the government-run Shanghai Film Company as an actress and became a member of the Communist Youth League—ties that would protect her for a time after the Red Guard invaded their home on an August night in 1966. Meiping was not at home when Nien heard the sounds of breaking furniture and shattered porcelain. Mao's revolutionaries, rampaging through Shanghai, were looting the house. They placed Nien under house arrest as a class enemy of the Revolution. She was forbidden to speak with her daughter and accused of being a spy for the Nationalist government.

In her autobiography, *Life and Death in Shanghai* (1987), Nien Cheng recalled the series of "struggle meetings" in which former friends and associates were forced to denounce her. Nien was repeatedly accused of plotting against the Communist government. Former staff members and friends from Shell Oil had to testify against her. "The men who got up to speak were frightened," she recalled, "and their hands holding the prepared statements shook. None of them looked in my direction." She refused to confess.

After a series of such confrontations, during which she was shoved violently and spat upon, Nien was taken to the political prison known as Shanghai's Number One Detention House and assigned the number 1806. She was placed in solitary confinement in a filthy cell and watched day and night through a peephole. The only reading material allowed was the Communist newspaper and the writings of Mao Zedong. Nien's greatest anxiety was for Meiping: word had recently reached her that her daughter and others at the film studio were being held prisoner there. No one would answer her questions.

Eventually the prison interrogator called her in and demanded that she write her life story. Her brief factual account was rejected and she had to write it again and again, explaining her visits to Hong Kong, her British friends, and her husband's involvement with the Nationalist Party. The interrogations became more frequent and more abusive. Once she became so angry that she banged on the table in front of the interrogator and a guard pulled a gun on her. "You may shoot me if you can prove me guilty with concrete evidence," she declared.

Prison officials were amazed at her defiance, and the "struggles" became more violent over the next three years. Nien Cheng suffered several near-fatal bouts with pneumonia along with sleep deprivation

and malnutrition. Never robust, she dwindled to a weight of eighty pounds. At the age of fifty-four, Nien Cheng was tortured. Her hands were handcuffed tightly behind her back and she was thrown into the windowless punishment cell without food or water. After eleven days even the guards were begging her to confess or to eat a little. When they finally removed the handcuffs, her fingers were the size of carrots and her wrists deeply infected. She feared she would lose the use of her hands, but she recovered slowly from the worst of her injuries.

During her sixth winter in prison, her clothes were so worn that she requested those that had been put aside for her when she was arrested. When the package arrived her heart sank: what had been sent by mistake were Meiping's clothes, hardly worn. What had happened to her daughter? Her determination to survive was eroded by her near-certainty that her only child was dead.

At last, word came that she was to be released on grounds that she had been "re-educated" and showed some degree of improvement in her thinking. Anger rallied her spirits and she refused to leave the prison "until a proper conclusion is reached about my case." Prison officials were aghast. This delicate woman who had become an embarrassment of the government by her resistance to every kind of pressure was refusing to leave the prison without "full rehabilitation and an apology for wrongful arrest."

They told her that she was out of her mind and expelled her forcibly from the outer gate. Outside the gate was her goddaughter Hean. At last she heard the news she had dreaded: Meiping was dead. It was reported that she had committed suicide by throwing herself from a ninth-floor window. Nien Cheng was sure that she had been murdered. Hean told her that Meiping had been put under enormous pressure to denounce her mother and had refused.

Despite her deep desire to leave China, Nien Cheng remained in Shanghai for seven more years, until Mao Zedong had died and the Cultural Revolution had been officially condemned by the new government. In the interim, she learned the truth about Meiping's death. She had, in fact been abducted and killed by revolutionaries because she refused to denounce her mother. Nien Cheng demanded justice from the new government, headed by Deng Xiaoping, and at last achieved some satisfaction. She was officially rehabilitated and declared a victim of wrongful arrest and persecution. Meiping's murderer was arrested and tried.

Shortly after leaving China, Nien Cheng settled in Washington, D.C., and began work on the manuscript of *Life and Death in Shanghai*. Written in English, the book was widely acclaimed, both as a personal testament and as a first-hand account of what millions had undergone during the Cultural Revolution. Since its publication in 1986, Nien Cheng has spoken to international audiences of her experiences and on human rights issues.

On becoming an American citizen in 1988 she said: "Here are Jewish survivors of the Holocaust, boat people from Vietnam, and political refugees from tyranny. Among people like these, I do not feel alone."

Robin Langley Sommer

Rachel Carson and Anita Roddick

lthough it would be difficult to imagine two more different personalities, it is arguable that Rachel Carson and Anita Roddick share the distinction of exerting a greater positive influence on environmental change than anyone else this century. Rachel Carson was a very private person, quiet, meticulous in her science and writing, with little appetite for the public attention she received after the publication of her books. Ms. Roddick, on the other hand, is a naturally gregarious self-publicist: she has an exuberant passion for life and a spirit of adventure which has apparently made a game of the business of commercial enterprise and raising human awareness.

Differences notwithstanding, it would be as impossible to envision a successful Body Shop of the 1930s as it would be to imagine Rachel Carson espousing the 1960s ideologies which so inspired Ms. Roddick. Both women thrived within their own chronological context and were able to inspire others because their message was both intelligible to their generation and ecologically timely. It is sobering to remember, for instance, that the words *environment* and *ecology* were known only to biologists when Rachel was born on May 27, 1907. The youngest of three children, she was raised on a Pennsylvania farm which fostered her natural love for the living world—particularly for the sea, for which she expressed a deep yearning. Sensitive, studious, and bookish, with a love of poetry and the precise use of language, she aspired to be a writer and majored in English at college until a compulsory biology course prompted her to switch to zoology.

She attained a temporary job at the Washington Bureau of Fisheries until the need to provide for her mother and two young nieces forced her to obtain permanent work. Although assured of her skills, she was naturally modest, and it is unlikely that she would otherwise have attempted the exam which led to the job of junior aquatic biologist—certainly she was the only female applicant. But apply she did and, on achieving top marks and thus the job, she worked there from 1931 until 1952. Happily, her work involved writing as well as marine research, and one of her first jobs was to produce twelve booklets entitled *Conservation in Action.*

Although for most of us the issue never arises, for some there comes a point at which a personal passion must give vent to a public action to defend what it loves. So it was for Rachel Carson, whose work opened her eyes to the damage to the living world by the hostile forces of man's destructive behavior. Although in no sense a crusader (she was most at home engaged in the stimulating pursuit of research, preferably from her seashore cottage in Maine) she felt obliged to speak out and wrote, "for all the people, the preservation of wildlife and wildlife habitat means also the preservation of the basic resources of the earth."

She was to write five books in all; the first three, *Under the Sea Wind* (1941), *The Sea Around Us* (1951), and *The Edge of The Sea* (1955), made her a publicly acclaimed figure (unwillingly so although, as one commentator observed, "once overboard she knew how to swim"). However it was her fourth book, *The Silent Spring* (1962), in which she condemned the blanket use of pesticides, that caused the greatest furor and had the most far-reaching effect on our attitude towards the environment and the use of chemical pollutants. It is partly because of her book that we take to be commonplace the sentence that so startled her readers in 1962: "Can anyone believe that it is possible to lay down such a barrage of poisons over the surface of the earth without making it all unfit for human life?" And, though we are now accustomed to the term "holistic," it was Rachel Carson who first introduced the notion by describing the problem that lies at the core of our current planetary malaise: "This is an era of specialists, each of whom sees his own problem and is unaware of or intolerant of the larger from into which it fits."

She deplored the prevalent attitude of scientific arrogance which deemed itself "in control of nature" and felt instead a sense of awe and wonder at man's place in the complex natural world. However, it was her redoubtable scientific skills that gave a caring authority to her defense of the living world and enabled her to awaken in her readers a sense of responsibility. At the same time, she communicated a sense of magic and joy.

The book was published to hugely favorable reviews and soon became an international best-seller, eventually forming the basis of pesticide legislation in several countries worldwide. However, the reactions from those whose interests were threatened was less than favorable, and the furor has been compared to that which followed the publication of Darwin's *Origin of the Species*. The National Agricultural Chemical Association responded by spending $250,000 on a campaign to improve its image. Miss Carson herself was attacked as a scaremonger and "a hysterical woman." There was even an attempt to ban the book while it was still being printed. The storm continued to rage until President John F. Kennedy set up a Pesticides Committee whose report eventually vindicated her views and prevented further denials that the problem existed.

Rachel Carson had no appetite for the controversy that raged around her book; a true scientist, she preferred to let the facts she had presented speak for

themselves. In any event, there can be little doubt that the success of *The Silent Spring* was as much due to the lyricism of its prose as its meticulous science, and the public approbation gladdened her. The thousands of letters she received seemed to bear witness to the awakening of a collective human conscience, and in 1963 she wrote, "a very strange thing is emerging—the reappearance of a sense of personal responsibility."

Sadly, she was having to face up to the fact that her own role in the complex interdependent system of nature was of limited duration. Her health had been failing for some time, and she was unable to take up the many offers she received to travel and speak worldwide. On April 15, 1964,

Rachel Carson died as she had lived, sensible to the fact that while all life is temporary and the end of life is natural, each individual can nevertheless exert a positive influence for itself, for its environment, and for future generations: "It is good to know I shall live on in the minds of many who do not know me and largely through association with things that are beautiful and lovely."

Rachel Carson died at the beginning of a decade in which the young Ms. Roddick was just finding her feet as a campaigner for nuclear disarmament. She had been born twenty years earlier of Italian parentage in Littlehampton on the Southern English coast, where she had worked as a youngster in her parents' café. Her upbringing fostered her independent spirit and natural zest for life. After abandoning a successful teaching career, she traveled the world for several years before meeting, on her return to Littlehampton, a young farm laborer, traveler, adventurer, and poet named Gordon Roddick. They enjoyed a whirlwind romance and set up home together, although it was not until Anita was pregnant with their second child that they decided to get married.

The couple ran a guest house in Littlehampton for a while until Gordon decided to fulfill a life's ambition to undertake a journey on horseback from Buenos Aires to New York, a trip that was scheduled to take two years. Scouting around for a way to make a living during her husband's absence, Anita hit on the idea of opening a shop selling cosmetics made from natural products. A few hasty plans were drawn up for the proposed scheme and, when she asked Gordon what she should do if the business failed while he was away, he replied, "Give it six months then pack it in and meet me with the kids in Peru."

As it turned out, it was Gordon who returned after just a year of traveling to find that The Body Shop was a thriving concern and that Anita had opened a second store. Several others followed—usually run as franchises—and within a few years The Body Shop had grown into the massive organization so familiar today.

Anita Roddick is a gifted saleswoman, and there can be no doubt that this salesmanship is among the most effective of the natural products on display in her six hundred shops. However, to launch an enterprise selling cosmetics, albeit of an eco-friendly nature, and turn it into a success is one sort of an achievement, and it is not for this that the Roddicks have made such an impact on the commercial and environmental worlds. What gives The Body Shop its remarkable staying power is more than its ability to market goods: it is a business with heart, upheld by the vision and impetus of its creator, in which the word "beauty" is banished and so is the advertising department; and a principle of honesty is sustained in its dealings with suppliers, customers, and staff. Ms. Roddick sees herself, with some justification, as a sort of modern-day Quaker, citing as a guiding principle in her business ethic Ralph Waldo Emerson's injunction that it is important "To Put Love Where Labor Is."

In spite of the accusations of her detractors (of whom there are many), there can be no doubt that The Body Shop is an example of what Ms. Roddick calls *enlightened capitalism*. For all its shortcomings it clearly provides for its staff, suppliers, and customers a profitable system of fair trade which is laudable and rare. Indeed it is probable that Ms. Roddick would have been remembered for this achievement alone had The Body Shop not gone public in 1984, turning the Roddicks overnight into millionaires and their business into a multi-million pound company.

There are those who feel that it is impossible to be both a capitalist and environmentalist, and they could doubtless present a solid theoretical case. But there are few who have had to steer a personal vision of a perfect world out of the safe harbor of coffee-table conversations and into the stormy waters of international commerce and the even rougher seas of anti-environmental government policy. This has been Anita Roddick's achievement. The success of their business forced her and Gordon to consider how best to use their wealth, power, and status and they decided, simply, to devote their energies to working for a better world. They linked first with Greenpeace, where they worked jointly on a Save the Whales campaign, and shortly afterwards with Friends of the Earth. Indeed their desire to campaign independently in recent years is largely because of Ms. Roddick's wish to be able to act more spontaneously in response to an international crisis (as she did after the collapse of the Rumanian government), and they now undertake two major campaigns a year and are devoted to a Trade Not Aid program.

Perhaps her most successful campaign thus far, typical of many other such endeavors, has been Stop The Burning, her vigorous persuasion of the Brazilian government to cease the razing of the rain forests.

Her contribution was not only to organize a vast one million-signature petition, while raising awareness of the problem among her customers, but also to journey to Brazil. Her aim was to establish trade links with the tribes whose livelihood was threatened by the destruction of the rain forest in such a way so as not to damage their way of life. She espouses three principles in her dealings with third world countries with whom she believes it would be beneficial to trade: she waits to be invited, she upholds the environment, and she rewards the primary producers.

Ms. Roddick's evaluation of her role is best summed up in her own words, "I am not rushing round the world like some kind of loony do-gooder; first and foremost I am a trader looking for trade." Modest at best, disingenuous at worst, her throwaway comments are arguably her only pieces of redundant packaging. Her achievements speak for themselves. Together with those of her predecessor Rachel Carson, they uphold the living world and inspire and sustain those who would follow in their footsteps.

Catherine Mooney

Anita Roddick, opposite, and below, in Africa

Maya Angelou

"I speak to the black experience, but I am always talking about the human condition—about what we can endure, dream, fail at, and still survive."

—MAYA ANGELOU

Throughout history there have been accounts of individuals who overcame unsurmountable odds to attain greatness in life. Maya Angelou is a living example of this achievement. Although she has often said that people are more alike than they are different, she is unusual for her level of success as a poet, autobiographer, playwright, screenwriter, dancer, actress, director, producer, university professor, lecturer, and civil rights activist.

Maya's life is chronicled in her autobiography *I Know Why The Caged Bird Sings* and her subsequent autobiographies; they tell of her richly varied life experiences and give insight into the depth of her being. A closer look, however, also reveals the presence of a prevailing force that constantly propels her forward to fulfill a seemingly predestined future.

Maya Angelou was born Marguerite Annie Johnson in St. Louis, Missouri, on April 4, 1928, to Bailey Johnson, a doorman and naval dietician, and Vivian Baxter Johnson, who was employed in a variety of positions, including card dealer, boardinghouse proprietor, and registered nurse. After her parents separated, Maya and her older brother, Bailey, Jr., were sent to live with their paternal grandmother, Annie Henderson, who owned and operated a general store in the small segregated town of Stamps, Arkansas. It was in Stamps that Maya first felt the pangs of despair associated with racism as she watched her

beloved grandmother proudly, but quietly, accept humiliating taunts from neighborhood youths.

Maya and Bailey, Jr., moved back to St. Louis to live with their mother in the mid-1930s. During this time, Maya was befriended by her mother's boyfriend. He later raped her. Maya was only eight years old at the time. Once the deed was discovered, she was forced to testify at her assailant's trial. A few days later, he was found beaten to death in an alley. Psychologically damaged by the tragedy and plagued by the guilt associated with her assailant's death, Maya decided she would stop talking. She did not speak again until 1940, five years later. It was during this time that she immersed herself in books and the study of the human voice.

Later, Maya and Bailey, Jr., rejoined their mother in San Francisco, and Maya went on to, among other things, work as a streetcar conductor (the first black female fare collector in San Francisco); graduate from high school; have a son, Clyde (Guy) Johnson; work as a madam and manage two prostitutes; marry and divorce a Greek sailor named Tosh Angelos; secure her first job as a dancer and singer; and tour Europe and Africa as a featured dancer in a State Department-sponsored production of *Porgy and Bess*. She also appeared in her first off-Broadway play; recorded her first album; joined the Harlem Writers Guild; wrote her first play; and worked as a civil rights activist.

During the 1960s Maya moved to Cairo, Egypt, with her second husband, a South African dissident lawyer named Vusumzi Make. It was during her stay in Cairo that she worked as an associate editor of the *Arab Observer*, an English-language newspaper. After her divorce from Make, she moved to Accra, Ghana, where her son Guy was attending the University of Ghana. There, Maya found work as a music and drama teacher at the University of Ghana, feature editor of the *African Review*, and writer for the *Ghanaian Times*. She also studied cinematography in Sweden.

It was upon her return to the United States that Maya was urged by James Baldwin and playwright and cartoonist Jules Feiffer to write the story of her life. In 1969 *I Know Why The Caged Bird Sings* was published.

In the proceeding years Maya wrote four more volumes of her autobiography: *Gather Together In My Name* (1974); *Singin' and Swingin' and Gettin' Merry*

Like Christmas (1976); *The Heart of a Woman* (1981); and *All God's Children Need Traveling Shoes* (1987). She has also published six volumes of poetry: *Just Give Me A Cool Drink of Water 'fore I Diiie* (1971); *The Poetry of Maya Angelou* (1975); *Oh Pray My Wings Are Gonna Fit Me Well* (1975); *And Still I Rise* (1978); *Shaker Why Don't You Sing?* (1983); and *I Shall Not Be Moved* (1990); in addition to a book of essays, *Wouldn't Take Nothing For My Journey Now* (1993).

Maya Angelou has written numerous plays, screenplays, and television scripts and has received countless awards. On January 20, 1993, she read her poem "On The Pulse of Morning," at the 1993 inauguration of President Bill Clinton, making her the first woman and African-American to read a poem at the inauguration of an American president in the history of the country.

Maya Angelou currently lives in Winston-Salem, North Carolina, and holds a lifetime appointment as a Reynolds Professor of American Studies at Wake Forest University.

Joan Halimah Brooks

Tina Turner

Tina Turner: a whirlwind of sensual energy with a volcanic alto, the Queen of Raunch Rock. From 1960 to 1976, she was the star of the combustible Ike and Tina Turner Revue, the hot, hip-shaking dance band that merged black rhythm and blues with soul, country blues, gospel, and rock 'n' roll. Janis Joplin called her the best performer in show business, and she is the person credited with teaching Mick Jagger to dance. But most of all, in a decade in which the plight of battered women is finally receiving public attention, Tina Turner is a survivor. Despite the hit records, her life was a living nightmare of mental and physical abuse. After sixteen years she finally walked out on Ike, her husband and musical collaborator, taking little from their partnership but her freedom.

Tina Turner was born Anna Mae Bullock on November 26, 1939, in Nutbush, Tennessee. The marriage of her father, a black farm overseer, and her mother, a spirited black Indian, was stormy. On and off, they left her and her older sister, Alline, in the care of relatives and friends. "I had no foundation in life," said Tina, "so I had to go out in the world and become strong."

When Anna Mae was sixteen, she moved to St. Louis, Missouri, to live with her mother and Alline. The sisters fequented the jumping juke joints in East St. Louis, where the hottest regional band was Ike Turner and the Kings of Rhythm. Once Ike heard Anna's voice, she regularly sang with the band. He bought her clothes and paid to have her teeth fixed. "He made me feel important," she explained. "For the first time in my life, I had a kind of family love."

In 1958 Anna recorded "Box Top," her first record with the Kings of Rhythm and had a son, Raymond Craig, fathered by a member of the band. Ike and his common-law wife also had a son, Ike, Jr., that year. But Ike dated many women, and soon his relationship with Anna was more than platonic. She quit her hospital job as a nurse's assistant and moved into his home, where many of his musicians lived and rehearsed.

In 1959 Ike and Lorraine's second son was born. By January 1960 Anna was also pregnant with Ike's child. In the spring of 1960, Tina sang the lead on their first single, "A Fool in Love," leading to a contract with Sue Records. Ike renamed Anna "Tina Turner"— after the character Sheena, Queen of the Jungle, a goddess with long, wild hair and a tattered provocative outfit. Tina donned her now trademark miniskirts and fishnet stockings, skintight black leather pants, high heels, and long flowing wigs. On the road, everyone thought Ike and Tina were married, but their Tijuana ceremony didn't take place until 1962.

When Tina hesitated about moving to California,

Ike beat her for the first time. From then on, she never knew when she was going to get hit. "I always had a black eye and a busted lip," Tina recalled. Over the years, Ike burned Tina with cigarettes and hot coffee, kicked and beat her, and fractured her ribs and jaw. "And then he would have sex with me. It was torture, plain and simple," Tina said.

In 1968 Tina left Ike, but he stopped her at a bus station. She terminated another pregnancy and survived a Valium overdose. "I was trapped in an endless cycle of overwork, touring, rehearsing, abuse, choking, punching… I was ready to die," she explained.

Slowly Tina's unique talent was noticed by her peers. In 1966 legendary pop producer Phil Spector asked her to do a solo recording of "River Deep—Mountain High." The record, proclaimed a masterpiece, became a hit in England. In 1975 Tina played "The Acid Queen" in the film version of The Who's *Tommy*.

To make life more bearable, Tina began chanting a Buddhist mantra daily, went for card readings, and studied reincarnation. Gradually she realized that all of their songs were Ike's vision. She is still embarrassed by her rendition of "I've Been Loving You too Long," choreographed by Ike and captured on the Rolling Stones' 1970 video *Gimme Shelter*, in which she makes obscene gestures with a microphone.

In 1966 The Revue toured with the Rolling Stones and their music soon reflected the influence of the then-popular white rock 'n' roll groups. Ike and Tina performed cover songs of the Stones' "Honky Tonk Women" and the Beatles' "Come Together." Their classic remake of Creedence Clearwater Revival's "Proud Mary" earned The Ike and Tina Turner Revue a 1971 Grammy Award.

In 1976 Tina walked out on Ike for good after a brutal punch-out which began at an airport and ended in a limousine. She escaped in a blood-stained white suit with just thirty-six cents and an oil company credit card. Until their divorce was final in 1978, she stayed with friends, lived in a rented house, used food stamps, and endured Ike's violent threats.

Tina borrowed money to start a new cabaret act and repay debts from canceled concert dates. Her new manager, Roger Davies, convinced her to hire a new rock 'n' roll band. Concerts in 1981 and 1983 at The Ritz in New York City led to duets and performances with Rod Stewart and the Rolling Stones and

a record contract with Capitol Records. Her 1983 single "Let's Stay Together" was a hit in England and the United States. Then in 1984, she recorded *Private Dancer* in London, the album that changed her life. Working with four producers, Tina combined rhythm and blues with reggae, electro-funk, hard rock, and heavy metal. It sold ten million copies, launched three hit singles, and won three 1984 Grammy Awards. The following year she starred with Mel Gibson in the hit movie *Mad Max Beyond Thunderdome*.

In 1991 Tina was inducted into the Rock Hall of Fame and moved to Europe. At the age of fifty-two, she embarked on a 121-show European tour. When *What's Love Got to Do With It* (the film based on her 1986 autobiography, *I, Tina*) and soundtrack were released in 1993, she toured the United States.

Tina now shares houses in the south of France and in Germany with Erwin Bach, thirty-nine, a record executive. In 1994 *Tina Turner—The Collected Recordings: Sixties-Nineties* was released. In the future, she hopes to act more than tour, and someday "teach and preach."

"I was a victim. I don't want sympathy," Tina insists. "Did I ever stand up for anything? Yeah. I stood up for my life."

Andrea Feld

Marian Wright Edelman

T his is a story about Marian Wright Edelman, a woman who will leave her mark on the twentieth century for many reasons. She grew up outside the national mainstream as a black female, but attained a position of international influence as an advocate for social reform. She has been true to the family values she learned as a child, accepting challenge and physical risk in order to defend social principles and attack injustices. As the founder and executive director of the Children's Defense Fund, she has become a leading advocate for children's welfare in the United States.

Marian Wright was born on June 6, 1939, in the small, segregated town of Bennettsville, South Carolina. She was the youngest of five children born to the Reverend Arthur Wright and his wife, Maggie. Reverend Wright and his Baptist pulpit shaped the family's life, particularly for the children in their early years. Although homework and excellence in school were the primary responsibilities for Marian and her brothers and sister, caring for the sick and needy and helping others were also priorities. After school, the children took turns visiting the homebound in their father's parish, and always put others ahead of themselves. When Reverend Wright saw a need for housing for the elderly in his parish, since none was available to them because of color restrictions, he built a home for elderly blacks which he ran until his death. His wife then managed the home, until long after she was older than most of the residents. As Reverend Wright lay dying shortly after the 1954 *Brown v. Board of Education* decision which banned school segregation, he told Marian, almost fifteen years old at the time, not to let anything get in the way of her education.

Determined to carry out her father's wishes, in 1956 Marian entered Spelman College in Atlanta, a prestigious liberal arts college for black students. Her goal was to study Russian and economics and ultimately to join the foreign service. In her senior year, however, she was inspired by the speeches of Martin Luther King, Jr., at that time an emerging leader in the civil rights movement, and by other rising black leaders such as Whitney Young and Dr. Benjamin Mays, president of Morehouse College (Atlanta). She volunteered at the local NAACP office and helped to organize sit-ins to protest the segregation in Atlanta. Very quickly she realized that black Americans had few advocates and legal representatives other than volunteers like her. At that moment, she decided to pursue law rather than the foreign service.

Marian graduated from Yale University Law School in 1963 and spent a year in the NAACP's New York City office as a staff attorney. She then went to Mississippi where, as director of the NAACP office in Jackson, Marian was the first black woman to be admit-

ted to the bar. These were dangerous times for anyone, regardless of color, who challenged segregation and the status quo of the old South. From 1964 to 1968, she traveled widely throughout rural Mississippi defending poor blacks; she introduced the Head Start program for preschoolers to prepare them for their formal education; and she connected with Senator Robert Kennedy by bringing to his attention the plight of the poor families of the Mississippi delta.

This relationship was significant for another reason: she met and fell in love with Kennedy's executive assistant, Peter Edelman. He, a white Jew, and she, a black Baptist, married and later would raise three sons in their interracial, intercultural, interfaith family. Teaching the values of their respective families of origin, Marian and her husband practiced a respect and tolerance of diversity. Their sons would later be bar mitzvahed in ecumenical services led by a Baptist preacher and a Rabbi.

Also during these years in Mississippi, Marian was to express her growing frustration with the civil rights movement. After the northern liberals (mostly white) returned north following their summer internships, she found an indifference among the southern blacks whose civil rights were so adversely affected.

By 1968, after the assassination of Martin Luther King, Jr., Marian was ready to move to Washington, D.C., where she believed she could be more effective as an advocate for change than as a litigator for the wronged and the indigent. With a small federal grant she began the Washington Research Project to study the condition of low-income people. The growing staff served as ombudsmen to monitor the federal funds which had been earmarked for the poor.

Marian discovered that by narrowing her focus to the specific needs of children rather than the general needs of all poor, she could attract a broader backing and constituency. By 1973, the Washington Research Project was rededicated as the Children's Defense Fund, with Marian as its founder and executive director. Through the CDF, Marian would demonstrate that children are a vulnerable class and a social and economic responsibility for the nation. Moreover, she would demonstrate that poverty knows no race nor class.

In the first twenty years, she increased the CDF's endowment to over eleven million dollars; funding came mostly from foundations, but also from corporations, private donors, publications, and special events. She also created CDF state and local offices and community programs in thirty-six states to provide a combination of services: they monitor the local implementation of policies affecting health, education, child welfare, mental health, child development, adolescent pregnancy prevention, family income, and youth employment, and they also provide information and support to a network of local advocates and service providers.

What made Marian Wright Edelman effective as an advocate for social reform for blacks, women, and children, particularly when she is a black woman in a country whose legislators and power brokers are predominately white men? The answers lie in the values of service she inherited from her parents, in her own life philosophy and spiritual faith, and in her special combination of pragmatism and idealism.

Marian Wright Edelman's life of advocacy has been recognized and celebrated worldwide. She is the beneficiary of over forty-five honorary awards including the Presidential Citation, over thirty honorary degrees, and positions on prestigious boards, commissions, and the United Nations. As the executive director of the Children's Defense Fund, she has demonstrated the archetype of an effective advocate for social reform, at the same time managing to balance the roles of wife and mother, idealist and pragmatist. Marian also models the life of one born outside the mainstream of a society who became a significant influence in the capital of the United States, which advocates equal opportunity for all. She often quotes one of her heroes, Dr. Morehouse, the former president of Morehouse College:

"It must be borne in mind that the tragedy of life doesn't lie in not reaching your goal. The tragedy lies in having no goal to reach. It isn't a calamity to die with dreams unfilled, but it is a calamity not to dream. It is not a disaster to be unable to capture your ideal, but it is a disaster to have no ideal to capture. It is not a disgrace not to reach the stars, but it is a disgrace to have no stars to reach for. Not failure, but low aim, is sin."

Holly Regier

Rigoberta Menchú and Aung San Suu Kyi

igoberta Menchú and Aung San Suu Kyi are two women whose struggles for human rights have become recognized internationally. Both have received Nobel Prizes for their commitment to the cause of freedom in their own countries and throughout the world, but their commitment arises out of very different backgrounds. They are not just symbols of the struggles for peace and for human rights, but active and dedicated women who speak now for justice and relief from oppression.

Rigoberta Menchú, small and reserved with a moon-shaped face and delicate gestures, is a woman of tremendous courage and strength. Her story begins with her peasant childhood in Guatemala and culminates in worldwide recognition with the 1992 Nobel Peace Prize for her work on behalf of Guatemala's Indians and peasants. Hers is a truly extraordinary story of bravery, perseverance, and pain.

In 1960, Rigoberta was born in the region of Quiché, the sixth child in what would become an eleven-member family. Her parents, Guatemalan Indians, were peasant workers. The very small plot of land they farmed high in the Altiplano mountains did not produce enough food to feed the family, let alone secure an income, so they traveled to the coast each year to work on large plantations.

Life on the plantation was brutal. The workers were crowded into open sheds with four to five hundred other Indians who spoke different languages. Rigoberta started her life as one of the many thousands of Indian children with no clean water, toilets, or soap. At the age of eight she began to work in the fields — children who did not work were not fed. Two of her brothers died

on the plantation, one apparently as a direct result of pesticides sprayed on the coffee fields while he was working, and another at the age of two from illness brought on by malnutrition. Without access to a doctor and unable to leave the fields, the family had to let this child die in the open shed.

The Altiplano is the heart and soul of Rigoberta's people: Their identity as Indians is nourished in the beauty and harshness of the mountain environment, and customs and rituals are enacted and preserved in the tiny, isolated villages. Rigoberta's mother and father felt particular pride in their Indian heritage and were elected leaders of the community. When government workers and plantation owners started to force villagers off their land, Vicente Menchú began a campaign to secure his land. He fully realized the danger he was putting himself in but saw no other option for the future of his family. He began a series of petitions, meetings, and

protests to save his community; in spite of repeated arrests and imprisonment he continued his work throughout many Indian villages. Rigoberta's greatest influence was her father, to whom she was deeply attached. She, too, organized and educated her *compañeros*, urging them to defend their land, their customs, and their rights. A country-wide peasant organization was formed in 1978 that led strikes and petitioned for better wages and working conditions.

In 1979 Rigoberta witnessed the brutal torture and death of her sixteen-year-old brother. He was taken by police and killed while his parents and siblings watched. Rigoberta then suffered the death of her father. He had organized a peasant march to the capital. His group of peasants occupied the Swiss embassy, several radio stations, and, finally, the Spanish embassy

which burned down with Vicente Menchú inside. The following year Rigoberta's mother died. She was kidnapped, raped, and tortured, then left to die, while her family watched but could not approach her for fear of being killed as well.

After the death of her mother, Rigoberta went into hiding and eventually left Guatemala for Mexico. She began what would be and endless journey around the world to recount her story. Rigoberta survived the horrors of her life and committed herself to improving the plight of her people. In her book, *I ... Rigoberta Menchu* (1984), she says, "My life does not belong to me. I've decided to offer it to a cause." She was so fearful of losing a family again that she decided not to marry or have children. While her sisters became guerrilla fighters in the mountains, Rigoberta chose the role of educator and leader. She has worked with international human rights groups and has spoken at forums in Europe, the United States, and at the United Nations. In 1992 she was awarded the Nobel Peace Prize for her campaign for social justice and for the rights of native peoples everywhere. Church bells could be heard ringing in her honor throughout Guatemala's villages.

Rigoberta Menchú has become a symbol of steadfast strength in the face of terror. She says, "That is my cause. As I've already said, it wasn't born out of something good, it was born out of wretchedness and bitterness. It has been radicalized by the poverty in which my people live. It has been radicalized by the malnutrition which I, as an Indian, have seen and experienced.... Therefore, my commitment to our struggle knows no boundaries or limits."

Rigoberta Menchú turned thirty-five years old in 1995. In her extraordinary life she has proven that a strong voice from a poor, illiterate Indian family can be heard and heeded in the corridors and loudspeakers of mighty institutions around the world. Her struggle continues.

It was a combination of

chance, destiny, and determination that catapulted Aung San Suu Kyi into the leadership role of the pro-democracy struggle in Myanmar (formerly Burma). The fifty-year-old writer returned to Burma after decades abroad and, by coincidence, a democratic movement was brewing in need of direction and a leader. Although her love and study of Burma had never included political aspirations, the people vividly remembered her legendary father and readily tied their hopes to his daughter. Against all odds and at great sacrifice, including nearly six years of house arrest and complete isolation, she continues to hold the people's hopes and dreams for a democratic Burma.

Aung San Suu Kyi left Burma as a young woman to pursue her education. For nearly twenty years she lived in the United Kingdom with her British husband, Michael Aris, and their two sons, Alexander and Kim. She was writing her doctoral thesis on Burmese Literature in 1988 when her mother became gravely ill and she rushed home to Burma. While nursing her mother at the family home in Yangon (formerly Rangoon), antigovernment protests erupted in the capital, setting the stage for her emergence as the leader of the pro-democracy movement.

Students were beginning to demonstrate to call for the resignation of General Ne Win, who for twenty-six years had presided over a government characterized by economic strife and political oppression. The protests multiplied, with ordinary citizens and Buddhist monks joining the students. Government forces opened fire on the crowds and arrested hundreds. Aung San Suu Kyi began holding mass rallies and openly criticizing the government, while the people's anger continued to mount. In a surprising move, General Ne Win announced his resignation with the promise of open, fair elections. Political parties were formed including the National League for Democracy (NLD) with Aung San Suu Kyi at the helm.

She traveled the countryside speaking to the people about the nonviolent struggle for human rights and ethnic unity the NLD represented. Armed with the principles of Mahatma Ghandi and Martin Luther King, Jr., she endured constant harassment from the ruling junta, proving continually that she was not afraid to stand up to the brutal government. Aung San Suu Kyi delivered a thousand speeches, wrote essays, and conducted interviews while the international community slowly became aware of her courage and the situation in Burma. Her compassion and dedication reminded the people of her father, Aung San, who had led the country to independence from British colonial rule in the 1940s and become Burma's beloved founding father. Aung San Suu Kyi's husband wrote, "In the daughter as in the father there seems an extraordinary coincidence of legend and reality, of word and deed." Her popularity swept the nation.

Aung San Suu Kyi, the person and the legend, posed too much of a threat to the regime and she was placed under house arrest on July 20, 1989. Her family home was fenced in and surrounded by guards and tanks. Supporters and associates in the NLD were arrested and jailed. Demanding only that she be imprisoned with her young supporters under the same miserable conditions, she embarked on a hunger strike. It lasted twelve days and ended after her supporters' well-being was assured.

In May 1990, elections were held and, despite months of isolation and the silencing of the NLD, her party won a landslide victory, claiming over eighty percent of the vote. Ignoring the results, the junta offered her release from house arrest with the contingency of permanent exile. She declined the offer.

Although she has not seen her family since 1989, her husband understands the depth of her commitment. He wrote, "From her earliest childhood, Suu has been deeply preoccupied with what she might

do to help her people. She never for a minute forgot that she was the daughter of Burma's national hero, Aung San."

In 1991 she won the Nobel Peace Prize for her "nonviolent means to resist a regime characterized by brutality" and for showing "one of the most extra-

ordinary examples of civil courage in Asia in recent decades." As she was unable to leave Burma, her family accepted the award on her behalf. She has also been awarded the Norwegian Thorolf Rafto Prize for Human Rights and the Sakharov Prize for Freedom of Thought in 1990.

She remains under house arrest and the Burmese people continue to wait for her release and for the transfer of power. Inadvertently, she has become a political martyr symbolizing the hope for democracy. In September 1994, the military regime opened talks with Aung San Suu Kyi and allowed foreign diplomats to visit her. Rumors of her release have electrified the people again as they hope for the future of Burma.

Ellen Williams and Annie Roberts

Selected further reading

Elizabeth I:
John Bennet Black, *The Reign of Elizabeth, 1558-1603*, (London: Readers Union, 1964)
Arthur Bryant, *The Elizabethan Deliverance*, (London: Collins, 1980)

Aphra Behn:
Janet Todd, *The Works of Aphra Behn*, (London: William Pickering, 1992)
Alastair Fowler, ed., *The New Oxford Book of Seventeenth Century Verse*, (Oxford and New York: Oxford University Press, 1991)

Catherine the Great:
Ian Grey, *The Romanovs: The Rise and Fall of a Russian Dynasty*, (David & Charles, 1970)

Mary Wollstonecraft:
Claire Tomalin, *The Life and Death of Mary Wollstonecraft*, (London: Weidenfeld and Nicolson, 1974; revised edition Penguin Books, 1992)

Susanna Moodie:
Margaret Atwood, *The Journals of Susanna Moodie: Poems*, (Oxford University Press, 1970)

Elizabeth Blackwell:
Rachel Baker, *The First Woman Doctor; the Story of Elizabeth Blackwell, M.D.*, (New York: J. Messner, 1944)
E. Blackwell, *Pioneer Work in Opening the Medical Profession to Women: Autobiographical Sketches*, (New York and London: Longmans, Green, and Co., 1895)
E. Grant, *Elizabeth Blackwell*, (London, 1974)

Grace Darling, Ida Lewis:
Jessica Mitford, *Grace had an English Heart*, (1988)

George Eliot:
J. W. Cross, editor, *George Eliot's Life* three volumes, (New York: Harper & Brothers, 1885; Grosse Pointe, MI: Scholarly Press, 1968)
Gordon S. Haight, *Eliot: A Biography*, (New York and Oxford: Oxford University Press, 1968)
Ruby Virginia Redinger, *George Eliot: The Emergent Self*, (New York: Knopf, 1975)
Phyllis Rose, *Parallel Lives: Five Victorian Marriages*, (New York: Knopf, 1983)

Abigail Scott Duniway:
Ruth B. Moynihan, *Rebel for Rights, Abigail Scott Duniway*, (New Haven: Yale University Press, 1983)

Mary Kingsley:
O. Campbell, *Mary Kingsley: A Victorian in the Jungle*, (1957)
S. Gwynn, *Life of Mary Kingsley*, (1932)
Elizabeth Longford, *Eminent Victorian Women*, (London: Weidenfeld and Nicolson, 1981)

The Pankhursts:
D. Mitchell, *Queen Christabel*, (London, 1977)
David Mitchell, *Women on the Warpath: The Story of the Women of the First World War*, (London: Cape, 1966)
Emmeline Pankhurst, *My Own Story*, (London, 1914; New York: Source Book Press, 1970)

Richard Pankhurst, *Sylvia Pankhurst: Artist and Crusader, an Intimate Portrait*, (New York: Paddington Press, 1979)
S. Pankhurst, *Life of Emmeline Pankhurst*, (London, 1935)
Anne Wiltsher, *Most Dangerous Women: Feminist Peace Campaigners of the Great War*, (London and Boston: Pandora Press, 1985)

Charlotte Despard:
Andro Linklater, *An Unhusbanded Life*, (London 1980)
Margaret Mulvihill, *Charlotte Despard: A Biography*, (London and Boston: Pandora Press, 1989)

Alexandra Kollontai:
Cathy Porter, *Alexandra Kollontai: A Biography*, (London: Virago, 1980)

Larissa Reisner:
Cathy Porter, *Larissa Reisner*, (London, Virago, 1988)

Radclyffe Hall:
Radclyffe Hall, *The Well of Loneliness*, (New York: Covici Friede, 1928; London: Virago, 1982)
Toni McNaron, *A Journey into Otherness*

Rosa Parks:
Brian Lanker, *I Dream a World: Portraits of Black Women Who Changed America*, (New York: Stewart, Tabori & Chang, 1989)
Myles Horton, with Herbert and Judith Kohl, *The Long Haul: An Autobiography of Myles Horton*, (New York: Doubleday, 1990)

Georgia O'Keeffe:
Maria Costantino, *Georgia O'Keeffe*, (New York: Smithmark, 1994; London: Grange Books, 1994)

Nien Cheng:
Robin Langley Sommer, *Nien Cheng: Prisoner in China*, (Woodbridge, CT: Blackbirch Press, 1992)

Rachel Carson:
Paul Brooks, *The House of Life: Rachel Carson at Work*, (New York: Houghton, Mifflin, 1989)

Anita Roddick:
Anita Roddick, *Body and Soul: Profits with Principles, the Amazing Success Story of Anita Roddick & The Body Shop*, (New York: Crown, 1991)

Clara Hale:
Brian Lanker, *I Dream a World: Portraits of Black Women Who Changed America*, (New York: Stewart, Tabori & Chang, 1989)

Rigoberta Menchú:
Rigoberta Menchú, translated by Ann Wright, *I, Rigoberta Menchú: An Indian Woman in Guatemala*, (London: Verso Editions, 1984)

Aung San Suu Kyi:
Aung San Suu Kyi, *Freedom From Fear and Other Writings*, (New York: Penguin Books, 1991)

Scholars disagree on the exact dates for some historical figures, even well-known ones, and factual information is scarce for more obscure individuals. Wherever possible, the editors of this book have used the *Encyclopedia Britannica* as a main source of information.

Every effort was made to obtain complete and accurate copyright information for the images used. If any errors or omissions have been made, please notify the publisher and the correction will be made in further printings of the book.

Acknowledgements

The publisher would like to thank the contributors to this anthology, the editors, the designer, and the following for their advice and assistance in the preparation of this book: Nancy Carter, Duncan Clarke, Ann Collins, Maureen Foster, Deborah Goodsite, Emily Head, Gloria Kan, Juliette Kennedy, Alain Levy, Sarah Partridge, Linda Peavy, Ursula Smith, Cindy Wooden, Sui Mon Wu. For supplying the illustrations:

AKG, London: pages 25, 26, 30, 34, 95
Australian Picture Library/J. Carnemolla: 70
The Bettmann Archive: 1, 9 (bottom), 12, 13, 16, 17, 18, 19, 21, 31, 32, 33, 35, 36, 38, 39, 40, 48, 49, 53, 56, 57, 58, 59, 60, 61, 63, 64, 67, 73, 75, 76, 77, 78, 86, 87, 89, 90, 99, 102, 103, 111, 116, 128, 132, front left endpaper, back right endpaper
Bibliothèque National de France: 51

The Body Shop: 148, 149
© Bruce Glassman: 145
Internationaal Informatiecentrum en Archief voor de Vrouwenbeweging, Amsterdam: 83
David King Collection: 145
Mary Evans Picture Library: 47, 65, 68
Mary Evans/Fawcett Library: 85, 97
Nevada State Museum: 80
Northwind Picture Archives (hand-coloring) 14, 43, 47, 50, 54, 80
Reuters/Bettmann: 4 (bottom), 8, 135, 143, 151, 152, 153
Scottish National Portrait Gallery: 23
Springer/Bettmann: 123, 150
UPI/Bettmann Newsphotos: 2 (top center), 2 (bottom right), 3 (center), 4 (center), 9 (top), 10, 79, 91 (both), 92, 93, 98, 101, 107, 109, 110, 113, 114, 117, 118, 119, 121, 124, 125 (both), 127, 129, 131, 134, 136, 137, 138, 139, 141, 142, 147, 154, front right endpaper

Index